Sociology: A New Approach

Edited by Michael Haralambos

Written by
Michael Haralambos
Frances Smith
James O'Gorman
and
Robin Heald

Causeway Books

Causeway Press Ltd
PO Box 13, Ormskirk, Lancashire L39 5HP

© Causeway Press Ltd.

British Library Cataloguing in Publication Data

Sociology.
1. Sociology
I. Haralambos, Michael
301   HM51

ISBN 0 946183 27 9
published 1983 (reprinted six times)
Second edition 1986,
Reprinted 1986, 1987 (twice), 1988, 1989, 1990, 1991, 1992

Typesetting by Bookform, Merseyside
Printed and bound by The Alden Press, Oxford

Preface to the First Edition

Sociology: A New Approach aims to provide an introduction to Sociology for GCSE and beyond. It offers an alternative to the traditional textbook. A comprehensive coverage of the GCSE syllabus is combined with a series of data response questions which are completely integrated with the text. In this respect it reflects the emphasis on data response and stimulus questions in GCSE Sociology examinations.

The book seeks to encourage the reader to become actively involved with the material and aims to provide a stimulating and effective learning experience. To this end material for the book has been selected not only for its relevance to Sociology but also for its intrinsic interest.

Sociology: A New Approach will also prove useful as a companion volume for 'A' level textbooks. It provides what they often lack – an opportunity for students to explore the subject by means of self-directed study. The section on methodology affords useful preparation for the stimulus questions on research methods in the AEB 'A' level Sociology examination.

Many people have contributed to the writing of this book. The authors would like to thank Ian Smith for his expert help with the section on population and Colin Wiggans for his valuable advice on the structure of the book and the construction of data response questions. We thank Andrew Allen whose care and skill in drawing the charts and diagrams and designing the cover has added to the quality of the book. We appreciate the help of Ian Hoyle, Eric Titterington, Barbara Valentine and Marian Whipp with material on social history which has added depth and colour in several places. The book owes much to the pointed and often amusing cartoons drawn by Antony Winterbottom. His work is much appreciated. Once again William Dickey and the staff of W. R. Tuson College Library provided invaluable assistance. As usual their help and interest went well beyond the call of duty. Catherine McGuffie deserves special thanks not only for her expert typing but also for her enthusiasm for the project.

Those who share the authors' lives probably find the experience of writing as difficult as the authors themselves. Frances Smith would like to thank Ian for practical support and cheerful encouragement at difficult moments. James O'Gorman would like to thank Joan and Maureen O'Gorman for their enthusiastic encouragement but most of all particular thanks to Judith Boxall, not just for her practical assistance and research skills, but also for the emotional support she provided. I should like to thank Pauline for her continued support and understanding. Any success the book enjoys will be due in part to her efforts.

Michael Haralambos
April 1983

Preface to the Second Edition

This edition has been extensively revised and updated to meet the requirements of GCSE syllabuses in Sociology. It includes some 120 pages of new material with additional sections on Race and Ethnicity, The Welfare State, Urbanization and Unemployment and the Future of Work and Leisure. In addition new material has been included in existing sections to reflect syllabus changes and changes in society during the 1980s. Statistical data have been updated throughout the book.

The authors would like to thank their spouses, children and friends without whose support, encouragement and forbearance this edition would not have appeared. Thanks are also due to Josina Gerard for the speed, skill and good humour with which she typed the manuscript. We are grateful to Allen Associates for the high quality artwork and to Antony Winterbottom for some further excellent cartoons. Finally may we take this opportunity to thank teachers and students for their many kind remarks about the first edition. We hope you enjoy the second.

Michael Haralambos
April 1986

Contents

Section 1: Culture and Socialization   1
1 Culture   1
2 Instinct   3
3 Animal behaviour   5
4 Culture and values   6
5 Culture and norms   9
6 Culture, status and role   10
7 Socialization (1)   12
8 Socialization (2)   15

Section 2: Social Control   19
1 The family   19
2 Religion   22
3 The peer group   25
4 Significant others   26
5 The mass media (1)   28
6 The mass media (2)   30
7 Racialism and social control   32

Section 3: Research Methods   39
1 Participant observation (1)   39
2 Participant observation (2)   43
3 Interviews (1)   46
4 Interviews (2)   48
5 Sampling procedures (1)   50
6 Sampling procedures (2)   52
7 Questionnaires   55
8 Pilot Studies   57
9 Secondary sources   59
10 Novels   63
11 Official statistics   66

Section 4: Social Stratification   69
1 The feudal system   70
2 The caste system   73
3 Social class — The Registrar-General's classification   76
4 Social class — A Marxist view   77
5 The distribution of income in the UK   80
6 The distribution of wealth in the UK   82
7 Inequality at the workplace   84
8 Social class and life chances   85
9 Social class subcultures   87
10 Embourgeoisement (1)   89
11 Embourgeoisement (2)   90
12 Social mobility   92
13 Does social class matter?   95

Section 5: Race and Ethnicity   97

1 The idea of race   97
2 The idea of ethnicity   100
3 Ethnicity and life chances   102
4 Racism and ethnic stratification   104
5 Ethnic subcultures   108
6 Afro-Caribbean subculture   110
7 Ethnicity and urban riots   113

Section 6: Poverty   119

1 Two views of poverty   119
2 Poverty in York, 1899   121
3 Absolute vs relative poverty   124
4 The culture of poverty   126
5 Poverty and class (1)   128
6 Poverty and class (2)   130
7 Poverty and the mass media   132

Section 7: The Welfare State   137

1 The origins of the welfare state   137
2 The foundations of the welfare state   140
3 The establishment of the welfare state   142
4 Voluntary organizations and self-help   146
5 A critical view of welfare   148
6 Welfare in the inner city   150

Section 8: Power and Politics   155

1 Democracy in Britain   155
2 Pressure groups   158
3 Power in Britain — A Marxist view   161
4 Television and political bias   164
5 Political socialization   166
6 Voting behaviour and social class (1)   170
7 Voting behaviour and social class (2)   172
8 Age, gender and voting behaviour   174
9 Opinion polls   176
10 The social background of MPs   179

Section 9: The Family   183

1 The family in pre-industrial society   184
2 Changing functions of the family   185
3 Family structure in early industrial society   190
4 The working class extended family   193
5 The symmetrical family   198
6 Conjugal roles   200
7 Family diversity (1)   202
8 Family diversity (2) Ethnicity   206
9 Marital breakdown   208

10 Women and divorce   211
11 A critical view of the nuclear family   213
12 Alternatives to the family   215

Section 10: Education   219

1   Education and society (1)   219
2   Education and society (2)   222
3   Social class and educational attainment   225
4   Poverty and educational attainment   227
5   Speech patterns   229
6   Compensatory education   232
7   Streaming   234
8   The self-fulfilling prophecy   236
9   Ethnicity and educational attainment (1)   239
10 Ethnicity and educational attainment (2)   242
11 Gender and educational attainment   245
12 Gender and schooling   247
13 The tripartite system   250
14 The comprehensive system   252

Section 11: Youth Culture   255

1   Initiation ceremonies   255
2   Youth in industrial society   257
3   Youth and social class   259
4   Is there a generation gap?   263

Section 12: Women and Society   267

1   Women in non-Western society   268
2   Women and industrialization   270
3   Socialization and the role of women (1)   273
4   Socialization and the role of women (2)   273
5   Housebound wives   276
6   Why women go to work   278
7   Women in the labour force (1)   280
8   Women in the labour force (2)   283
9   Women in the labour force (3)   285

Section 13: Population   289

1   Population and the Third World   289
2   The death rate in England and Wales   292
3   Birth and fertility rates in England and Wales (1)   297
4   Birth and fertility rates in England and Wales (2)   300
5   Why do women live longer than men?   304
6   The age structure of the population   307
7   Migration   311
8   Population changes — United Kingdom   314
9   The social effects of the fall in mortality   316

Section 14: Urbanization 319
1 Urbanization in Britain 319
2 The 'loss of community' 324
3 Internal migration and de-urbanization 326
4 The inner city 330

Section 15: Work and Leisure 335
1 Assembly line production 335
2 Craft technology 337
3 Micro-chip technology 339
4 Deskilling 343
5 Alienation 345
6 Industrial sabotage 347
7 Work, leisure and family life 348
8 Work and patterns of leisure 350

Section 16: Unemployment and the Future of Work and Leisure 353
1 Unemployment – definition and measurement 353
2 Who are the unemployed? 356
3 Changes in employment patterns 359
4 The effects of unemployment 363
5 Women and unemployment 365
6 Youth unemployment 367
7 The future of work 370
8 The future of leisure 373

Section 17: Crime and Deviance 375
1 Deviance and culture 375
2 Official statistics on crime 378
3 Victim studies 379
4 The crime rate 382
5 Crime and social class 385
6 White collar crime 387
7 Labelling theory (1) 389
8 Labelling theory (2) 392
9 Crime and ethnicity 393

Section 18: Religion 397
1 Religion and society 397
2 Religion and social order 399
3 Religion — The opium of the people 401
4 Secularization 403

Index 407

Acknowledgements

We are grateful to the following for permission to reproduce copyright material (details in text).

Batsford Academic and Educational Ltd. p. 225 (table)
Tony Benn pp. 164–166
Cambridge University Press pp. 141–142, 157 (table), 191 (table)
Community Care pp. 130–132
The Controller of Her Majesty's Stationery Office for tables pp. 203, 239–240, 245–246, 329, 355, 356
Corgi Books pp. 60–63
Professor C. B. Cox p. 251
The Critical Quarterly Society p. 251
J. M. Dent pp. 64–66
Gower Publishing Company Ltd. p. 379
The Guardian pp. 95, 164–166, 273, 275–276
Harper & Row, Publishers, Inc. pp. 33–36
Heinemann Educational Books pp. 158–161
Holt, Rinehart & Winston pp. 237–238
Human Sciences Press pp. 30–32
Sir Keith Joseph p. 95
Professor Sir Edmund Leach pp. 213–215
The Listener pp. 213–215
Longman Group Ltd. pp. 121–124
Macdonald & Co. (Publishers) Ltd. in association with Rathbone Books Ltd. pp. 70–73
Methuen & Co. Ltd. p. 237
New International Publications Ltd. pp. 187–189, 290–292
New Science Publications pp. 340–341
New Society pp. 84 (table), 102 (table), 132–134, 179–181, 200–202, 304 (table)
The Observer pp. 116, 248–249, 278–279, 280–282, 341–342
Penguin Books Ltd. pp. 116, 125 (table), 150–151, 152–153, 189, 250–251, 268, 269, 331–332, 333, 347–348
Pluto Press for tables pp. 361, 362
Politics Pal p. 102 (table)
Jacqueline Penrose pp. 273, 275–276
Routledge & Kegan Paul Ltd. pp. 43–44, 46, 47–48, 51–52, 53 (tables), 58, 194–197, 268–269
Souvenir Press Ltd. pp. 335–336
Times Newspapers Ltd. pp. 243–244 (table), 274, 283–285
United States Government Printing Office p. 381 (table)
University of Chicago Press pp. 40–42, 184–185, 337–338

Acknowledgements

We are grateful to the following for permission to reproduce photographs and artwork.

Allen Lane, Penguin Books Ltd. for photographs on p. 14 (from **The Wolf Children** by Charles Maclean, London, 1977)

BBC Hulton Picture Library for photographs on pp. 120, 207, 261, 331

BBC Publications for chart on p. 383

The Controller of Her Majesty's Stationery Office for charts on pp. 81, 311, 315, 358

Dover Publications Inc. for drawings on pp. 78, 296, 320 (from **Graphic Works of George Cruikshank**, selected and with an introduction and notes by Richard A. Vogler, New York, 1979)

Format Photographers and Val Wilmer for photograph on p. 111

Free Association Books for cartoons on pp. 54, 328 (from **Is Anybody Out There** by J. F. Batellier, London, 1984)

Lancashire Library, Preston District for drawing on p. 24 (from **The Political Alphabet** by George Cruikshank)

Library of Congress for photograph on p. 34

Manchester Studies Unit for photograph on p. 192

The Mansell Collection for engraving on p. 138 and picture on p. 146

Mirror Group Newspapers for cartoon on p. 44

John Murray Ltd. for advertisements on pp. 186, 271 (from **The Wonderful World of American Advertisements 1865–1900** by Leonard de Vries and Ilonka Van Amstel, London, 1973)

Museum of the American Indian, Heye Foundation for photographs on p. 7

National Museum of Labour History for drawing on p. 69, photograph on p. 195 and engraving on p. 322

National Museums of Canada for photograph (neg. 73462) on p. 62

Network Photographers for photographs on pp. 151, 360

The Photo Source for photographs on pp. 94, 364

Pluto Press for charts on pp. 83, 329

Popperfoto for photograph on p. 390

Punch for cartoon on p. 143

Rex Features for photographs on pp. 109, 115, 340, 377

Times Newspapers Ltd. for chart on p. 93

United Nations for photograph on p. 291

United States Government Printing Office for chart on p. 380

Antony Winterbottom, Spiral Studios, for cartoons on pp. 21, 45, 100, 163, 178, 201, 204, 221, 224, 249, 284, 336, 373, 401

Wolverhampton Council and David Peters for photographs on p. 368

xii

To
Pauline, Kate and Jane
Ian, Timothy and Matthew
Jude
Ben

Section 1 Culture and Socialization

This section looks at some of the basic ideas or concepts that sociologists use to understand human behaviour. It begins with the idea of culture, the learned, shared behaviour of members of society. Comparisons are then made between human and non-human societies in order to develop an understanding of the importance of culture for human behaviour. Some of the main aspects of culture – values, norms, statuses and roles – are then examined. The section ends by showing the importance of socialization – the process by which people learn the culture of their society. Throughout the section comparisons are made between Western and non-Western society in order to illustrate the variety of human behaviour.

1 Culture

Human beings learn how to behave. They share much of their behaviour with other members of the society to which they belong. The learned, shared behaviour of members of a society is known as culture. The following passage examines the importance of culture for human society.

> Many living creatures do not learn how to behave. They have not been taught by their parents, they have not copied older brothers and sisters or imitated adult members of their society. They do not have to learn their behaviour because their actions are directed by instinct. Instincts are instructions about how to behave which are biologically inherited. They guide the salmon's return from the sea to spawn and die in fresh water. They direct the migration of birds and

organize the complex society of ants and bees.

The instinctive behaviour of living creatures belonging to the same species is very similar. For example blackbirds build similar nests at the same time of year. All human beings belong to the same species but studies of various human societies show considerable differences in behaviour. This suggests that the way of life of men and women is learned rather than biologically inherited. If their actions were based on instinct, human beings, as members of the same species, should behave in much the same way.

The following examples of customs concerning marriage and family life indicate the variety of human behaviour. In traditional China, a woman's father or one of her brothers is responsible for finding a husband for her. If a woman does not marry, her entire family is disgraced. When unmarried female missionaries came to China from the West, they were thought to be escaping from the shame brought about by the failure of the men of their household to find them a husband. For a Koryak woman of Siberia, sharing a husband with other wives is an ideal system. It reduces her workload and provides her with company. She cannot understand how Western women could be so selfish as to restrict their husbands to a single wife. Amongst the Cheyenne Indians a son-in-law is expected to provide food for his mother-in-law. However he must never speak to her. Should he find himself alone in her presence, he must cover his head with a buffalo robe.

The above examples are taken from three societies which have different ways of life. Sociologists use the term culture to refer to the way of life of members of a society. Culture includes the values, beliefs, customs, rules and regulations which human beings learn as members of society. People need culture to meet even the most basic of human needs. For example they have no instincts to tell them what is edible and how to prepare food and eat it. They learn these lessons from the culture of their society.

It is essential that culture is not only learned but also shared. Thus without a shared language members of society could not communicate and cooperate effectively. Without rules applying to everybody, there would be disorder in society. Imagine the chaos and confusion that would result in today's society if there were no road traffic regulations. Rules must be both learned and shared.

   Culture then is the learned shared behaviour of members of a society. Without culture human society would not exist.

(adapted in part from **Sociological Perspective** by Ely Chinoy, Random House, New York, 1968 and **The Individual and Culture** by Mary E. Goodman, Dorsey, Homewood, 1967)

1. What is instinctive behaviour?   (4)
2. How does behaviour based on instinct differ from behaviour based on culture?   (4)
3. Why do the examples of different customs concerning marriage and the family suggest that human behaviour is learned rather than instinctive?   (5)
4. Human beings spend considerable time and effort teaching young people the culture of their society. Why do they do this?   (7)

2 Instinct

Many living creatures apart from human beings live in social groups. An understanding of human behaviour can be developed by an examination of non-human societies. The following passage gives a brief description of the social life of honeybees. It shows how a society can be organized on the basis of instinct rather than culture.

   Like human beings, the honeybee lives in societies. It is a social insect. A hive consists of one queen, a few hundred male drones and between twenty and sixty thousand female worker bees. Each honeybee has a part to play in the running of the hive. The queen specializes in the production of eggs. This is her only job and she lays up to 200,000 a year. The male drones have the sole task of fertilizing the queen. They receive food from the worker bees and help themselves from the stores of honey in the hive. In the autumn, at the end of the breeding season, the workers refuse to feed them or allow them access to the stores of honey. The starving drones drop to the bottom of the hive and are pulled out by the workers and left to die.

The worker bees spend the first three weeks of their lives performing household tasks. They build and repair the honey combs from their wax producing glands and feed the newly hatched youngsters from their food producing glands. They clear out the hive removing debris and dead bees which have collected at the bottom. For the remaining two weeks of their lives most worker bees become field bees, foraging for nectar and pollen.

Honeybees live a highly ordered and organized social life. Each bee specializes in particular tasks and has set duties to perform. However, they have not **learned** how to behave. They have not been taught by older members of the colony, they have not imitated other bees. Instead, their behaviour is directed by instinct, by instructions contained in the genes which they inherit from their parents. The behaviour of honeybees is therefore inborn. This can be shown by the ways in which honeybees communicate. When a worker bee discovers a source of food it passes this information on to other bees by dancing on its return to the hive. The dance indicates the distance and direction of the food from the hive. One study suggests that the distance is indicated by the speed at which the bee turns. If the food is 300 yards away it turns 28 times a minute. If it is 3,000 yards away it turns nine times a minute. Worker bees who have never had any contact with other workers can both perform and interpret the dance. These skills are therefore instinctive. Since the bees have had no opportunity to learn from others, their ability to understand and perform the dance must be inborn.

(adapted from **Bees and Beekeeping** by A. V. Pavord, Cassell, London, 1975)

1. Name the three types of honeybees and briefly outline the tasks they perform.   (6)
2. Explain why honeybees do not have to learn the parts they play in society.   (4)
3. What evidence is given in the passage which can be taken as proof that the behaviour of honeybees is based on instinct?   (4)
4. Without instinct the society of honeybees could not exist. Explain this statement.   (6)

3 Animal behaviour

The closer we approach man in the animal kingdom, the less important instincts are for directing behaviour and the more important learned behaviour becomes. It was once thought that the behaviour of all creatures apart from man was based on instinct. A large number of studies, particularly of apes and monkeys, has shown that this view is incorrect. The following study on macaque monkeys illustrates this point.

> For a number of years Japanese scientists have been studying the behaviour of macaque monkeys on islands in northern Japan. On one island the macaques lived in the forest in the interior. The scientists tried to discover whether they could change the behaviour of the monkeys. They began by dumping potatoes in a clearing in the forest. The macaques picked them up, sniffed them inquisitively and tasted them. Gradually they changed their eating habits and potatoes, a food previously unknown to them, became their main diet. The scientists then began moving the potatoes towards the shoreline and the macaques followed. The potatoes were regularly dumped on the beach and the troupe took up residence there rather than in the forest. Then, without any encouragement from the scientists, a number of brand new behaviour patterns developed. Some of the macaques began washing potatoes in the sea before eating them, a practice which was soon adopted by the whole group. Some of the younger monkeys began paddling in the sea then took the plunge and learned how to swim. Their elders followed suit and swimming became normal behaviour for the whole troupe. Finally, some of the more adventurous youngsters began diving into the sea from rocks on the shoreline. Other members of the troupe imitated them but some of the older macaques decided that this time they would not follow the lead of the youngsters.

(adapted from **Sociology: Themes and Perspectives** by Michael Haralambos with Robin Heald, University Tutorial Press, Slough, 1980)

1. List three new behaviour patterns which developed in the macaque troupe. (3)

2. Give three examples of learned behaviour in animals other then macaques. (3)
3. Give one similarity between the ways in which macaques and human beings learn their behaviour. Provide examples to illustrate your answer. (4)
4. Why did the Japanese scientists argue that much of the behaviour of macaque monkeys is learned rather than instinctive? (5)
5. The learned behaviour of monkeys and apes is simple and limited compared with that of human beings. Show briefly with examples that this is the case and suggest why it is so. (5)

4 Culture and values

Values form an important part of the culture of a society. A value is a belief that something is good and worthwhile. It defines what is worth having and worth striving for. Values often vary considerably from society to society. The following description of the major values of traditional Cheyenne society provides a sharp contrast with the values held today in the West.

> The Cheyenne Indians lived on the Great Plains of the United States of America, west of the Mississippi River and east of the Rocky Mountains. The following account describes part of their traditional way of life which came to an end at the close of the last century when they were defeated by the US army and placed on reservations.
> The Cheyenne believe that wealth, in the form of horses and weapons, is not to be hoarded and used by the owner. Instead it is to be given away. Generosity is highly regarded and a person who accumulates wealth and keeps it for himself is looked down upon. A person who gives does not expect an equal amount in return. The greatest gift he can receive is prestige and respect for his generous action.
> Bravery on the battlefield is one of the main ways a man can achieve high standing in the eyes of the tribe. Killing an enemy, however, does not rank as highly as a number of other deeds. Touching or striking an enemy with the hand or a weapon, rescuing a wounded comrade or charging the enemy

Cheyenne warriors

Men in front of lodge during a religious ceremony

Photographs courtesty Museum of American Indian, Heye Foundation alone while the rest of the war party looks on are amongst the highest deeds of bravery. The Cheyenne developed war into a game. Killing large numbers of the enemy is far less important than individual acts of courage which bring great respect from other members of the tribe. The brave deeds of a warrior are recounted at meetings of the warrior societies and sung about by the squaws. They may lead to his appoint-ment to the tribal council and to the position of war chief which means others will follow him into battle and respect his leadership.

The values of Cheyenne society provide goals for its members to aim for and general guidelines for their behaviour. Values, like culture in general, are learned and shared by members of society. Some sociologists argue that shared values form the basis for social unity or social solidarity. They help to bind people into a close knit group. Because they share the same values, members of society are likely to see others as 'people like themselves'. They will therefore have a sense of belonging to a social group, they will feel a part of the wider society. In this respect shared values form the basis for unity in society.

(adapted from **The Cheyennes** by E. Adamson Hoebel, Holt, Reinhart and Winston, New York, 1960)

1. What are the two major values of Cheyenne society?   (2)
2. Identify two major values from your own society.   (2)
3. How do the Cheyenne express the values of their society in their behaviour?   (4)
4. Give three rewards a Cheyenne warrior might receive for being successful in terms of the values of his society.   (3)
5. How does the Cheyenne attitude towards wealth differ from that in your own society?   (4)
6. a Why are shared values beneficial to society?   (2)
   b How might it be harmful to society if people held a wide range of differing values?   (3)

5 Culture and norms

Values provide general guidelines for conduct. Norms are much more specific. They define appropriate and acceptable behaviour in particular situations. A society may value privacy but this value provides only a general guide to behaviour. Norms define how the value of privacy is translated into action in particular situations and circumstances. Thus in British society norms relating to privacy state that a person's mail must not be opened by other people. An individual's house must not be entered without his permission. A person's 'private life' is his own concern and others must not pry into his personal affairs. In this way a series of norms direct how people should behave in terms of the value of privacy.

Norms guide behaviour in all aspects of social life. There are norms of dress which define the types of clothing appropriate for members of each sex, age group and social situation. There are norms governing behaviour with family, friends, neighbours and strangers. There are norms which define acceptable behaviour in the home, classroom and workplace, at a party, wedding and funeral, in a cinema, supermarket and doctor's waiting room.

As a part of culture, norms are learned, shared and vary from society to society. This can be seen clearly from norms concerning food. Amongst the Bedouin of North Africa, sheep's eyes are regarded as a delicacy whereas in the West they are not even considered fit to eat. The Bedouin eat with their fingers and a loud and prolonged burp at the end of a meal is a compliment to the host. In the West such behaviour would be considered the height of bad manners. Or, as a sociologist would say, it would not conform to Western norms of eating behaviour.

Norms provide order in society. Imagine a situation in which 'anything goes'. The result is likely to be confusion and disorder. This can sometimes be seen in the classroom if teacher and students fail to establish a set of rules for conducting a lesson. Norms help to make social life predictable and comprehensible. If there were no norms stating how people should express pleasure or irritation, warmth or hostility it would be difficult to understand how others felt, to predict their behaviour and respond to them in appropriate ways. Norms also provide practical solutions to everyday problems. Take an apparently simple operation like cooking, cracking open and eating a boiled egg. There are norms directing the whole operation. Social life would be much less efficient if such methods had to be constantly re-invented by trial and error.

Lacking instincts, human beings need norms to guide and direct their actions. In a thousand and one areas of social life norms define appropriate and acceptable behaviour.

(adapted in part from **Sociology** by Leonard Broom and Philip Selznick, Harper and Row, New York, 1977)

1. It has often been claimed that a high value is placed on human life in Western society. Describe three norms which direct behaviour in terms of this value.   (6)
2. Briefly outline the norms which define acceptable behaviour at a party and in a doctor's waiting room and indicate how they differ.   (6)
3. Using your own examples, outline two ways in which norms are useful for the operation of human society.   (8)

6 Culture, status and role

All the world's a stage
And all the men and women merely players.

In these lines Shakespeare makes the point that in society people have certain positions and play certain parts. In sociological terminology, they hold statuses and play roles. For example in Western society there are occupational statuses such as bricklayer, nurse, clerk and solicitor and family statuses such as father, mother, brother and sister. A status can be ascribed or achieved. An ascribed status is largely fixed and unchangeable, the individual having little or no say in the matter. Many are fixed at birth such as the gender statuses of male and female. In pre-industrial society status was often ascribed, a boy taking on the status of his father, a girl that of her mother. Thus most Cheyenne males automatically became hunters and warriors like their fathers before them while females became wives and mothers and gathered roots and berries as their mothers had done. In present day British society, aristocratic titles provide an example of an ascribed status. Prince Charles is heir to the throne simply because he is the eldest son of the reigning monarch. There are however, occasions when an ascribed status can be changed. A monarch can abdicate as in the case of Edward VIII who was forced to give up the English throne in 1936 because he intended to marry an American divorcee.

An ascribed status is imposed upon a person. There is little he or she can do about it. An achieved status, on the other hand, involves some degree of choice and direct and positive action. A person chooses to get married and adopt the status of a married man or woman. There is often an element of choice in selecting an occupation in modern industrial societies. An achieved status, as the name suggests, results partly from individual achievement. To some extent a person achieves his or her job as an architect, librarian or joiner on the basis of ability and effort.

Each social status is accompanied by a role. Roles define the expected and acceptable behaviour for those occupying particular statuses. Thus the role of doctor states how a doctor is expected to behave. It is a collection of norms defining how the part of a doctor should be played. Roles are a part of culture and often differ considerably from society to society. In traditional Cheyenne society the role of women is mainly domestic – caring for children, preparing and cooking food and making clothing. Hunting is left to the men. However hunting formed an important part of the female role amongst the Australian aborigines of Tasmania. The women hunted seals and opossums (small tree-dwelling animals).

Roles are performed in relation to other roles. Thus the role of teacher is played in relation to the role of student, the role of husband in relation to the role of wife. Tasks can often be accomplished more effectively if those concerned adopt their appropriate roles. Thus a doctor can do his job more efficiently if he and his patients stick to their roles rather than also playing the part of old friends or courting couples. Roles provide social life with order and predictability. If teacher and student play their roles, they know what to do and how to do it. Knowing each others' roles they are able to predict and understand what the other is doing. Like other aspects of culture roles guide and direct behaviour in human society.

(adapted from **Sociological Perspective** by Ely Chinoy, Random House, New York, 1968 and **Sociology: Themes and Perspectives** by Michael Haralambos with Robin Heald, University Tutorial Press, Slough, 1980)

1. List your own statuses and identify which are ascribed and which are achieved. (2)
2. a Give one example of an ascribed status that can be changed. (1)
   b Briefly outline the difficulties that such a change might create for the individual concerned. (3)
3. Select one occupational status in modern industrial society and suggest how it is achieved on the basis of ability and effort. (4)
4. Roles are learned rather than instinctive. How do the roles of Cheyenne and Tasmanian women provide evidence to support this statement? (4)
5. Outline, with your own examples, two ways in which roles are useful for the operation of human society. (6)

7 Socialization (1)

In view of the importance of values, norms, statuses and roles, it is essential for the wellbeing of society that culture is effectively learned by its members. The process by which people learn the culture of their society is known as socialization. Socialization begins at birth and continues throughout a person's life. During its early years, the child learns many of the basic behaviour patterns of its society. This is the period of primary socialization, the first and probably the most important part of the socialization process. In practically every society the family bears the main responsibility for primary socialization. As the child moves into the wider society, secondary socialization begins. During this process the child learns from a wider range of people and institutions. Thus in modern industrial societies, schools play an important part in secondary socialization.

Something of the importance of the socialization process may be seen from the following extract. It describes the behaviour of two girls who, for a large part of their short lives, had been isolated from other human beings.

In 1920 two girls were reportedly discovered in a wolf den in Bengal, India. Aged about two and eight years, they were taken to an orphanage where they were looked after by the Reverend J. A. L. Singh and his wife. The younger child, Amala died soon after she arrived at the orphanage, the elder girl, Kamala, remained in the orphanage until 1929 when she too died. Despite the fact that Amala and Kamala were called 'wolf-children' and found in a wolf's den, there is no evidence that they were actually raised by wolves. The Reverend Singh wrote the following description of their behaviour in 1926.

At the present time Kamala can utter about forty words. She is able to form a few sentences, each sentence containing two, or at the most, three words. She never talks unless spoken to, and when spoken to she may or may not reply. She is obedient to Mrs Singh and myself only. Kamala is possessed of very acute hearing and evidences an exceedingly acute animal-like sense of smell. She can smell meat at a great distance. Never weeps or smiles but has a 'smiling appearance'. Shed a single tear when Amala died and would not leave the place where she lay dead. She is learning very slowly to imitate. Does not now play at all and does not mingle with other children. Once both Amala and Kamala somewhat liked the company of an infant by the name of Benjamin while he was crawling and learning to talk. But one day they gave him such a biting and scratching that the infant was frightened and would never approach the wolf-children again. Amala and Kamala liked the company of Mrs Singh, and Kamala, the surviving one of the pair, is much attached to her. The eyes of the children possessed a peculiar glare, such as that observed in the eyes of dogs or cats in the dark. Up to the present time Kamala sees better at night than during the daytime and seldom sleeps after midnight. The children used to cry or howl in a peculiar voice neither animal nor human. Kamala still makes these noises at times. She is averse to all cleanliness, and serves the calls of nature anywhere, wherever she may happen to be at the time. Used to tear her clothes off. Hence a loin cloth was stitched to her in such a fashion that she could not open or tear it. Kamala used to eat and drink like a dog, lowering her mouth down to the plate, and never used her hands for the purpose of eating or drinking. She would gnaw a big bone on the ground and would rub it

Kamala and Amala soon after they were brought to the orphanage

Kamala receiving a biscuit from Mrs Singh

at times in order to separate the meat from the bone. At the present time she uses her hands for eating and walks straight on two legs but cannot run at all.

(letter quoted in **Human Societies** edited by Geoffrey Hurd, Routledge & Kegan Paul, London, 1973, pp. 95–96)

1. The children had apparently spent much of their lives isolated from other human beings. Why did this prevent them from behaving in ways which would be considered normal in the society into which they were born?   (4)
2. List four items of Kamala's behaviour which suggest that she was beginning to act in ways considered normal in human society.   (4)
3. a Briefly compare what Kamala had learned by the age of fourteen after six years in the orphanage with what most children have learned by the age of five.   (3)
   b Why does this suggest that primary socialization is vital to effectively learn the culture of society?   (3)
4. a Give three possible reactions by people in the wider society to Kamala's behaviour which would make it difficult for her to cope outside the orphanage.   (3)
   b Suggest why people would respond to her in these ways.   (3)

8 Socialization (2)

The socialization of young people can be seen as a series of lessons which prepare them for their adult roles. During childhood people learn many of the basic skills they will require in adult life. This is clearly seen from the following description of children's games and activities in the society of the Mbuti pygmies.

The Mbuti pygmies live in the tropical rain forest in the north-east corner of Zaire in central Africa. They are hunters and gatherers, the men being mainly responsible for hunting and the women for gathering edible fruit, berries and roots. Nets are often used for hunting. They are stretched into a long arc and women and children drive game such as antelope into the nets where they are killed by the men with spears and bows and arrows. Arrows, usually tipped with poison, are also used to kill birds and monkeys. The pygmies favourite food is honey. For two months of the year they spend considerable time and effort breaking into hives in the trees to extract honey. They are almost as much at home in the trees as they are on the ground. They take to the trees to avoid dangerous animals such as the forest buffalo and to chase game.

Women are mainly responsible for cooking. They roast plantains – a banana-like fruit – in hot ashes and make stews of meat, mushrooms and chopped leaves. They gather wood for the fire and carry water to the camp site. Women make the huts from a framework of saplings – young trees – thatched with broad leaves. They also make the carrying baskets which are used for transporting food and equipment.

Pygmy children enjoy their early years. They love climbing trees and swinging on vines. Some children actually begin climbing trees before they can walk. One of their favourite games involves half a dozen climbing to the top of a young tree and bending it over until the top touches the ground. Then they all jump off together. If anyone is too slow, he goes flying upwards as the tree springs back. His friends are highly amused and laugh and jeer as he swings in the air.

Like children in all societies, pygmy children like to imitate older people. Their parents encourage them to do this. Fathers make tiny bows for their sons with blunt arrows made of softwood. They may also give their sons a strip of hunting net. Mothers weave tiny carrying baskets for their daughters much to the enjoyment of all concerned. Boys and girls often 'play house', building a miniature house from sticks and leaves. The boys shoot their arrows at plantains and ears of corn and proudly carry them back to the play house. They are then cooked and eaten in a serious and solemn manner.

Hunting is a favourite childhood game. Boys stretch out their pieces of hunting net while girls beat the ground with bunches of leaves driving an old frog towards the net. If a frog cannot be found, a grandparent will be asked to imitate an antelope. He is chased round the camp and finally driven into the net. The children then jump on the unfortunate grandparent and playfully pound him with their fists.

(adapted from **The Forest People** by Colin M. Turnbull, Jonathan Cape, London, 1961)

1. What evidence does the extract contain to indicate the role of parents in the socialization process?   (4)
2. How do the games of pygmy boys help to prepare them for their adult roles?   (6)
3. How do the games of pygmy girls help to prepare them for their adult roles?   (6)
4. Select one children's game from your own society and suggest how it might prepare young people for adult life.   (4)

Section 2 Social Control

Every society has methods of making its members toe the line, of making sure that they stick to the straight and narrow. These methods are known as mechanisms of social control. They ensure that most of the people most of the time conform to society's norms and values. Section 1 indicated the importance of culture. It must be learned and shared for human society to operate effectively. But learning culture is one thing, acting in terms of it is another. Every society requires some mechanisms of social control to make sure its members follow the guidelines of their culture. For social order to exist norms and values are necessary and conformity to them must be enforced.

The ultimate and most obvious form of social control is physical violence. In one form or another it exists in every known human society. Under certain circumstances some have the right to use physical violence against others in an attempt to control their behaviour. The police and armed forces are obvious examples in modern industrial societies. Other forms of social control are less obvious. Few would regard the family, the peer group, religion and the mass media as powerful instruments of social control. Yet many sociologists would see them as far more important and effective than the whole state system of control which ranges from Parliament which enacts the law to the police, judiciary and prison service which enforce it.

1 The Family

The importance of the family in the socialization process was discussed in Section 1. This point is now re-examined focussing on the family as an agency of social control.

> Without the support of older members of its species, a newborn human baby could not survive. Alone it cannot meet

basic human needs, such as the need for food, or learn the necessary knowledge and skills for living in human society. Most young people are raised in families. During its early years the child is largely dependent upon its immediate family and as a result its parents have considerable power to direct its behaviour. The child is at its most impressionable during infancy. This means that its behaviour can be more easily shaped and moulded than in later life. In view of these factors, the family can be a powerful mechanism of social control.

For society to operate effectively its members must learn social norms and values. But simply knowing the culture of their society does not necessarily mean that people will act in terms of it. There is much more likelihood of them doing so if they actually want to conform to their culture. During primary socialization within the family many children not only learn the basic norms and values of their society but also become committed to them. They therefore feel that the norms and values are right and proper and experience guilt if they depart from them. In other words they develop a conscience which is rather like an 'inner policeman' preventing or punishing behaviour which deviates from accepted patterns with feelings of guilt and remorse. The child's behaviour will therefore be guided by internal controls – the voice of its conscience.

The family has often been seen as ideally suited to developing a conscience in new members of society. Once a deep emotional bond has been established between the child and its parents, any threat to that bond fills the child with anxiety. Rather than risk the loss of love, the child adopts the norms and values taught by its parents. It develops feelings of guilt and anxiety at the thought of deviating from the behaviour approved by its parents.

Parents use a wide variety of techniques for controlling the behaviour of their children. The Cheyenne do not tolerate babies crying, partly because it could give away the position of the camp to an enemy but also because they dislike anyone forcing their attention and demands on others. Infants are kept in cradleboards carried on their mothers' backs. When they cry they are taken away from the camp and the cradleboard is hung on a bush until the crying stops. After a few hours the squawling infant realizes that its noisy behaviour leads to complete rejection by its parents and soon learns to change its tune. Cheyenne babies are never struck, scolded, or threatened for bad behaviour. However good behaviour is consistently rewarded with praise, love and affection. Parents constantly encourage their children to be brave, generous, honest, hardworking and respectful to their elders.

A contrast to Cheyenne child training practices is provided by some of the methods used by many English working class parents. Threats and teasing are often used as the following statements from mothers indicate.

I say, 'A policeman will come and take you away, and you'll have no Mummy and Daddy.'
I tell her God will do something to her hand if she smacks me.
I've told him I'll have to put him in a home if he's naughty.
She picks her nose – I tell her it's dirty and her nose will fall off.

Children's behaviour is not simply shaped by responding to the rewards and punishments handed out by their parents.

Much of the time they simply copy their mothers and fathers. They often identify with their parents and as a result want to be like them. Mothers provide role models for their daughters, fathers for their sons. The constant example provided by someone they want to be like is a powerful control over the child's behaviour.

Lessons learned during the child's early years often last a lifetime. As the following quotation suggests, this may well be essential for the wellbeing of human society.

Every day society is submitted to a terrible invasion: within it a multitude of small barbarians is born. They would quickly overthrow the whole social order and all the institutions of society if they were not well disciplined and educated (R. Pinot – quoted in Goodman, 1967, p. 128).

(adapted from **The Individual and Culture** by M.E. Goodman, Dorsey, Homewood, 1967; **The Cheyennes** by E.A. Hoebel, Holt, Rinehart & Winston, New York, 1960 and **The Family and its Future** by J. and E. Newson, J.A. Churchill, Edinburgh, 1970)

1. Why do parents have considerable power to control the behaviour of their children? (5)
2. Why is the development of a conscience often seen as a far more effective means of social control than institutions such as the police and armed forces? (4)
3. Why is the method used by Cheyenne mothers to prevent their babies from crying so effective? (3)
4. The threats used by English mothers sometimes involve backing up the mother's authority with that of an outside authority figure. With reference to two of the outside authority figures mentioned, suggest why their use might be an effective means of controlling the child's behaviour. (4)
5. 'Like mother, like daughter, like father, like son.' What evidence is provided in the passage to explain how this might happen? (4)

2 Religion

Religion may be defined as a belief in some form of supernatural power which influences or controls people's lives. Thus Melford

Spiro defines religion as 'beliefs in superhuman beings and in their power to assist or harm man'. Religion promises rewards such as everlasting bliss to those who follow its teachings and punishments such as eternal damnation for those who do not. In this respect it can be seen as a mechanism of social control. Often religious teachings and commandments are similar to the values of society. This means that people are more likely to conform to social values. In such cases religion strengthens and reinforces the values of society. Religious beliefs may also help to maintain the structure of society. They may, for example, support the position of men and women and reinforce the power of princes and kings. In doing so religion acts as a mechanism of social control. The following extracts illustrate these points.

> You shall not kill.
> You shall not commit adultery.
> You shall not steal.

(Three of the Ten Commandments of the Christian religion).

1. Which social values do the above commandments support?   (3)
2. How do religious commandments strengthen and reinforce social values?   (5)

> Neither was the man created for the woman; but
>   the woman for the man.
> Wives, submit yourselves unto your own
>   husbands, as it is fit in the Lord.

(St. Paul's interpretation of early Christian beliefs about the relationship between men and women).

3. Briefly explain the position of women in society contained in the above quotations.   (3)
4. How can the fact that these beliefs are religious give them power to control the behaviour of women?   (5)

> In ancient Egypt from about 2700 to 2000 BC, the pharaohs or kings were regarded as gods. State officials such as magistrates, tax collectors and governors of the regions of

The divine right of kings – The church gives its blessing to royal power

Egypt were directly responsible to the pharaoh. They were his representatives. They voiced his wishes and commands and therefore spoke with divine authority. After their lives as gods and men ended, the pharaohs lived on as gods. They were placed in pyramids, their eternal homes, whose grandeur reflected their status.

(adapted from **The Culture of Ancient Egypt** by John A. Wilson, Phoenix Books, Chicago, 1956)

5. How can being a god as well as a king strengthen the position of a monarch. Use information from the above passage in your answer.   (4)

3 The peer group

A peer group is a group whose members share a similar status in society. Members of peer groups are often of a similar age such as children's play groups and teenage gangs. They usually share a similar social situation such as workers on the shopfloor and teachers in the classroom. Peer groups are important agencies of social control. Because most people want to be accepted by members of their group, they will usually conform to peer group norms. If they do not they risk rejection by the group. The following passage indicates the power of the peer group to control the behaviour of its members and to enforce group norms.

From 1927 to 1932, a famous study of workers' behaviour was conducted at the Hawthorne works of the Western Electric company in Chicago. What follows is a small part of the findings of this research. One work group, made up of fourteen men, connected and soldered wires to terminals, which formed components for telephone equipment. The men were paid a basic wage plus a bonus if they produced more than a certain number of completed units. The bonus was shared out equally amongst all members of the group. The managers thought that the bonus scheme would result in the men working as hard as they could so as to earn as much money as possible. In practice this did not happen.

Members of the work group established their own norm for output. It was below the level that could have been reached if each man worked as hard as he could. The men believed that if they worked flat out then the supervisors would begin to expect a much higher output. This might lead to the level at which bonus was paid being raised. They also felt that if they reduced their output too much it would give supervisors a reason to 'bawl them out'. To avoid these problems the workers produced roughly the same amount from week to week.

The norm regulating the workers' output was enforced in various ways. Anybody working too fast was ridiculed as a 'speed king' or a 'ratebuster'. Those producing too little were called 'chiselers'. What the men called 'binging' was one way of slowing people down or speeding them up. This involved hitting a worker on the upper arm. As one man said to a 'speed king'. 'If you don't quit work I'll bing you'. He then struck his workmate and chased him round the shopfloor.

The work group also developed a norm about relationships between workers and their supervisors. It stated that a man should not give information to supervisors which might get one of his workmates into trouble. Anyone who did so was labelled as a 'squealer'.

(adapted from **The Management and the Worker** by F. J. Roethlisberger and W. J. Dickson, Harvard University Press, Cambridge, 1939)

1. Identify two ways in which workers were punished for failing to conform to the group norm for output. (4)
2. Suggest two further ways in which workers might have been punished for breaking the output norm. (4)
3. Suggest two rewards a worker might receive for conforming to the norms of the work group. (4)
4. Members of peer groups often insist on strong group loyalty and try to protect each other from outsiders. What evidence of this type of behaviour is contained in the passage? (4)
5. Why do the rewards and punishments of peer groups usually provide effective control over the behaviour of their members? (4)

4 Significant others

Significant others are people who matter to an individual. They usually include his or her immediate family, friends, neighbours and workmates. People are concerned about what significant others think about them. Their approval makes them feel good, their disapproval upsets them. Because the opinion of significant others is held so highly, they can play an important part in controlling the behaviour of an individual. People often conform to social norms in order to gain the approval of significant others and to avoid their disapproval. The following extracts illustrate these points. They are taken from the autobiography of Long Lance, a Blackfoot Indian.

The Blackfoot Indians lived on the plains of Western Canada. Children were taught the skills of horse riding from an early age. One of Long Lance's earliest recollections was falling off a horse. He was picked up by his eldest brother and planted firmly on the horse's back. His brother said, 'Now, you stay there! You are four years old, and if you cannot ride a horse, we will put girls' clothing on you and let you grow up a woman.'

1. Why was this remark effective in controlling the young boy's behaviour? Note in your answer the possible reactions of significant others to the boy if his brother's threat had been carried out.　　　(5)

Fathers were responsible for the physical training of the Blackfoot boys. They wanted to harden their bodies and make them brave and strong. Fathers used to whip their sons each morning with fir branches. Far from disliking this treatment, the youngsters proudly displayed the welts produced by the whipping. Sometimes they were whipped in public and they competed to see who could stand the most pain. Some would endure until all the branches were worn away. Their fathers would then 'hand them the stub, which we would keep and display with considerable pride during the rest of our young lives'.

2. With some reference to the extract, suggest how the desire for respect from significant others is an important factor in social control.　　　(5)

When he was about six years old, Long Lance would play a game with his friends. They would place burning pine needles on the backs of their hands to see who could let them burn down to ashes. 'If there was anyone among us who could not stand the pain, we would ridicule him.'

3. The childhood peer group is one example of an individual's significant others. With some reference to the extract, suggest how the peer group controls the behaviour of its members.　(5)

Blackfoot mothers spent long hours telling their children the legends of the tribe. Long Lance recalls that, 'We had a legend for everything that was good, and the more we youngsters lived up to the legends which our mothers told us the more highly respected we were in the tribe.' Children were told stories about the 'great shame' befalling those who told lies and the prestige which results from courage and brave deeds. Long Lance states, 'We had no Bible as the white boys have; so our mothers trained us to live right by telling us legends of how all the good things started to be good.'

(adapted from **Long Lance** by Chief Buffalo Child Long Lance, Corgi Books, London, 1956)

4. Using information from the extract, suggest the part played by significant others in reinforcing the message and moral of the legends and stories.   (5)

5 The mass media (1)

The mass media refer to means of communicating with large numbers of people without direct personal contact. They include television, radio, newspapers, magazines, comics, books, films and advertising billboards. The mass media are a major source of information and ideas. These can shape people's attitudes and so to some degree direct their behaviour. Many researchers have seen the mass media in modern industrial society as instruments of social control. In particular they are seen to support the status quo, the established order in society and to oppose any threat to that order. The following passage examines the BBC in the light of these views.

In Britain the BBC in its broadcasts on radio and TV aims to be 'impartial', 'neutral' and to present balanced views. An internal BBC circular on 'Principles and practice in news and current affairs' lays down a number of guidelines. Broadcasts should not 'offend against good taste or decency, or be likely to encourage crime and disorder, or be offensive to public feeling'. Producers of radio and television programmes should stay 'not only within the Constitution (but also) within the consensus (i.e. general public agreement) about basic moral values'.

There are, however, certain things which do not merit neutral and impartial treatment. IRA 'extremism' in Northern Ireland is a case in point. Interviews with IRA representatives can only be broadcast 'after the most serious consideration' and in such a way as to make it clear that the BBC is opposed to their 'indiscriminate terrorist methods'. The rules governing broadcasting mention Lord Reith's (the then Director-General of the BBC) refusal in 1926 to transmit anything which 'might have prolonged or sought to justify the General Strike while still providing authentic, impartial news of the situation'. This example is used in the circular to illustrate the general approach which should be taken by the BBC.

As a general rule BBC programmes are controlled by BBC employees – producers, directors, etc. – who are bound by the rules. The man in the street has few opportunities to broadcast his views to the nation. However in 1973 the BBC began a television series entitled 'Open Door' which gave voluntary groups a chance to put out their own programmes. Yet limits were placed on their freedom of expression. They were not allowed to 'promote a political party or group, or to pursue an industrial dispute'.

(adapted from **Class in a Capitalist Society** by John Westergaard and Henrietta Resler, Penguin, Harmondsworth, 1976, pp. 269–71)

1. What evidence is contained in the first paragraph to support the view that radio and television are mechanisms of social control?

(6)

2. What evidence does the passage contain to suggest that the BBC will oppose threats to the established order in society? (5)

3. In view of the evidence in the passage, can the BBC be seen as 'neutral' and 'impartial'? (5)

4. Can the 'Open Door' series be seen as a rejection of the view that the BBC supports the established order in society? (4)

6 The mass media (2)

The following extract summarizes the results of research conducted in the USA on the portrayal of women in television commercials. The general conclusion from these studies is that TV commercials reinforce the traditional role of women in society. In this respect they can be seen as an instrument of social control since they may well be a means of keeping women 'in their place'.

> Woman...
> We insult her every day on TV
> And wonder why she has no guts or confidence.

Media portrayal of women has been a concern of the women's movement since the 1960s. Early criticism focussed on commercials.

Women understood the spirit in which advertisements were singled out for criticism. Each advertisement was more than an affront in itself; it symbolized the use of women as commercial props.

Television is the most pervasive medium. Children in their pre-school years watch about 24 hours a week. Older children and adults spend even more time with television. By the time a student finishes high school, she or he has seen more than 350,000 commercials. What do these commercials say about women and men?

The studies reviewed in this section document five aspects of commercials: voice-overs (offscreen narrators), roles, activities, settings, and the ages of women and men. Between 1972 and 1978, at least 11 studies reported the percentage of female and male voice-overs. Each of the voice-over studies was conducted by different researchers sampling different commercials in different years. Yet they agree that the voice of authority that tells us what to buy is male. Overall, the studies indicate that about 90% of the voice-overs are male and only 10% are female. Five studies provide evidence on the number and kinds of roles that women and men portray. The finding by Dominick and Rauch that commercials show women in considerably fewer roles than men (18 roles for women and 43 roles for men) has been confirmed by the research group known as Women on Words and Images (21 roles for women and 40 roles for men). The most common role for a woman is that of family member – wife, mother, grand-mother, or daughter. Data from five studies show that an average of 60% of the women are shown in family roles while only 18% of the men are shown in comparable roles. Closely related is the finding that men are more often shown as employed than women (67% of those employed were males). Men are also given the high-status jobs (60% of the men and 14% of the women had high-status jobs). Women are often shown doing housework or being concerned with their physical appearance. Summing up the results of several studies, we find that about 38% ot the women and only 11% of the men are involved in cleaning, washing, and cooking. Women on Words and Images found that nine women and one man did the cooking on the set of commercials they monitored. When not occupied with domestic chores, women are shown striving to improve their physical appearance. But what about men? Men are the beneficiaries of women's activities. They eat the food, wear the laundry, enjoy their homes and their wives' appearance, and are nursed back to health.

Findings concerning the settings of commercials complete the pattern. Women work inside the home and men work outside. According to three studies, approximately 43% of the women and 18% of the men are shown working in the home and 32% of the women and 63% of the men are shown working outside. Contrary to the statistical fact that more than 50% of American women are over 40 years old, television commercials show only about 25% of the women as over 40. Although the average age of women in the popula-tion is somewhat higher than that of men, television reverses this fact and shows about 45% of the men as over 40. For example, Alice Courtney and Thomas Whipple found that 16% of the women and 44% of the men in the commercials they monitored were over 40. Our society has long emphasized youthfulness, but it is women in the 1970s who must forever be young. Television reinforces this in two ways; actresses are young, and they sell the concept of youthful appearance in products such as Oil of Ulay and Liquid Ivory Soap. Television tells women that they should be young and offers them many ways to imitate the image they see.

Commercials broadcast during children's programming were monitored in four studies that document two important aspects of the commercials children see on Saturday mornings: roles portrayed by women and men and the relative presence of women and men.

When a little girl watches television on Saturday morning, she may wonder about her place in the world. Not only is she not seen at all in the exciting action commercials, she is not seen very much in any of the commercials. Two studies found that women and girls were about 34% of all characters in commercials while men and boys were about 66%. Other studies analysing the relative presence of girls and boys alone or together in commercials show that boys and men are much more visible than girls and women.

(from **Women and the Mass Media** edited by Matilda Butler and William Paisley, Human Sciences Press, New York, 1981, pp. 68, 69, 70, 71, 76)

1. What do the authors mean when they state that, 'Television is the most pervasive medium'? (3)
2. Why are researchers particularly concerned about the effects of television on children in their pre-school years? Make some reference to the extract in your answer. (4)
3. Most studies of the mass media suggest that they reinforce existing attitudes and opinions rather than changing them.
   a What traditional views of women might be reinforced by the commercials analysed in the extract? (8)
   b How might this help to maintain the position of women in society? (5)

7 Racialism and social control

Introductory sociology courses often present social control systems in a very positive light. They are seen as a good thing. Social control is said to be beneficial for society because it enables its members to work together and co-operate in relative peace and harmony. However there is another side to the picture. Many aspects of social control can be seen as harmful both to society and to its members. One such system which would probably be seen as unacceptable by most members of present day Western society is described in the following extract. It is taken from the autobiography of Richard Wright which was first published in 1937. Wright, a black American, describes how he experienced the 'Jim Crow system', in the southern states of the USA. This system of racial prejudice and discrimination kept the majority of black Americans on the lowest level of society. It employed a variety of mechanisms of social control to keep them 'in their place'. Often blacks encouraged other blacks to 'know their place' fearing that friends and relatives might be beaten up, jailed and even lynched for stepping out of line.

The back yard of Richard's house was paved with cinders. He and his friends used to have great fun throwing them at each other. One day Richard's gang got into a fight with a group of white boys. The black boys threw cinders but the whites replied with a barrage of broken bottles. One caught Richard behind the ear opening a deep gash which needed three stitches. He was furious. It wasn't fair to fight with broken bottles. All a cinder could do was leave a bruise. When Richard told his mother what had happened he was astonished at her reaction. She grabbed a barrel stave, dragged me home, stripped me naked, and beat me till I had a fever of one hundred and two. She would smack my rump with the stave, and while the skin was still smarting, impart to me gems of Jim Crow wisdom. I was never to throw cinders any more. I was never to fight any more wars. I was never, never, under any conditions, to fight white folks again. And they were absolutely right in clouting me with the broken milk bottle. Didn't I know she was working hard every day in the hot kitchens of the white folks to make money to take care of me? When was I ever going to learn to be a good boy? She couldn't be bothered with my fights. She finished by telling me that I ought to be thankful to God as long as I lived that they didn't kill me.

All that night I was delirious and could not sleep. Each time I closed my eyes I saw monstrous white faces suspended from the ceiling, leering at me.

Richard got his first job with an optical company in Jackson, Mississippi. He recalls the interview. The morning I applied I stood straight and neat before the boss, answering all his questions with sharp yessirs and nosirs. I was very careful to pronounce my **sirs** distinctly, in order that he might

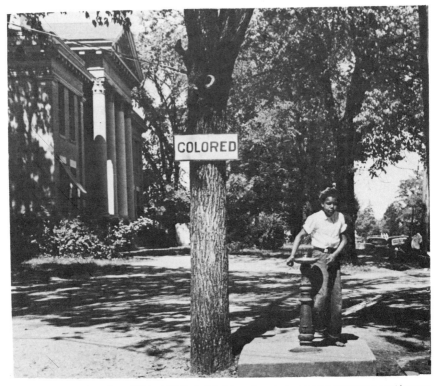

Halifax, North Carolina, USA, 1938. A drinking fountain on the county courthouse lawn for blacks only.

know that I was polite, that I knew where I was, and that I knew he was a **white** man. I wanted that job badly.

'Boy, how would you like to learn something around here?' he asked me.

'I'd like it fine, sir,' I said, happy. I had visions of 'working my way up'. Even Negroes have those visions.

'All right,' he said, 'Come on.'

I followed him to the small factory.

'Pease,' he said to a white man of about thirty-five, 'this is Richard. He's going to work for us.' Pease looked at me and nodded. I was then taken to a white boy of about seventeen.

'Morrie, this is Richard, who's going to work for us.'

'Whut yuh sayin' there, boy!' Morrie boomed at me.

'Fine!' I answered.

The boss instructed these two to help me, teach me, give me jobs to do, and let me learn what I could in my spare time. My wages were five dollars a week.

I worked hard, trying to please. For the first month I got along O.K. Both Pease and Morrie seemed to like me. But one thing was missing. And I kept thinking about it. I was not learning anything and nobody was volunteering to help me. Thinking they had forgotten that I was to learn something about the mechanics of grinding lenses, I asked Morrie one day to tell me about the work. He grew red.

'Whut yuh tryin' t' do, nigger, get smart?' he asked.

'Naw; I ain' tryin' t' git smart,' I said.

'Well, don't, if yuh know whut's good for yuh!'

I was puzzled. Maybe he just doesn't want to help me, I thought. I went to Pease.

'Say, are yuh crazy, you black bastard?' Pease asked me, his grey eyes growing hard.

I spoke out, reminding him that the boss had said I was to be given a chance to learn something.

'Nigger, you think you're **white**, don't you?'

'Naw, sir!'

'Well, you're acting mighty like it!'

'But, Mr. Pease, the boss said . . .'

Pease shook his fist in my face. 'This is a **white** man's work around here, and you better watch yourself!'

From then on they changed toward me. They said good-morning no more. When I was a bit slow performing some duty, I was called a lazy black son-of-a-bitch.

Richard's days at the optical company were now numbered. He had stepped over the line. Pease and Morrie made his life at work unbearable. Richard finally called it a day when they threatened to beat him up with a steel bar. He was surprised at his family's reaction. When I told the folks at home what had happened, they called me a fool. They told me that I must never again attempt to exceed my boundaries. When you are working for white folks, they said, you got to 'stay in your place' if you want to keep working.

This lesson was hammered home to Richard on his next job. He was slowly but surely learning how blacks were expected to behave.

My Jim Crow education continued on my next job, which was portering in a clothing store. One morning, while polishing brass out front, the boss and his twenty-year-old son got out of their car and half dragged and half kicked a Negro woman into the store. A policeman standing at the corner looked on, twirling his night-stick. I watched out of the corner of my eye, never slackening the strokes of my chamois upon the brass. After a few minutes, I heard shrill screams coming from the rear of the store. Later the woman stumbled out, bleeding, crying, and holding her stomach. When she reached the end of the block, the policeman grabbed her and accused her of being a drunk. Silently, I watched him throw her into a patrol wagon.

When I went to the rear of the store, the boss and his son were washing their hands in the sink. They were chuckling. The floor was bloody and strewn with wisps of hair and clothing. No doubt I must have appeared pretty shocked, for the boss slapped me reassuringly on the back.

'Boy, that's what we do to niggers when they don't want to pay their bills', he said, laughing.

His son looked at me and grinned. 'Here, hava cigarette,' he said.

Not knowing what to do, I took it. He lit his and held the match for me. This was a gesture of kindness, indicating that even if they had beaten the poor old woman, they would not beat me if I knew enough to keep my mouth shut.

'Yes, sir,' I said, and asked no questions.

After they had gone, I sat on the edge of a packing box and stared at the bloody floor till the cigarette went out. That day at noon, while eating in a hamburger joint, I told my fellow Negro porters what had happened. No one seemed surprised. One fellow, after swallowing a huge bite, turned to me and asked:

'Huh! Is tha' all they did t' her?'

(Abridged excerpt from pages 4–9 of **Uncle Tom's Children** by Richard Wright. Copyright, 1937 by Richard Wright. Renewed 1965 by Ellen Wright. By permission of Harper & Row, Publishers Inc.)

1. What evidence does the extract contain to indicate that the status of blacks is lower than that of whites?   (5)

2. How did Richard's family encourage him to accept his place in the Jim Crow system?   (5)
3. How can the reaction of the black porters be seen as further encouragement to Richard to accept the situation?   (5)
4. What evidence does the extract contain to show that whites worked together to keep blacks 'in their place'?   (5)

Section 3 Research Methods

Sociologists use a wide variety of information or data in their research. Some of this material comes from existing sources such as official statistics, newspapers and historical documents. These are known as secondary sources and are examined in the second part of the section. However sociologists themselves collect much of the data they use in their research. The first part of the section deals with some of the more important methods of data collection.

1 Participant observation (1)

Many sociologists claim that an effective study of human behaviour requires as full and complete a picture as possible of the life of a social group. Some argue that the best way to obtain such a picture is by directly observing people in their normal, everyday activities. A method known as participant observation has been developed for this purpose. It involves the observer directly participating in the activities of the group he is studying. For example he may join a group of workers on the shopfloor or a group of unemployed men on the street corner.

Participant observation offers the sociologist an opportunity of seeing life as it is actually lived. However, as a research method, it has a number of disadvantages. It is very time consuming – many researchers spend a year or more studying a group. Also the number of people that can be directly observed is small – the researcher can only be at one place at a time and cannot watch and listen closely to large numbers of people. It is therefore not possible to generalize from the findings of participant observation studies. For example, the researcher would not be justified in making the generalization that all factory workers are bored from a study of twenty men. In addition there is a danger that the presence of an outsider will influence and change the behaviour of those he observes. In such a case he would not obtain an accurate picture of their way of life. Despite these disadvantages, participant observation does offer the opportunity to see life as it is lived and to appreciate the point of view of those who live it.

The following extract is taken from a study of an Italian American street corner gang in a low income district of south Boston. It was conducted by William Foote Whyte who spent three and a half years in the area as a participant observer. He gave the name 'Cornerville' to the area, the 'Norton Street gang' to the group and 'Doc' to the gang leader.

The spring of 1937 provided me with an intensive course in participant observation. I was learning how to conduct myself, and I learned from various groups but particularly from the Norton Street gang.

As I began hanging about Cornerville, I found that I needed an explanation for myself and for my study. As long as I was with Doc and vouched for by him, no one asked me who I was or what I was doing. When I circulated in other groups or even among the Nortons without him, it was obvious that they were curious about me.

I soon found that people were developing their own explanation about me: I was writing a book about Cornerville. This might seem entirely too vague an explanation, and yet it sufficed. I found that my acceptance in the district depended on the personal relationships I developed far more than upon any explanations I might give. Whether it was a good thing to write a book about Cornerville depended entirely on people's opinions of me personally. If I was all right, then my project was all right; if I was no good, then no amount of explanation could convince them that the book was a good idea.

Of course people did not satisfy their curiosity about me simply by questions that they addressed to me directly. They turned to Doc, for example, and asked him about me. Doc then answered the questions and provided any reassurance that was needed.

I learned early in my Cornerville period the crucial importance of having the support of the key individuals in any groups or organizations I was studying. Instead of trying to explain myself to everyone, I found I was providing far more information about myself and my study to leaders such as Doc than I volunteered to the average corner boy.

My relationship with Doc changed rapidly in this early Cornerville period. At first he was simply a key informant – and also my sponsor (a person who makes himself responsible for and supports another). As we spent more time together, I ceased to treat him as a passive informant. I discussed with him quite frankly what I was trying to do, what problems were puzzling me, and so on. Much of our time was spent in this discussion of ideas and observations, so that Doc became, in a very real sense, a collaborator (partner) in the research.

Doc found this experience of working with me interesting and enjoyable and yet the relationship had its drawbacks. He once commented: 'You've slowed me up plenty since you've been down here. Now, when I do something, I have to think what Bill Whyte would want to know about it and how I can explain it. Before, I used to do things by instinct.'

In my interviewing methods I had been instructed not to argue with people or pass moral judgements upon them. This fell in with my own inclinations. I was glad to accept the people and to be accepted by them. However, this attitude did not come out so much in the interviewing, for I did little formal interviewing. I sought to show this interested acceptance of the people and the community in my everyday participation.

I learned to take part in the street corner discussions on baseball and sex. This required no special training, since the topics seemed to be matters of almost universal interest. I was not able to participate so actively in discussions of horse racing. I did begin to follow the races in a rather general and amateur way. I am sure it would have paid me to devote more study to the **Morning Telegraph** and other racing sheets, but my knowledge of baseball at least insured that I would not be left out of the street corner conversations.

Sometimes I wondered whether just hanging on the street corner was an active enough process to be dignified by the term 'research'. Perhaps I should be asking these men questions. However, one has to learn when to question and when not to question as well as what questions to ask.

I learned this lesson one night in the early months when I was with Doc in Chichi's gambling joint. A man from another part of the city was regaling us with a tale of the organization of gambling activity. I had been told that he had once been a very big gambling operator, and he talked knowingly about many interesting matters. He did most of the talking, but the others asked questions and threw in comments, so at length I began to feel that I must say something in order to be part of the group. I said: 'I suppose the cops were all paid off?'

The gambler's jaw dropped. He glared at me. Then he denied vehemently that any policemen had been paid off and immediately switched the conversation to another subject. For the rest of that evening I felt very uncomfortable.

The next day Doc explained the lesson of the previous evening. 'Go easy on that "who", "what", "why", "when", stuff, Bill. You ask those questions, and people will clam up on you. If people accept you, you can just hang around, and you'll learn the answers in the long run without even having to ask the questions.'

I found that this was true. As I sat and listened, I learned the answers to questions that I would not even have had the sense to ask if I had been getting my information solely on an interviewing basis. I did not abandon questioning altogether, of course. I simply learned to judge the sensitiveness of the question and my relationship to the people so that I only asked a question in a sensitive area when I was sure that my relationship to the people involved was very solid.

When I had established my position on the street corner, the data simply came to me without very active efforts on my part. It was only now and then, when I was concerned with a particular problem and felt I needed more information from a certain individual, that I would seek an opportunity to get the man alone and carry on a more formal interview.

(from **Street Corner Society** by William F. Whyte, revised edition, University of Chicago Press, Chicago, 1955, pp. 300–305)

1. How did 'Bill' (William Whyte) gain acceptance within the group? (5)
2. Whyte states, 'I tried to avoid influencing the group because I

wanted to study the situation as unaffected by my presence as possible.' What evidence does the extract contain which suggests that a) he was successful and b) he was unsuccessful?

(3, 3)

3. Those involved in 'street life' are often suspicious of outsiders.
   a What evidence for this is contained in the extract? (3)
   b With some reference to the extract suggest why, particularly in this type of situation, participant observation is a more effective method of obtaining accurate data than interviews or questionnaires. (6)

2 Participant observation (2)

Social Relations in a Secondary School by David H. Hargreaves is a study of the behaviour of teachers and students in a secondary modern school in an industrial town in northern England. Part of the information came from participant observation. Hargreaves stayed for a year in the school and spent many hours observing the behaviour of teachers and students in the classroom. In the following extract he examines his role as a participant observer.

The method of participant observation leads the investigator to accept a role within the social situation he studies: he participates as a member of the group as well as observing it. In theory, this direct participation in the group life permits an easy entrance into the social situation by reducing the resistance of group members; decreases the extent to which the investigator disturbs the 'natural' situation; and permits the investigator to experience and observe the group's norms, values, conflicts and pressures, which (over a long period) cannot be hidden from someone playing an in-group role. The fact that I had three years' experience of teaching and that I was to spend a third of my time in the school teaching classes allayed (reduced) many of the fears teachers felt about my presence in the school. If I had been a teacher, the argument seemed to run, and I was going to do some teaching in the school, then surely I must be looking at the school from **their** point of view.

One aspect of my participant observation in the school was

to sit at the back of a form during an ordinary lesson. Whereas initially most of the teachers happily ascribed a teacher-role to me on the basis of my past experience and current teaching within the school, to observe them within the confines of their own classrooms involved a disruption of their usual autonomy (freedom) and upset their ascription of a teacher-role to me. In exceptional circumstances teachers do see their colleagues at work but for the most part the assessment any teacher may make of his colleagues' competency depends upon more indirect information, such as examination results, noise from the classroom, attitude of pupils outside the classroom and gossip. As soon as I became an observer of the classroom situation, I could no longer be regarded as a teacher. Instead my role became more that of the Inspector. A few teachers reacted with some kind of withdrawal. Whenever I went into a lesson conducted by Mr. H., he made the boys work quietly out of text books, talked in a whisper to boys at his desk so that I could not hear from the back and declined to speak to the class as a whole unless this became unavoidable. With other teachers, the changes my presence effected took more subtle forms. Mr. O. usually set the form some written work and then joined me at the back of the room, where he chatted with me or told me jokes. Mr. F. never refused to let me observe but if he could he decided to read a story to the form or directed a lesson in which the boys played a passive and silent role. Mr. L. invariably sent boys to the back of the room with their books for me to examine and comment on, although when I had seen every book several times this practice declined. Many of the teachers appeared to behave quite naturally and act as if I was not in the room at all, and it is difficult to check on the extent of the changes my presence produced. Sometimes the teachers would themselves indicate the effects of my presence. In the lower streams in particular the boys are caned comparatively frequently, if the conversations over lunch and in the common room are any measure of this. But it was notable how very rarely a teacher caned a boy when I was in the room.

A further check came from conversation with the boys, who revealed changes which might otherwise have not been at all obvious.

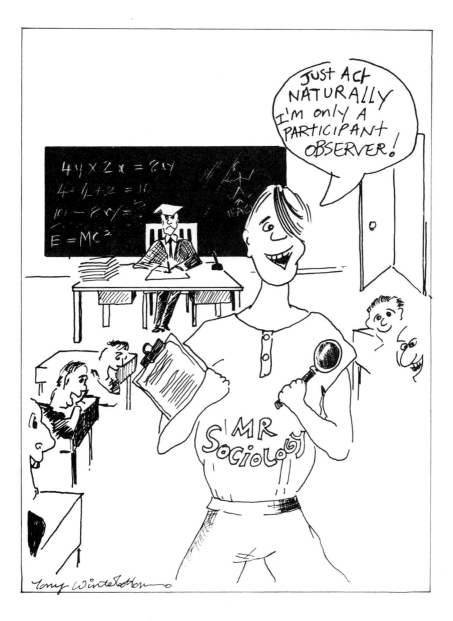

When you're in he tries to act calmly as though he's a little angel and all that.

Did you notice when you were in Mr. M's – he called me by my first name. But when you're on the field (games) he calls you by your second name.

They put on a show for you. They put the good act on, smiles and all that, and when you've gone out...

Like if Mr. O's getting mad 'cos someone's ripped a book or something, but if you're in he seems to drop it. If you weren't there he'd get real mad.

Initially my presence also caused changes in the boys' behaviour though I am convinced that these are of less importance, for once the boys became accustomed to me, they behaved normally.

(from **Social Relations in a Secondary School** by David H. Hargreaves, Routledge & Kegan Paul, London, 1967, pp. 193–4, 195–7)

1. In your own words outline two of the advantages of participant observation discussed by Hargreaves.   (6)
2. If participant observation is to succeed, the observer must be accepted by the group.
   a Why is this so?   (2)
   b Why was Hargreaves accepted, at least at first, by the teachers he was observing?   (2)
3. Why did some of the teachers change their behaviour in the classroom when observed by Hargreaves?   (5)
4. Why was Hargreaves worried about his presence as an observer in the classroom affecting the behaviour of teachers and students?   (5)

3 Interviews (1)

Compared with participant observation, interviews are cheap and fast. An interview can be completed in an hour or so. As a result the number of people studied is usually larger than in research based on participant observation. However, interviews do not allow sociologists to directly observe people in their normal, every-day settings. What people say in an interview can be very different from what they actually do. Without other methods, sociologists are unable to adequately check the accuracy of interview data. In addition, the answers people give are often strongly influenced by the interviewer.

In the following extract Hannah Gavron describes the way she conducted interviews for her book, **The Captive Wife**. She interviewed 96 mothers with one or more children under the age of five. Like many interviewers she was worried about directing the respondent – the person being interviewed. Often the interviewer expects or hopes for a certain answer and this can influence the respondent's reply. Sometimes interviewers ask 'leading questions' which direct the respondent to a particular answer. In the hope of avoiding these problems, Gavron used the technique of 'non-directive' interviewing which gives the respondent some freedom to direct the interview herself.

> Each interview was allowed to develop naturally, enabling the respondent to direct the conversation along her own lines and filling in the schedule to suit her own order. This meant that the answers to many questions were obtained without any direct demand. For example every wife said something about her methods of bringing up her children. This was then recorded in the appropriate section of the schedule, and **then** she was asked whether she found any difference between her own ideas and those of her husband, and those of her parents. In this way identical schedules were obtained from each person, which could then be compared, but at the same time each woman interviewed had been given a fair degree of freedom to express her own views in her own way.
>
> To some degree being one's own interviewer both increases and decreases the difficulties. There is no problem of misunderstanding or misinterpretation of the schedule, nor of different questions being given varying importance. Any bias is constant throughout so that the schedules, when complete, have a degree of uniformity. The main disadvantage, however, is that if the interviewer is also the author of the research, as in this case, the very expectations that led to the promotion of the research may determine some of the responses given. It is difficult to see how this can be avoided completely, but awareness of the problem plus constant self control can help. In circumstances such as these, it is probably

best to employ the kind of 'non-directive' interviewing that has been used in this research.

(from **The Captive Wife: Conflicts of Housebound Mothers** by Hannah Gavron, Routledge & Kegan Paul, London, 1966)

1. What is 'non-directive' interviewing?   (4)
2. With some reference to the extract outline the advantages and disadvantages on 'non-directive' interviewing as a method of gathering information.   (5)
3. What is the main problem of the author of the research being his or her own interviewer?   (3)
4. What are the advantages of the author of the research being his or her own interviewer?   (5)
5. Why did Gavron want 'identical schedules' from each person interviewed?   (3)

4 Interviews (2)

One of the main disadvantages of interviews is the problem of 'interviewer bias'. This means that in some way the interviewer influences and directs the answer given by the respondent or interviewee. Thus the respondent may modify or change his or her answer depending on the age, sex, ethnicity or nationality of the interviewer. The interviewer may expect or hope for certain answers. This may be transmitted to the respondent and influence his or her reply. The following passages illustrate some of the effects of 'interviewer bias'.

In 1914, 2,000 destitute men ('down and outs' with no means of support) were questioned by two interviewers. They were asked, among other things to explain their situation. One of the interviewers was a strong supporter of prohibition – forbidding by law the manufacture and sale of alcoholic drinks. There was a strong tendency for the men he interviewed to blame their situation on alcohol. The second interviewer was a strong supporter of socialist political views. He believed that private industry should be nationalized and that making a profit should take second place to the welfare (well-being) of the workers. The men that he interviewed were much more likely to explain their misfortune in terms of the industrial situation.

(Discussed in 'On errors in surveys' by W. E. Deming in **Research Methods** edited by B. J. Franklin and H. W. Osborne, Wadsworth, Belmont, 1971, p. 347)

1. How can the idea of 'interviewer bias' be used to explain the different results obtained by the two interviewers?   (6)

In the early 1960s a series of interviews were conducted with 840 black Americans in North Carolina. All the interviewers were women, thirteen were black and nine white. There were important differences between the results obtained by black and white interviewers. For example, a higher proportion of those interviewed by blacks as compared with those interviewed by whites, said that they approved of civil rights demonstrations and school desegregation (ending all-white and all-black schools). In addition, more respondents refused to give any answers to these questions when faced with a white interviewer.

(adapted from 'Interviewer – respondent interaction' by J. Allan Williams Jr. in **Research Methods** edited by B. J. Franklin and H. W. Osborne, Wadsworth, Belmont, 1971)

2. Suggest an explanation for the different results obtained by black and white interviewers.   (7)

During the 1960s many black Americans rejected the idea that 'white is right' and stopped trying to copy white Americans. Being black became something to be proud of rather than ashamed. The author of the following research believed that this outlook was reflected in black American 'soul' music. The extract quotes a small part of an interview with Jay Butler, a black disc jockey from Detroit.

Interviewer	The song **Take me as I am** by Solomon Burke. What's it about?
Jay Butler	It's just about a guy and his woman an' he's telling her not to try and change him, to take him as he is.
Interviewer	But don't you think it could have a deeper meaning, that it's saying accept me as a black man, not as a poor substitute for a white man.
Jay Butler	Yeah. You got a point there. The black community wants to be accepted as black American. I don't wanna be a white American, I wanna be a black American. It's like the Detroit Emeralds' song **I'm an ordinary man, take me the way I am**. There's a two-fold meaning in all these soul songs. Take Solomon Burke's **Take me as I am**. This song might be about a guy and his girl, but it means more at this period of time. Back in the 1950s we were trying to be accepted by white Americans on their terms. Now accept me as I am, accept my nappy hair, accept me period.

(from **Right On: From Blues to Soul in Black America** by Michael Haralambos, Eddison, London, 1974, p. 146, with additional material from the author's unpublished notes)

3. How might the idea of 'interviewer bias' help to explain the development and result of this interview?   (7)

5 Sampling procedures (1)

Sociologists cannot study everybody. They have neither the time nor the money. They therefore select a sample of those they wish to study. The sample may be of the population as a whole, or of a particular section within the population such as the working class, women, teenagers, factory workers, managers and so on. The aim of sampling is to select a number of people who are representative of the particular section of the population under investigation. If, for example, a representative sample of 10% of the student population of a comprehensive school was taken, the sociologist would feel some justification in claiming that his results applied to all students in the school. In other words he would be able to generalize from the data he obtained from his sample. One of the most frequently used sampling procedures is the 'random sample'. A number is given to each individual in the group under investigation and a set of random numbers is then used to select the members of the sample. The nearest everyday equivalent is to give each individual in the group to be studied a number and then to pick these numbers out of a hat. By means of a random sample the researcher can predict with some assurance that his sample is representative of the group as a whole.

The following extract outlines the way in which Hannah Gavron selected the sample for her study entitled **The Captive Wife: Conflicts of Housebound Mothers**. The Group Practice mentioned refers to a health centre from which a group of doctors operate.

> The working class wives were all drawn from the practice lists of the Caversham Centre, a Group Practice in Kentish Town (London). Selection was made as follows. An alphabetical list was taken from the files of all the wives who fell into the right categories, that is, (a) married (b) at least one child under five (c) born in or after 1930. 70 were selected at random from the list, but 20 had to be eliminated as being ineligible. The method of approach was to call at the address, explain my introduction from the doctor, and ask if they would be willing to assist in the work. In fact two refused and 48 agreed.
>
> Selection of 48 middle class women proved more difficult. The practice at the Caversham Centre had very few middle class patients, and the doctors felt they were not in any way representative of the middle classes in general. It was decided that the advantages of an introduction such as the one obtained at the Caversham Centre were sufficiently great to try to repeat this with the middle class sample. However, it proved very difficult to find a doctor who had a large number of middle class patients in the right categories, and who were willing to assist in the research. Advice was sought from the College of General Practitioners, and one doctor in West Hampstead offered to assist. In fact a study of his files revealed only 35 names which fulfilled all the right conditions. An initial introduction to the 35 women selected

was obtained through a letter from the doctor explaining the purpose of my research. Subsequently I telephoned to ask their assistance and arranged a visit. In no case was there a refusal. The remaining 13 were selected from the London lists of the 'Housebound Wives' Register. This is an informal association, begun after a letter in the **Guardian**, of women with children. It has groups all over the country and discussion with the area organizer in North London revealed that its membership covered a wide variety of people. It is fully realized that to select from an organization such as this involves a degree of bias, mainly due to the fact that the women have selected themselves, i.e. joined the group, and that this bias is probably a greater one than that incurred by selecting from a doctor's practice.

(from **The Captive Wife: Conflicts of Housebound Mothers** by Hannah Gavron, Routledge & Kegan Paul, London, 1966)

1. The working class wives in the sample were selected randomly from doctors' lists. Why do researchers such as Gavron use random samples? (4)
2. Why was Gavron concerned about selecting part of her middle class sample from the 'Housebound Wives' Register? (4)
3. Gavron's sample was made up of 96 women. In view of this why does she state that 'large-scale generalizations' cannot be made from her study? (4)
4. Briefly suggest why Gavron selected both middle and working class wives for her sample. (4)
5. Gavron's selection of her sample was influenced by 'the advantages of an introduction'.
   a Why might an introduction from a doctor be useful to a researcher? (2)
   b What evidence is contained in the extract to suggest that such introductions were advantageous? (2)

6 Sampling procedures (2)

The Family and Social Change: A Study of Family and Kinship in a South Wales Town by Colin Rosser and Christopher Harris is a study of family life in Swansea. Part of the information used in the research came from a random sample made up of 2% of the population of the County Borough of Swansea. In order to make sure that the sample was representative, it was compared with information from the census. Table 1 shows the age and sex distribution of the Swansea sample compared to that of the census which gives the percentage of males and females in various age groups for the population as a whole. Table 2 compares the social class distribution of the sample with information from the census which shows the percentage of the national population in each social class.

Table 1 Age-Sex distribution

Age Group	Sample		Census	
	Men %	Women %	Men %	Women%
20–29	11.9	14.8	18.8	16.4
30–39	20.5	19.0	21.0	18.2
40–49	22.1	20.2	20.2	19.2
50–59	21.6	18.0	19.2	18.8
60–69	14.7	15.7	13.0	15.2
70–79	7.8	8.8	6.3	9.1
80–89	1.3	3.2	1.5	2.9
90 +	.1	.3	.09	.2
% of Men & Women	49	51	48	52

Table 2 Occupational Class

Registrar-General's Occupational Class	Sample %	Census %
I	5.2	3.0
II	15.8	12.4
III	52.8	50.4
IV	13.2	13.0
V	12.3	21.2
Not known	.7	–

(from **The Family and Social Change: A Study of Family and Kinship in a South Wales Town** by Colin Rosser and Christopher Harris, Routledge & Kegan Paul, London, 1965, p. 326)

1. Why did Rosser and Harris compare their sample with information from the census? (6)
2. In the age group 20 to 29 which gender group (men or women) in

A cross-section of society.

the sample appears more representative of the nation as a whole? Briefly explain your choice. (3)

3. Which two social classes in the sample appear least representative in terms of the social class distribution of the national population? Briefly explain your choices. (3)

4. Rosser and Harris state that it is 'likely that there was a slight exaggeration of occupational status by our informants' (i.e.

those who made up the sample). How might this partly explain the differences between the social class distribution in the sample and the census?   (4)
5. The sample was taken in 1960. The census was taken in 1951. Rosser and Harris state that 'there is a long-term trend away from unskilled to skilled and semi-skilled employment'. How might this help to explain some of the differences between the social class distributions in the sample and the census?   (4)
(Class V – unskilled manual, Class IV – semi-skilled manual, Class III – skilled manual and clerical and minor supervisory occupations).

7 Questionnaires

A questionnaire is simply a list of questions. Questionnaires are often used for gathering data for social surveys. A social survey involves the collection of the same type of information from all members of the sample. Thus they may be given an identical set of questions and requested to answer them. Questionnaires provide a relatively cheap, fast and efficient method for obtaining large amounts of information from relatively large numbers of people. The data produced by questionnaires are often easily quantified which means they can be put into a numerical form. For example, a questionnaire completed by factory workers might show that 58% belonged to trade unions and 60% supported the Labour Party. When data is put into this form it is possible to measure the strength of the connection between different factors. Using the above example, it might be found that 90% of trade union members supported the Labour Party. Putting the data in the form of numbers makes it possible to measure the importance of the link between trade union membership and Labour Party support.

Those who support the use of questionnaires argue that they produce comparable data. Since everybody is answering exactly the same questions, it is claimed that different answers will indicate real differences between the respondents. Different answers in an interview, however, might reflect differences in the way a question is phrased or different reactions to the interviewer.

However there are a number of disadvantages involved with the use of questionnaires. The following passages examine some of the problems that have resulted from the use of questionnaires in social surveys.

> Postal questionnaires are a relatively inexpensive method of obtaining information. The questionnaires are mailed to members of the sample who are asked to complete and return them. However the response rate is frequently low. Often only a small per cent of the sample return postal question-naires. Those who do may have a special reason for doing so and may therefore be untypical of the sample as a whole. In 1977 a nationwide survey of the sexual behaviour of American women known as the **Hite Report** was published. 100,000 postal questionnaires were sent out but only 3,000 were returned. Thus only 3% of the sample replied.
>
> (adapted from **Scientific Method** by D. Crossland, R. Park and N. Lowe, National Extension College, Cambridge, 1978, p. 33)

1. Suggest two reasons why the response rate in the Hite Report was low.   (4)
2. Why should any generalizations about the sexual behaviour of American women based on the findings of the Hite Report be regarded with caution?   (4)

> Magazines sometimes produce questionnaires and invite their readers to complete them. For example in the mid-70s in Britain **Woman's Own** produced a questionnaire on love and marriage which was completed by some 10,000 women. However, as the following example shows, there are problems with making generalizations and predictions from this type of survey. In 1936 the **Literary Digest**, an American magazine with a mainly middle class readership, asked its readers a series of questions with the aim of predicting the results of the US presidential election. The survey forecast a Republican president whereas a Democrat was elected to the White House. In addition the number of votes predicted for each presidential candidate were subtantially different from the election results. (The nearest British equivalent to the

Republicans is the Conservative Party, to the Democrats, the Liberal Party.)

(adapted from **Research Methods** edited by B. J. Franklin and H. W. Osborne, Wadsworth, Belmont, 1971, p. 162).

3. Suggest why the survey failed to predict the election results. (4)
4. Why would a random sample of the US voting population have been more likely to provide an accurate prediction? (4)

Great care must be taken with the wording of questionnaires. It is important that the questions have the same meaning for all members of the sample. It is also important that questions have the same meaning for the researcher who designed the questionnaire and those who answer it. The following example illustrates this point. A Gallup poll survey in 1939 found that 88% of a sample of the US population described itself as middle class, a result which surprised the researchers. Members of the sample were offered a choice of three alternatives, 'upper', 'middle' and 'lower class'. The survey was repeated shortly afterwards and the term 'lower class' was replaced by 'working class'. Now 51% of the sample described itself as working class.

(adapted from **Introducing Sociology** by Peter Worsley, Penguin, Harmondsworth, 1977, p. 428)

5. How can the large differences between the results of the two surveys be explained? (4)

8 Pilot studies

Many researchers begin with a 'pilot study' before starting their main study. Often they obtain valuable information which can then be used in the main part of the research. The first extract describes the pilot study undertaken by Willmott and Young in their research on working class family life in the East End of London. The second extract describes what Hannah Gavron learned from the pilot study which preceded her investigation of the problems of housebound wives.

> As well as taking care in choosing a sample, and trying to interview as many of the people selected, it is also important to ensure that one asks sensible and clear questions, of the kind which will produce meaningful answers. What people say in an interview may not correspond with what they actually do, as we warn the reader in the Introduction to this book. Their memory may be faulty, they may be muddled, or they may for some reason deliberately mislead the interviewer, but in organizing a survey one can reduce errors of this sort by framing the questions carefully, and by providing a number of opportunities to check on the consistency of people's answers, either in the course of the interview or by calling back later on for some fuller information. These problems help to explain why most investigators undertake a 'pilot' survey before proceeding to the main inquiry. In Bethnal Green and Greenleigh we carried out just over 100 'pilot' interviews, to help us decide upon the design of the inquiry, the questions to ask, and how to put them.

(from **Family and Kinship in East London** by Michael Young and Peter Willmott, Routledge & Kegan Paul, London, 1957)

> The pilot study had revealed two things. Firstly that a considerable degree of rapport (understanding) was necessary for a satisfactory interview on this subject (which involved attitudes and emotions as well as facts), and secondly that if the respondent was allowed to follow her own train of thought, many questions would be answered without the necessity of asking them specifically, although in some cases it might be valuable to check back later. For these reasons some time was spent at the beginning of each interview establishing a kind of relationship by exchanging small pieces of conversational information. Once some degree of rapport had been established the conversation ceased, leaving the respondent confident and at ease, and allowing the interview to develop.

(from **The Captive Wife: Conflicts of Housebound Mothers** by Hannah Gavron, Routledge & Kegan Paul, London, 1966)

1. With reference to the first extract, briefly discuss the problems involved in constructing questions for an interview.   (6)
2. a What do Young and Willmott mean by checking on 'the consistency of people's answers'?   (3)
   b How is it possible to do this in the course of an interview?   (3)
3. a Gavron was investigating the problems and feelings of house-bound mothers. Why did she feel that 'a considerable degree of rapport was necessary for a satisfactory interview on this subject'?   (4)
   b How did she achieve this rapport?   (2)
   c Once she achieved this rapport, what effect did it have on her respondents?   (2)

9 Secondary sources

So far the extracts in this section have looked at ways in which sociologists collect their own information. These sources of information are known as primary sources; the material collected by means of participant observation, interviews and question-naires is known as primary data. However there is a vast range of existing information which is available for sociological research. It ranges from historical material such as parish records, legal docu-ments, letters, diaries, novels and autobiographies to modern material such as official statistics, newspapers, books, television programmes, recorded music and films. These sources of information are known as secondary sources, the information itself as secondary data.

There are many examples of the use of modern secondary sources in this book. For instance they have been used to analyse how gender roles (the roles of women and men) are created and reinforced. Section 2:6 looks at the way women are portrayed in television commercials. Section 12:3 examines the presentation of gender roles in children's reading books such as the **Janet and John** series.

Historical sources are also used throughout this book. Section 9:3 shows how the use of historical documents provides a picture of family life in the past. It examines Peter Laslett's research on family life from the 16th to the 19th century which was based on parish records and Michael Anderson's study of families in Preston based on the results of the 1851 census. Social change is one of the major concerns of sociologists. Without historical material they would be unable to document and explain how societies have changed, they would be unable to compare the present with the past.

However there are a number of problems involved in using secondary sources for sociological research. As Section 3:10 shows, official statistics must be used with caution since it is often far from clear what they are actually measuring. Written material such as newspaper articles, novels and autobiographies cannot be taken at face value. They are written from a particular standpoint, to support an argument, make a point and reflect a political, religious or moral belief. They cannot be seen as balanced, unbiased, objective accounts.

Despite these problems secondary sources are immensely valuable. In particular historical sources are all we have for under-standing the past. Sociologists have only been around for some 150 years. The history of the human race stretches back well over a million years. Clearly we cannot rely on primary sources for understanding human society.

The following extract looks at an example of historical material. It is taken from **Long Lance**, the autobiography of Chief Buffalo Child Long Lance written in 1928. It is a unique record of the traditional way of life of the Blackfoot Indians who lived on the Canadian prairies – a way of life that has all but disappeared.

> We youngsters were given daily lectures on how to live, by twelve of the oldest men of the tribe. Because they had lived to such remarkable ages it was considered that they knew better how to live than anyone else. Every morning just before sunrise, while the camp still lay on their pallets in their teepees, one of these old men would take his turn in getting up early and walking through the camp shouting out his lecture on how to live to be old and his advice on morals, courage, and personal bravery. His voice would awake us, and we would lie still and listen intently to every word he said. At that time of the morning, just as we had awakened from a night's rest, his words seemed to pierce deep into us; we remembered every word he said, and all during the day his advice would keep coming back into our minds, and we would try to live up to it.

All of these men were great warriors who had many scalps to their credit, and we respected our old people above all others in the tribe. To live to be so old they must have been brave and strong and good fighters, and we aspired to be like them. We never allowed our old people to want for anything, and whenever any one of them would stop as he made his silent, dignified way through the camp, and put his arm across our shoulders and utter a little prayer for us to the Great Spirit, we would feel highly honoured. We would stand quietly, and when he was through we would remain in our tracks, respectful and silent, until he had disappeared. We looked upon our old people as demigods of a kind, and we loved them deeply; they were all our fathers.

*   *   *   *

When they received this news of the coming of the minister, all of the Indians painted their faces and put on all of their best medicine clothes. The medicine-man got out his drum, and soon we were all ready to receive him.

When we saw the minister coming, the medicine-man started to beat his tom-tom and sing one of his medicine songs; for he thought that would please the visitor who represented the white man's 'medicine' and Great Spirit. Our chief went out and met the minister and shook his hand, and then he took him over to meet our minister, the medicine-man.

After they shook hands, the minister made a speech. He told our medicine-man that he was preaching something not worthwhile. He said:

'I didn't mean for you people to fix up like this; I meant for you to wash the paint off your faces and put your medicine drums away. There is only one God in Heaven, and I am here to tell you about Him.'

Indians never interrupt anyone when he is talking, even if he should talk all day – that is an ancient courtesy among Indians – so everyone stood and listened to the minister while he told us of the white man's God. He made a long speech. He said that the Indians must lay down their arms and live peaceably alongside the white man who was coming into his country.

Blackfoot Indians performing a religious ceremony.

When the missionary finished his speech, our chief arose and addressed him. He said:

'Why do you tell us to be good? We Indians are not bad; you white people may be, but we are not. We do not steal, except when our horses have been raided; we do not tell lies; we take care of our old and our poor when they are helpless. We do not need that which you tell us about.'

'But,' said the missionary, 'there is only one God, and you must worship him.'

'Then if that is true,' said our chief, 'we Indians are worshipping the same God that you are – only in a different way. When the Great Spirit, God, made the world He gave the Indians one way to worship Him and He gave the white man another way, because we are different people and our lives are different. The Indian should keep to his way and the white man to his, and we should all work with one another for God and not against one another. The Indian does not try to tell you how you should worship God. We like to see you worship

Him in your way, because we know you understand that way.'
'But the Great Spirit you speak of is not the same one that we worship', said the missionary.

(from **Long Lance** by Chief Buffalo Child Long Lance, Corgi Books, London, 1956, pp. 41–42, 131–132)

1. Sociologists must use secondary sources if they are to understand human society. Briefly explain why. (4)
2. If you were studying present day Blackfoot society how might Long Lance's autobiography be useful for your research? (4)
3. Studying other societies helps us to understand our own.
   a Briefly compare attitudes to the elderly in modern British society and traditional Blackfoot society. (3)
   b Suggest why these attitudes differ. (3)
4. a Why were there misunderstandings between the missionary and the Blackfoot? (3)
   b What can we learn from this about how to approach people with cultures different from our own? (3)

10 Novels

A good novel can bring a time, a place and the people who live there to life. It can offer a deep understanding of their world. Thus it has been claimed that George Orwell's novel, **The Road to Wigan Pier**, provides greater insight into working class family life than many sociological studies. Even science fiction, at first sight far removed from this world, can offer a great deal to the study of society. Ursula Le Guin's magnificent science fiction novel **The Dispossessed** presents one of the finest accounts of capitalism, communism and anarchism ever written. Read alongside some of the writings of Karl Marx it would provide an excellent introduction to some of the main concerns of sociology.

Novelists do not often present balanced objective accounts. However, this does not prevent their work from providing understanding and insight. This can be seen from the following extract from **Uncle Tom's Cabin** by Harriet Beecher Stowe, first published in 1852. At that time slavery was still legal in the United States. Ms. Stowe tried to present a picture of slavery as a 'living dramatic reality', something more suited to a novel than a sociological report. She was passionately opposed to slavery and researched the novel by talking to escaped slaves in the anti-slavery headquarters in Boston.

The following extract is a conversation between Marie, the wife of St. Clare, a southern plantation owner and Miss Ophelia, a visiting relative from New England in the north. Mammy is Marie's lady's maid, she is black and a slave. The novel is set in the USA in the early 19th century.

'Now, Mammy has a *sort* of goodness,' said Marie; 'she's smooth and respectable, but she's selfish at heart. Now, she never will be done fidgeting and worrying about that husband of hers. You see, when I was married and came to live here, of course I had to bring her with me, and her husband, my father couldn't spare. He was a blacksmith, and, of course, very necessary; and I thought and said, at the time, that Mammy and he had better give each other up, as it wasn't likely to be convenient for them ever to live together again. I wish now I'd insisted on it, and married Mammy to somebody else; but I was foolish and indulgent, and didn't want to insist. I told Mammy at the time that she mustn't ever expect to see him more than once or twice in her life again, for the air of father's place doesn't agree with my health, and I can't go there; and I advised her to take up with somebody else; but no—she wouldn't. Mammy has a kind of obstinacy about her, in spots, that everybody don't see as I do.'

'Has she children?' said Miss Ophelia.

'Yes; she has two.'

'I suppose she feels the separation from them?'

'Well, of course, I couldn't bring them. They were little dirty things—I couldn't have them about; and, besides, they took up too much of her time; but I believe that Mammy has always kept up a sort of sulkiness about this. She won't marry anybody else; and I do believe now, though she knows how necessary she is to me, and how feeble my health is, she would go back to her husband to-morrow, if she only could. I *do*, indeed,' said Marie; 'they are just so selfish, the best of them. . . . I hold to being *kind* to servants—I always am; but you must make 'em *know their place*. Eva [Marie's daughter] never does; there's no getting into the child's head the first beginning of an idea what a servant's place is! You heard her offering to take care of me nights, to let Mammy sleep! That's just a specimen of the way the child would be doing all the time, if she was left to herself.'

'Why,' said Miss Ophelia bluntly, 'I suppose you think your servants are human creatures, and ought to have some rest when they are tired?'

'Certainly, of course. I'm very particular in letting them have everything that comes convenient—anything that doesn't put one at all out of the way, you know. Mammy can make up her sleep, some time or other; there's no difficulty about that. She's the sleepiest concern that ever I saw; sewing, standing, or sitting, that creature will go to sleep, and sleep anywhere and everywhere. No danger but Mammy gets sleep enough. But this treating servants as if they were exotic flowers or china vases is really ridiculous,' said Marie, as she plunged languidly into the depths of a voluminous and pillowy lounge, and drew towards her an elegant cut-glass vinaigrette. 'You don't know what a provoking, stupid, careless, unreasonable, childish, ungrateful set of wretches they are.'

Marie seemed wonderfully supported, always, when she got upon this topic; and she now opened her eyes, and seemed quite to forget her languor.

'You don't know, and you can't, the daily, hourly trials that beset a housekeeper from them, everywhere and every way. But it's no use to complain to St. Clare. He talks the strangest stuff. He says we have made them what they are, and ought to bear with them. He says their faults are all owing to us, and that it would be cruel to make the fault and punish it too. He says we shouldn't do any better, in their place; just as if one could reason from them to us, you know.'

'Don't you believe that the Lord made them of one blood with us?' said Miss Ophelia, shortly.

'No, indeed, not I! A pretty story, truly! They are a degraded race.'

'Don't you think they've got immortal souls?' said Miss Ophelia, with increasing indignation.

'Oh, well,' said Marie, yawning, 'that of course—nobody doubts that. But as to putting them on any sort of equality with us, you know, as if we could be compared, why, it's impossible! Now, St. Clare really has talked to me as if keeping Mammy from her husband was like keeping me from mine. There's no comparing in this way. Mammy couldn't have the feeling that I should. It's a different thing altogether—of course, it is; and yet St. Clare pretends not to see it. And just as if Mammy could love her little dirty babies as I love Eva! Yet St. Clare once really and soberly tried to persuade me that it was my duty, with my weak health, and all I suffer, to let Mammy go back, and take somebody else in her place. That was a little too much even for *me* to bear. I don't often show my feelings. I make it a principle to endure everything in silence; it's a wife's hard lot, and I bear it. But I did break out, that time; so that he has never alluded to the subject since. But I know by his looks, and little things that he says, that he thinks so as much as ever; and it's so trying, so provoking!'

(from **Uncle Tom's Cabin** by Harriet Beecher Stowe, J.M. Dent, London, 1961, pp. 173, 176, 177, 178)

1. In view of Harriet Beecher Stowe's beliefs, why is Miss Ophelia presented as a much nicer person than Marie?   (4)
2. Many slave owners saw blacks as a 'lower race' which could not be judged by the same standards as whites. What evidence does the extract provide to illustrate this point?   (6)
3. Slavery as a system of social control was justified by a set of beliefs.
   a What does this mean?   (3)
   b Briefly show how some of Marie's beliefs can be used to justify slavery.   (3)
4. What are the problems of using the type of material in the above extract as sociological data?   (4)

11 Official statistics

Official statistics are one of the most important secondary sources available for sociological research. They are produced in ever increasing numbers by local and national government bodies. Each year Her Majesty's Stationery Office publishes the **Annual Abstract of Statistics** and **Social Trends** both packed with a mass of statistical information on births and deaths, marriage and divorce, income and wealth, employment and unemployment, health, crime, education and housing. These and many other areas contained in their pages make up a large part of the subject matter of sociology.

Although official statistics are widely used by many sociologists, they cannot be used uncritically, they cannot be taken at face value. Some of the problems of using official statistics are examined in the following passage.

To produce statistics you must first define what you are looking at and then measure it in terms of this definition. Take the case of unemployment. The unemployed are officially defined as those claiming unemployment benefit. Using this definition the Department of Employment publishes monthly statistics which show the extent of unemployment. But if other definitions were used the figures might be very different. The unemployed could be defined as those wishing to find paid employment. This would include many people not entitled to unemployment benefit such as young people on the Youth Training Scheme and many married women. Measuring unemployment in terms of this definition would give a much higher figure than that provided by official statistics (see Section 16:1).

Poverty provides another example of this type of problem. The poor are officially defined as those receiving supplementary benefit. This pays a minimum income to meet basic needs such as food, clothing and housing. However many researchers argue that people are poor if they are unable to afford a reasonable standard of living, not just the bare necessities. In terms of this definition many people whose incomes are well above the supplementary benefit level would be poor. The extent of poverty would therefore be much greater than that provided by official figures (see Section 6:6).

Thus, before they can make use of official statistics sociologists need to know exactly what is being measured. Even with this knowledge official statistics must be used with caution since they may well be inaccurate. They may not even produce accurate figures in terms of their own definitions of what they are measuring. Each year the Inland

Revenue publishes statistics on the distribution of income in the population. These figures are based on income tax returns. Yet the returns are sometimes falsified by people trying to evade income tax. Suicide provides another example of the problem of accuracy. Official figures are based on coroners' decisions that particular deaths are suicides. Often this involves a difficult judgement. Many deaths officially certified as accidental or due to natural causes may well be suicides.

Finally sociologists need to know why official statistics are compiled and produced in certain ways. Why do government departments define and measure unemployment and poverty in one way and not another? Why do coroners tend to define certain types (e.g. deaths in motor vehicle crashes) as accidental? Answers to these questions are needed before official statistics can be properly understood and used in sociological research.

(adapted in part from **Demystifying Social Statistics** edited by J. Irvine, I. Miles and J. Evans, Pluto, London, 1979)

1. Do you find official definitions of unemployment and poverty reasonable? Explain your answer. (6)
2. Suggest why governments have not adopted the alternative definitions of unemployment and poverty given in the passage. (4)
3. a Before they can use official statistics sociologists need to know exactly what is being measured. Briefly explain why. (5)
   b Even with this knowledge, official statistics have to be treated with caution. Why? (5)

Section 4 Social Stratification

People might be equal in the sight of God but they are far from equal in society. In every known human society there is some form of social inequality. In particular, some people have more wealth, power and prestige than others. In many societies there are fairly clearcut divisions between social groups. Thus in Western societies people can be divided into social classes. Class is one form of social stratification. Social stratification may be defined as a system of social groups which can be ranked, one above the other, usually in terms of wealth, power and prestige.

There are many forms of social stratification. This section concentrates on social class in Western society but it also considers the feudal system of Medieval Europe and the caste system of traditional India. Social class is a relatively 'open' system of social stratification. This means that there is a fairly high rate of social mobility or movement from one level or stratum to another. Thus it is by no means unusual for a person born into the working class to become upwardly mobile and spend his adult life as a member of the middle class. By comparison the feudal and estate systems are 'closed'. There is relatively little social mobility and most people remain members of the stratum into which they were born.

1 The feudal system

The feudal pyramid

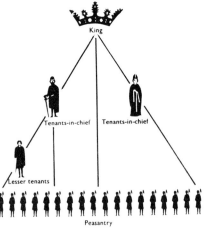

Peasantry

By AD 1000, Europe was emerging from the upheavals of Dark Age migrations and Viking raids. But warfare among powerful families continued to form part of everyday life. Endless fighting created a need for two distinct social classes: highly trained warriors; and a protected peasantry, whose chief duty was to keep the warriors well fed and clothed.

Thus arose the social order called feudalism. This pattern of society developed differently in different places, and it endured much longer in some areas than in others. (It survived, for instance, until the 20th century in much of Eastern Europe.) But it held its greatest sway during the Middle Ages.

The word 'feudalism' comes from the medieval Latin feudum, meaning a piece of land granted in return for services. Such grants date back to the years when Roman rule was collapsing. Because Roman law no longer protected small landowners from invading barbarians, the landowners sought protection from powerful neighbours. The neighbours supplied military aid in return for farm produce and services. In contrast, big landowners who needed military help paid for it by granting some of their land to knights-at-arms.

This practice also found favour with the Germanic peoples. By the 10th century, force of arms had raised many barbarian chiefs to kingship. Equipped with the powers of lawmaker, judge and general, they brought feudal government to wide areas of Western Europe – first France, then Germany, England and Scandinavia. Common to all systems was this main feature: the king, regarded as the owner of all land, granted estates ('fiefs') to his vassals. These were either nobles who inherited their estates, or people to whom the king actually granted land in return for a given number of warriors. The greatest vassals were dukes, counts and abbots; and these in turn were likely to have vassals of their own. At the base of the pyramid stood thousands upon thousands of peasants and serfs. There was little social mobility in the feudal system. Kings and nobles were usually succeeded by their eldest sons. Peasants and serfs had little opportunity to rise in the social hierarchy and most plodded on in their fathers' footsteps.

Ownership and control of land formed the basis of the feudal system. Land was the main form of wealth and the source of power and prestige. Medieval Europe was an agricultural society therefore land formed the foundation of the economy. Its importance can be seen from the demands of the followers of William, Duke of Normandy, who conquered England in 1066. In the words of the historian, M. Bloch, 'We want lands, said the Norman lords who refused the gifts of jewels, arms and horses offered by their duke.'

Our most detailed knowledge of medieval feudal rule comes from England's Domesday book a census made by William I (1066–87). Though in name William owned all England, he kept only part of it for himself. He granted the rest to 1500 chief nobles and churchmen (known as tenants-in-chief), who swore loyalty and undertook to perform two important services for him. First, they advised him in his council. Secondly, they provided knights and men-at-arms for his army. To provide these troops the tenants-in-chief found it necessary to subdivide most of their lands among some 8000 lesser tenants, notably knights-at-arms. In exchange for their land, the knights promised military service. In turn, the knights split some of their lands among peasant farmers.

Medieval law recognized two sorts of peasants: freemen and serfs. Freemen often held their land in return for part-time military service as men-at-arms. But it was the serfs who made up the vast majority – as much as 95% – of Europe's population. Unlike the freemen, serfs were not allowed to work or travel where they pleased. Oaths of life-long obedience tied them to their landholding. They and their descendants had to farm their lord's land and pay him special dues. They even required their lord's permission to marry.

In spite of these obligations, serfs were not slaves. They had rights dating back to the time when they first accepted serf-dom in return for military protection. For example, they had a right to graze their cattle on common lands that – strictly speaking – belonged to the lord and to send their pigs to feed in his forest.

In short, an intricate web of rights and duties bound serf, freeman, knight, noble and king to one another. Under this feudal system, everyone got some benefits. But the peasants benefited least. Though owed military protection in return for servitude, they often suffered from the nobles' quarrels; one lord was likely to annoy another by assaulting his peasants. So there were frequent peasant revolts. The lords feared such uprisings more than anything else. In fact, peasant revolt was often the only thing that could temporarily make the nobles stop fighting one another and close ranks.

(from **History: Civilization from its Beginnings** edited by Alan Bullock, Macdonald, London, 1962, pp. 156–7)

1. Which of the following terms describes status in the feudal system, a) ascribed b) achieved? Briefly explain your choice. (2)
2. Which of the following terms describes the feudal system of stratification, a) open b) closed? Briefly explain your choice. (2)
3. In the feudal system each man had his lord. Explain this statement with reference to the extract. (4)
4. Why was land so important in the feudal system? (4)
5. Why is land much less important in social class systems of stratification? (4)
6. What is the connection between military power, military service and land in the feudal system? (4)

2 Caste

In India the caste system has existed for several thousand years. Even today its influence is still strong, particularly in rural areas, though in towns and cities it is tending to break down. The system is based in part on Hindu religious beliefs which provide justification and support for this form of social stratification. The following passage describes the caste system in Cochin, a state on the Malabar coast in south-west India.

A caste is a group of families bearing a common name and claiming descent from a common ancestor. Each caste is divided into a number of sub-castes or jatis each of which specializes in a particular occupation – there are carpenter jatis, goldsmith jatis, potter jatis and so on. People's position in the system is fixed or ascribed at birth. They automatically belong to the same caste and usually follow the same occupation as their parents. Castes are endogamous social groups which means that a person must marry within his or her caste.

The castes of Cochin form a system of social stratification with those at the top having more wealth, power and prestige than those at the bottom. In Hindu society the higher castes are believed to be more pure in religious terms than the lower castes. Members of the lowest stratum are defined as unclean, base and impure. These beliefs are reflected in the jobs people do and in the social relationships between members of different castes. For example those at the base of the system perform unclean and degrading tasks such as the disposal of dead animals. Members of the higher castes regard contact with such people as polluting. They may even call out as they walk along the road so that low caste members will move to one side and not pollute the air they breathe.

The highest stratum in Cochin society is the Khshatriya caste. It is made up of members of the royal family who rule the state. They are relatively few in number but are extremely wealthy, owning large estates.

The Brahmin caste forms the second level of the caste system. The Brahmins are holy men whose high social standing comes from the belief that they are religiously pure. Many devote their lives to prayer and study and are regarded as the source of wisdom and truth. Because of this Brahmins act as advisers to the royal household.

The third caste is known as the Nayar. Traditionally members of this caste were the warriors of Cochin. They trained their sons in the use of the sword and the lance and served the royal family. Nowadays they are usually land-owners, earning their living by farming. Differences in prestige and purity are clearly seen from the way a Nayar addresses a Brahmin. He refers to his own house as a dung heap, to his clothes as spiders' webs and to his food as raw rice. But he refers to the Brahmin's house as a noble residence, to his food as ambrosia (food of the gods) and to his teeth as pearls.

Members of the fourth caste perform personal services for the Brahmins and Nayars. This service caste includes teachers, barbers, washermen and weavers. They are able to approach members of higher castes without polluting them.

The Untouchables form the base of the caste system. They are the largest social grouping and include agricultural labourers, fishermen, potters and a wide variety of manual workers. Contact with Untouchables pollutes members of higher castes. Even if the shadow of an Untouchable falls across the food of a Brahmin it will render it unclean. Untouchables are despised by their social superiors and their occupations are considered degrading and impure.

The caste system is reflected in living arrangements. The magnificent palaces of the royal family stand in sharp contrast to the squalid huts of the Untouchables. In a typical settlement the houses of the Brahmins and Nayars are set apart in their own compounds. They are grouped around the temples and ceremonial baths. Members of the service caste live nearby. However, the Untouchables are segregated from other members of the caste system. They live on the outskirts of villages or in their own communities often in the middle of paddy fields.

(adapted from **Habitat, Economy and Society** by C. Daryll Forde, Methuen, London, 1963)

1. What determines a person's caste position? (2)
2. Assuming that the rules of the caste system are strictly obeyed, how much social mobility would there be? Briefly explain your answer. (3)
3. What are the differences in the way a person obtains his or her occupational role in Hindu society and modern Britain? (3)
4. Draw a diagram to represent the caste system. (2)
5. What advantages does an individual enjoy as a result of being born into a higher caste? (3)
6. What is the connection between religion and social status in the caste system? Give two examples from the extract in your answer. (3)
7. How does the location of people's homes reflect the caste system? Suggest possible similarities between this and the connection between housing location and social class in Britain. (4)

3 Social class – The Registrar-General's classification

Class is the main system of social stratification in Western industrial society. There is no one accepted way of defining social class. Many researchers use occupation as the main indicator of a person's class position. Some use the status or prestige of occupations as the basis for assigning them to classes. Others place more emphasis on the economic rewards of different occupations and allocate them to social classes on this basis. The following chart gives a brief outline of the Registrar-General's classification of occupations in terms of social classes. The basis for assigning particular jobs to particular classes is 'the general standing within the community of the occupations concerned'. The Registrar-General's social classification is widely used in government reports and surveys.

The Registrar-General's social classification

	Social class	Examples of occupations in each class
	Class 1 Professional	Accountant, doctor, dentist, solicitor, university lecturer.
Middle Class	**Class 2** Managerial and technical	Manager, teacher, librarian, nurse, farmer.
	Class 3 (Non-manual) Clerical and minor supervisory	Clerk, shop assistant, policeman, draughtsman, sales representative.
	Class 3 (Manual) Skilled manual	Electrician, tailor, bus driver, printer, cook.
Working Class	**Class 4** Semi-skilled manual	Agricultural worker, postman, telephone operator, fisherman, barman.
	Class 5 Unskilled manual	Railway porter, labourer, lorry driver's mate, window cleaner, office cleaner.

1. Explain in your own words how the Registrar-General constructs his classification of social classes. (4)
2. Place the following occupations in the appropriate social classes using the guidelines provided by the Registrar-General.
   a bricklayer
   b architect
   c typist
   d telephone supervisor
   e dishwasher (5)

3. In view of the principle used by the Registrar-General for classifying occupations, why is the line dividing the middle and working classes drawn between Class 3 (Non-manual) and Class 3 (Manual)? (3)
4. The Registrar-General notes that the 'general standing' of occupations is linked to a number of other social inequalities including education and economic factors. What does he mean by this? Give examples in your answer of the links between occupation, education and economic factors. (8)

4 Social class – A Marxist view

> Let the ruling classes tremble at a communist revolution. The proletarians have nothing to lose but their chains. They have a world to win. Working men of all countries unite.
> (from **Manifesto of the Communist Party** by Karl Marx and Friedrich Engels)

Karl Marx (1818–1883) provides a very different view of social class. He saw only two social classes in Western industrial societies, the ruling class or bourgeoisie made up of a minority of the population and the subject class or proletariat to which the majority belonged. The power of the ruling class comes from its ownership of the 'forces of production'. In an industrial society these include the factories and the machinery and raw materials used for manufacturing goods. Members of the proletariat own only their own labour which they hire out to the owners of industry in return for wages. The bourgeoisie is a non-producing class – it doesn't actually produce anything. Wealth in the form of manufactured goods is produced by the labour of the proletariat or working class. However much of this wealth is taken from them by the owners of industry in the form of profits. Marx argued that the proletariat is exploited by the bourgeoisie. The bourgeoisie use them for their own benefit and harm the interests of the proletariat in the process.

Marx believed that members of the proletariat would eventually realize that they were being exploited and oppressed. They would then join together to overthrow the bourgeoisie either by force or

Profits on their way to the bank. George Cruikshank's view of the exploitation of workers in the clothing industry in 1846

by voting their own representatives into government. They would then set up a communist society which means that the forces of production would be communally owned, that is jointly owned by all members of society. Goods produced would be shared equally and everyone would work for the benefit of society as a whole.

Marx's views on class are part of his more general theory of the history of human society. Some sociologists argue that they are more appropriate to nineteenth century Europe and have little relevance today. However in recent years Marx's ideas have had considerable influence within sociology.

The following extract presents some of Marx's ideas in the form of a conversation. A group of workmen sit drinking tea. One of

them, a man named Owen, gives his explanation of the stark inequalities which he sees around him.

> Employers, or rather exploiters of labour, profit-seeking
> shareholders, thieves, swindlers, bishops, financiers, capital-
> ists, none of these people produce anything themselves, but
> by means of cunning and scheming they contrive between
> them to obtain possession of a very large proportion of the
> things produced by the labour of others.
>
> The other class in society is those people who are engaged in
> useful work – the production of the benefits of civilization,
> the refinements and comforts of life. These are the
> productive people, the working class.
>
> Now we proceed to the 'share out' of those things produced.
> The people in division one are universally considered to be the
> most worthy and deserving, we give them two-thirds of the
> whole. The remainder is shared between the working people.
> You must not run away with the idea that in this class it is
> shared out equally between them. Some get more than their
> fair share, some get little, some get none at all. It is here that
> the 'battle of life' rages most fiercely.
>
> And all those people in this class are so fully occupied in this
> dreadful struggle to secure a little that but few of them pause
> to enquire why there are not more of the things they are
> fighting for, or why it is necessary to fight at all.

(adapted from **The Ragged Trousered Philanthropists** by Robert Tressall,
Grant Richards Press, 1914)

1. Briefly compare Marx's view of class with the Registrar-
   General's social classification.   (5)
2. Why does Owen talk about employers, thieves and swindlers in
   the same breath?   (5)
3. Why do most members of the proletariat or working class tend
   to accept their position without question?   (4)
4. How can the idea of 'divide and conquer' applied to the proletariat help to explain why the bourgeoisie rules successfully? (3)
5. Why does Marx urge working men to unite?   (3)

5 The distribution of income and wealth

All researchers recognize that social class involves economic in-equalities. Whereas Marxists give primary importance to inequalities in the distribution of wealth, particularly wealth in the form of ownership of the forces of production, other sociologists place equal if not more emphasis on income inequalities.

Table 1 shows the distribution of income before taxation and benefits. Households receive income from various sources – from employment, from occupational pensions, from investments and from other households e.g. alimony payments and gifts. Total income from these sources makes up **original income**.

Table 2 shows the distribution of income after taxation and benefits. The addition to original income of benefits paid by the state such as retirement pensions and supplementary benefit and the deduction of income tax payments and national insurance contributions gives **disposable income**.

Tables 1 and 2 are constructed in the following way. The income received by everyone is added together. Those with the highest income are placed at one end of the scale, those with the lowest at the other end. They are then divided into five equal groups with the richest fifth at one end and the poorest fifth at the other.

Table 3 shows the 'average value of benefits in kind and super-annuation contributions' for five occupational groups. These are benefits on top of pay provided by employers. Superannuation contributions are payments made by employees to a pension scheme organized by their employer.

Table 1   Distribution of original household income 1983

Percentage of income

(from figures in **Social Trends 16**, HMSO, London, 1986, p. 91)

Table 2 Distribution of disposable household income 1983

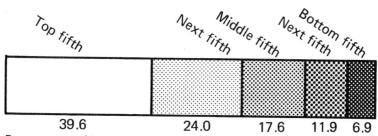

39.6   24.0   17.6   11.9   6.9

Percentage of income

(from figures in **Social Trends 16**, HMSO, London, 1986, p. 91)

Table 3 Average value of benefits in kind and super-annuation contributions for five occupational groups

Factory superintendent — 18% on top of salary

Works manager — 29%

Manufacturing manager — 33%

General manager — 37%

Managing director — 36%

Average salary received, July 1978 (including bonuses, commission, holidays, sickpay)

Average value of benefits in kind and superannuation contributions

(from **An A to Z of Income and Wealth**, HMSO, London, 1980, p. 16. Chart reproduced with the permission of the Controller of Her Majesty's Stationery Office)

1. What percentage of a) original income and b) disposable income does the richest fifth receive. (2)
2. Give one reason why official figures on the distribution of income may be inaccurate. (2)
3. What effects do taxation and benefits have on the distribution of income. Provide evidence from Tables 1 and 2 to support your answer.

4. In general the more a person earns, the greater the value of the benefits he receives from his employer in addition to pay. What evidence does Table 3 provide to support this statement?   (2)
5. Give two examples of 'benefits in kind' which a senior manager might receive from his employer.   (4)
6. With reference to the evidence in the tables, show why it is possible to reject the claim that the UK is a classless society.   (7)

6 The distribution of wealth in the UK

Inequalities in the distribution of wealth are considerably greater than inequalities in the distribution of income. It is difficult to define what should be counted as personal wealth. The definition used to compile the following figures sees wealth as 'marketable assets', that is assets that can be bought or sold. Examples of personal wealth therefore include houses, land and company shares which are owned by individuals. Table 1 shows the distribution of wealth among the adult population (aged 18 and over) in 1983. Table 2 shows the amount of various types of wealth at four different levels of wealth. Table 3 shows the proportion of company shares, overseas investments and land (by value) owned by these four groups.

1. What is the difference between income and wealth?   (4)
2. What share of personal wealth is owned by the wealthiest 10%?   (2)
3. What share would this group own in a society in which wealth was distributed equally?   (2)
4. a What accounts for over half the wealth of those with wealth holdings between £10,000 and £49,999?   (1)
   b What accounts for over a quarter of the wealth of those with wealth holdings over £200,000?   (1)
5. a What proportion of overseas investments is owned by those with wealth holdings below £10,000?   (1)
   b What percentage of the adult population do they form?   (1)
   c What proportion of land (by value) is owned by those with wealth holdings over £200,000?   (1)
   d What percentage of the adult population do they form?   (1)
6. From the evidence presented in the tables, what support can be provided for the Marxist view that there is a ruling class in Britain?   (6)

Table 1   The distribution of wealth 1983

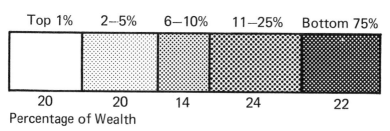

Top 1%	2–5%	6–10%	11–25%	Bottom 75%
20	20	14	24	22

Percentage of Wealth

(based on figures on **Social Trends 16**, HMSO, London, 1986, p. 92)

Table 2   How wealth is made up at different levels 1981

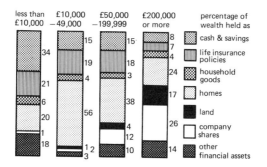

(adapted from table in **The State of the Nation** by S. Fothergill and J. Vincent, Pan, London, 1985, p. 20)

Table 3   Privately owned company shares, overseas investments and land 1981

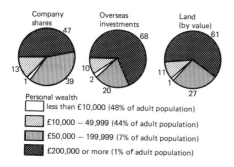

(adapted from table in **The State of the Nation** by S. Fothergill and J. Vincent, Pan, London, 1985, p. 20)

7 Inequality at the workplace

The distribution of income is closely related to social class defined in terms of occupation. In general, non-manual or white collar and professional occupations receive significantly higher wages than manual or blue collar jobs. Less obvious inequalities are directly linked to a person's occupation. Many of these have an important effect on his or her economic circumstances. This is shown clearly in the following table which is based on research by Wedderburn and Craig. It examines the terms and conditions of employment of different occupational groups in various manufacturing industries. The passage that follows, based on Peter Townsend's research into poverty in the UK, reveals further job related inequalities.

Selected differences in terms and conditions of employment

	Percentage of establishments in which the condition applies		
	Manual workers	clerical workers	Senior managers
Holiday: 15 days +	38	74	88
Choice of holiday time	35	76	88
Normal working 40 + hours per week	97	9	22
Sick pay—employers' scheme	57	98	98
Pension—employers' scheme	67	90	96
Time off with pay for personal reasons	29	83	93
Pay deductions for any lateness	90	8	0
Warning followed by dismissal for persistent lateness	84	78	41
No clocking on or booking in	2	48	94

(adapted from 'Workplace Inequality' by Dorothy Wedderburn, **New Society**, 9 April 1970, p. 593 and reproduced with permission)

Peter Townsend writes, 'Inequality at the workplace is systematically related to occupational class. There are major differences in the character, security, conditions and fringe benefits at work as between manual and non-manual grades.' In general the lower a person's social class, the greater the disadvantages directly related to his or her occupation. Manual jobs have a higher rate of injury. Townsend quotes the following examples, 'I had a heavy job and was doing a lot of lifting. I slipped a disc and had to have an operation ' – Man, aged 53, builder's labourer; now registered disabled. 'I was a foundry worker. The boiler blew up and injured me' – Man, 58; now a labourer in a metal works. Manual workers have less secure employment than non-manual workers. They have a greater risk of redundancy, unemployment, lay-offs and short-time working. Manual workers are more likely to work unusual and anti-social hours. Townsend quotes a 22-year-old bus driver who states, 'I got ulcers or some kind of stomach trouble through irregular meals.'

(adapted from 'Inequality at the workplace: How white collar always wins' by Peter Townsend, **New Society,** 18 October 1979, pp. 120–123)

1. Which occupational group works the longest hours? (1)
2. Which occupational group has the longest holidays? (1)
3. Which occupational group is most closely supervised? Give two reasons for your choice? (4)
4. In terms of the information in the above table, which occupational group enjoys the greatest economic benefits? Explain your choice with reference to three pieces of evidence from the table. (7)
5. How might the work related inequalities shown by Townsend's study result in loss of income for manual workers? (7)

8 Social class and life chances

The German sociologist Max Weber (1864–1920) made the observation that a person's class position influences many areas of his life. In particular his class has an important effect on his 'life chances', that is his chances of obtaining those things defined as desirable and of avoiding those things defined as undesirable in his society. According to Gerth and Mills, life chances include, 'Everything from the chance to view fine arts, the chance to remain healthy and grow tall, and if sick to get well again quickly, the chance to avoid becoming a juvenile delinquent and very crucially, the chance to complete an intermediary or higher educational grade.' In general, the higher a person's class position, the better his life chances and the greater his opportunity to obtain and experience those things defined as desirable in his society. The relationship between social class and life chances is indicated in the following tables.

Infant mortality rates by social class – England and Wales 1981

	Social Class					
	1	2	3	4	5	6
Infant mortality rate	8.2	9.7	9.8	11.7	13.2	15.5

(Manual occupations begin with class 4. The infant mortality rate is deaths of infants under one year of age per thousand live births)

(Table compiled from figures in **Social Trends 15**, HMSO, London, 1985, p. 104)

Table 2   Percentage reporting long-standing illness and limiting long-standing illness by social class and sex 1982

	Social class					
	1	2	3	4	5	6
Long-standing illness						
Males	23	25	27	29	33	35
Females	21	26	31	29	38	42
Limiting long-standing illness						
Males	11	14	15	17	20	23
Females	10	14	17	18	25	30

(People defined illness as 'limiting' if they believed it limited their activities compared with people of their own age.)

(Table compiled from figures in **General Household Survey 1982**, HMSO, London, 1984, pp. 165, 166)

Table 3   Type of house by social class 1977

Type of house	Social class						
	1	2	3	4	5	6	All
Detached	43	37	16	12	8	5	17
Semi-detached	28	31	33	36	30	25	33
Terraced house	15	16	23	32	35	38	28

(The figures refer to the percentages of each social class living in the three types of houses. The figures do not add up to 100% because people also live in other types of accommodation e.g. flats)

(Table adapted from **Social Class Differences in Britain** 2nd edition by Ivan Reid, Grant McIntyre, London, 1981, p. 192)

1. Which social class has the highest rates of infant mortality?   (1)
2. Summarize the relationship between social class and infant mortality rates.   (3)

3. Briefly suggest why there are class differences in rates of infant mortality. (5)
4. Which social class has the lowest rates of long-standing illness and limiting long-standing illness? (1)
5. Briefly suggest how a person's class position can affect his health. (5)
6. Members of which social class are most likely to live in semi-detached houses? (1)
7. Briefly suggest reasons for class differences in housing. (4)

9 Social class subcultures

In all stratification systems there is a tendency for members of each stratum or level to develop their own way of life which differs to some extent from that of other members of society. In socio-logical terminology, they develop their own subculture, that is certain norms, attitudes and values which are distinctive to them as a social group. Subcultures tend to develop when some members of society share certain circumstances and problems which are not shared by all members. As this section has indicated, there are important differences between the circumstances of manual and non-manual workers. Many sociologists argue that this has resulted in distinctive middle and working class sub-cultures.

An important aspect of a subculture is the general view of life or 'perspectives' held by its members. The following chart outlines some of the main aspects of traditional working class and middle class perspectives. The information is a summary of the findings of studies on workers living in close-knit communities and employed in long-established industries such as mining, docking and ship-building. The information on middle class perspectives is based mainly on studies of middle class family life. Recent research suggests that traditional working class perspectives are tending to disappear. However, many sociologists believe that there are still important differences between working and middle class attitudes and outlooks on life.

Traditional working class perspective	Middle class perspective
1. Society is divided into 'us' and 'them'.	1. Society is divided into a series of levels or strata. Society is like a ladder with many rungs.
2. There is little chance of any of 'us' becoming one of 'them'.	2. There are many opportunities for individuals to improve their social position.
3. What happens if life is largely due to luck or fate.	3. What a man achieves depends largely on what he 'makes of himself'.
4. The only way we can improve our situation is by joining together and taking collective action.	4. Improving one's situation depends on individual effort and personal qualities such as perseverence and determination.
5. Live for today, enjoy yourself and accept your situation.	5. Look to the future, plan ahead and make sacrifices for future reward.

(adapted from **The Affluent Worker in the Class Structure** by J. H. Goldthorpe, D. Lockwood, F. Bechhofer and J. Platt, Cambridge University Press, Cambridge, 1969, pp. 116–121)

1. Which of the following views indicate traditional working class perspectives and which indicate middle class perspectives? Briefly explain your choices.
   a 'Que sera sera, whatever will be will be.' (2)
   b You can make it if you try. (2)
   c Save and prosper. It's worth it in the long run. (2)
   d The poor have only themselves to blame. (2)
   e Live for today because tomorrow might never come. (2)
2. In terms of these perspectives suggest why trade union membership is more typical of manual rather than non-manual workers. (4)
3. Suggest how these differing perspectives might partly account for the fact that students from middle class backgrounds attain higher educational qualifications than those from working class backgrounds. (6)

10 Embourgeoisement (1)

What is the shape of the class system in modern Western societies? Which occupational groups should be placed in which social classes? Where should the line be drawn dividing the middle and working classes? How is the shape of the class system changing? These and similar questions have formed the basis for considerable research in sociology. Part of this research has been concerned with the question of embourgeoisement which means becoming middle class. The following passage examines this question.

During the 1950s there was a general increase in prosperity in Western industrial societies. Living standards rose steadily and in particular, many manual workers now earned wages equal to and even above those of white collar workers in the lower middle class. Studies of poverty, for example Rowntree's study in 1950, suggested that poverty was rapidly disappearing. It appeared that the widespread poverty of the earlier years of the century was now a thing of the past.

A number of sociologists writing in the 1950s believed that a process of embourgeoisement was occurring. They argued that large numbers of relatively highly paid manual workers, for example workers in the car industry, were becoming middle class. These workers became known as affluent workers. It was claimed that their entry into the middle class was leading to a change in the shape of the stratification system. The majority of the population was increasingly moving into the middle range of the class system. This would result in a 'middle mass society'.

The affluent worker was seen to be becoming middle class in more than just economic terms. A number of sociologists believed that he was also becoming middle class in social terms. This means that he would identify with the middle class and adopt middle class attitudes, norms and values.

(adapted from **The Affluent Worker in the Class Structure** by J.H. Goldthorpe, D. Lockwood, F. Bechhofer and J. Platt, Cambridge University Press, Cambridge, 1969, pp. 1–29)

1. If embourgeoisement was occurring, which of the following would represent the shape of the class system? Briefly give reasons for your choice.

a ☐   b △   c ▽   d ⋈   e ◇   (4)

2. Which of the above shapes would represent an outline of the class system before embourgeoisement was supposed to have begun? Briefly give reasons for your choice.   (4)

3. Select one of the following phrases to describe the social movement of the affluent worker if embourgeoisement was occurring.
   a horizontal social mobility
   b upward social mobility
   c downward social mobility   (1)

4. Name one white collar occupational group which would be included in the lower middle class.   (1)

5. What is an 'affluent worker'?   (3)

6. What does the phrase, 'identify with the middle class' mean? (3)

7. Give two examples of middle class attitudes, norms or values which the affluent worker may have adopted.   (4)

11 Embourgeoisement (2)

In the early 1960s a team led by John Goldthorpe and David Lockwood conducted a study in Luton to discover whether or not embourgeoisement was occurring. The research was based on a sample of 229 affluent workers and 54 clerical workers. Goldthorpe and Lockwood argued that if embourgeoisement was occurring then there would be little difference between the affluent workers and clerks in economic and social terms.

The results of Goldthorpe and Lockwood's research showed that affluent workers saw their work mainly in terms of money. Most had chosen their jobs because they were highly paid with the aim of improving their living standards. They did not expect or find much interest and satisfaction in their work. They did not expect or seek promotion. Few had close friends at work and few attended the social clubs provided by their firms. By comparison the white collar workers look for more than money. They expect and find more satisfaction from work. They hope and work for promotion. They make more friends at work and the firms' social clubs are mainly filled with white collar workers.

Many affluent workers (57% of the sample) were home owners or buyers. They lived on estates made up of both manual and white collar workers. However, they showed no desire to mix with their white collar neighbours. The friends they made in the neighbourhood were nearly always manual workers like themselves. Many of the material goods owned by affluent workers, e.g. cars, washing machines, household furnishings, were very similar to those of their white collar neighbours. However the affluent workers did not appear to regard such possessions as middle class status symbols. Rather they saw them as practical ways of improving their style of life and standard of living.

Most affluent workers (80% of the sample) voted Labour in the 1959 election. According to Goldthorpe and Lockwood, 'Labour was typically seen (by affluent workers) as the party of the working classes, as the party for which the manual worker would naturally vote.' Research has shown that around two-thirds of the working class and about one-fifth of the middle class regularly vote Labour in British general elections.

(adapted from **The Affluent Worker in the Class Structure** by J. H. Goldthorpe, D. Lockwood, F. Bechhofer and J. Platt, Cambridge University Press, Cambridge, 1969)

1. Why are white collar workers more likely than affluent workers to participate in works' social clubs? (4)
2. What changes would be expected in the attitudes of affluent workers towards their work if embourgeoisement was occurring? (5)
3. What evidence does the extract contain which suggests that affluent workers neither seek nor value middle class status? (5)
4. a If embourgeoisement was occurring what proportion of affluent workers would be expected to vote for the Labour Party? (2)
   b What evidence does the passage contain which suggests that in terms of his political views the affluent worker is not becoming middle class? (4)

12 Social Mobility

Social mobility refers to movement from one stratum to another in a system of social stratification. Social mobility can be either upward, for example moving from the working to the middle class, or downward. The most common way of measuring social mobility is to compare the status of sons with that of their fathers. Thus if the son of an unskilled manual worker becomes a labourer he is not socially mobile, but if he becomes an accountant he is upwardly mobile. In terms of the Registrar-General's classification he has moved from Class 5, the class into which he was born, to Class 1. The following passage examines some of the findings of the most recent large scale study of social mobility in England and Wales.

In 1980, a group of sociologists at Nuffield College, Oxford, published the results of a study of social mobility in England and Wales. The 'Oxford Mobility Study' was conducted in 1972 and based on a sample of 10,000 men. Occupation was used to indicate a person's class with the main emphasis being given to the economic rewards of occupations. The authors identified seven classes which they then simplified into a three class system.

1. **The Service Class**: people with well paid jobs with career prospects in the professions, national and local government, senior management and higher technical jobs.

2. **The Intermediate Class**: people with routine non-manual jobs, clerks, sales personnel, self-employed with small businesses, supervisors, lower-grade technicians.

3. **The Working Class**: Skilled, semi-skilled and unskilled manual workers, including farm labourers.

One aim of the study was to discover whether Britain had become a more open society. Have, for example, the chances for a working class boy to reach the service class improved over the years. The study compared the social mobility rates of men born between 1908–1917 with those born between 1938–1947. Findings on the first group are shown in Table 1 as 'then', those for the second group as 'now'.

The findings of the Oxford Mobility Study may be simply expressed as the 1:2:4 Rule of Relative Hope. This rule states that whatever the chance of a working class boy of reaching the service class, a boy from the intermediate class has twice

Table 1   ## Table 2

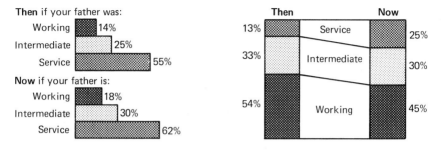

Your chance of ending up in service class

Then if your father was:
Working 14%
Intermediate 25%
Service 55%

Now if your father is:
Working 18%
Intermediate 30%
Service 62%

Then   **Now**
13%   Service   25%
33%   Intermediate   30%
54%   Working   45%

(adapted from **The Sunday Times**, 13 January 1980, p. 13)

the chance and a boy from the service class four times the chance.

The 1:2:4 rule applies to both groups of men in the survey (i.e. those born 1908–1917 and those born 1938–1947). Table 1 compares the chances of the two groups of reaching the service class. Although the percentage of working class boys entering the service class has risen (from 14% to 18%) so has the percentage of those from the intermediate and service classes. The relative chances of children from each social class background has remained unaltered at approximately 1:2:4.

At first glance this might not make sense. How can considerably more people enter the service class over the years? This is due simply to a change in the occupational structure. During the period covered by the survey the number of service class occupations has nearly doubled. These changes are shown in Table 2. As a result of changes in the occupational structure there is far more room at the top of the class system.

(adapted from 'The 1:2:4 rule of class in Britain' by P. Kellner and P. Wilby, **The Sunday Times**, 13 January 1980, p. 13)

1. Outline the changes in the occupational structure during the period covered by the study.   (4)

There's more room at the top now but the odds are still against the working class boy

2. What are the chances of those born into the intermediate class in a) 1908–17 and b) 1938–47 of reaching the service class?   (2)
3. If Britain were a completely open society, would the chances of those born into the working class of entering the service class be, a) the same b) better or c) worse than those born into the service class? Briefly explain your answer.   (4)
4. Why are more working class boys entering the service class in recent years?   (2)
5. The relative chances of boys from each social class of reaching the service class has remained unchanged. Show that this is the case with reference to the figures in the chart.   (4)
6. Briefly suggest why those born at the top have the greatest chance of obtaining service class jobs.   (4)

13 Does social class matter?

The following extracts present the views of two Conservative MPs, Sir Keith Joseph and Norman St. John Stevas, on the class system.

The heart of the class concept is that human beings are automatically changed by owning wealth. But this is palpably (obviously) not a sufficient description of the variety of human beings... There are many things that resources cannot buy. You cannot become an MP these days by the ownership of money. You certainly can't become a successful poet or historian or novelist by the ownership of money. You can't be loved because of the ownership of money. You can't enjoy life because of the ownership of money...

If I tell you that a man is a worker, or that a man is a wage earner, or that a man has capital, what more do you know about him? You don't know about his private life, you don't know about his day-dreams, you don't know about the degree to which he is a good husband or she's a good wife. You don't know anything about their capacity as parents, you don't know about their serenity, you don't know about the state of their soul. You know one set of facts only, that there is some more choice in some range of activities given by the ownership of money than by not owning money.

(Sir Keith Joseph MP, 1979, then Secretary for Industry. Quoted in **The Guardian**, July 18, 1979, p. 7)

I think that class is largely an irrelevancy in contemporary British society. Some people may use it as an excuse for their own failures, but I think we have very largely a mobile society, a society open to talent. The talented child or young person is able to reach the top of any profession or any activity to which that child sets his or her mind, provided that ability is there. I think we're a much more mobile society, for example, than the United States. We talk a lot about class in British society, but I think its significance socially is very small.

(Norman St. John Stevas MP, 1980, then Leader of the House of Commons. Quoted in **Social Class Differences in Britain** 2nd Edition by Ivan Reid, Grant McIntyre, London, 1981, p. 298)

1. Discuss the above views in the light of the evidence presented in this section. (20)

Section 5 Race and Ethnicity

The previous section looked at various forms of social stratification – the feudal system, caste and social class. This section is concerned with ethnic stratification. It begins with the idea of race arguing that this idea is not particularly useful for understanding the position of non-white minority groups in society. Instead it argues that such groups are more usefully seen as ethnic groups. The section examines the idea of ethnicity and the case for and against ethnic subcultures. It looks at the various aspects of racism and the evidence for racism in British society. Ethnic stratification is then examined in terms of the life chances of members of ethnic minority groups. The section closes with an analysis of the riots in English cities during the first half of the 1980s.

1 The idea of race

The following passage looks at some of the ways in which the term race has been used. From a sociological viewpoint race is a social definition, a social construction – a race is simply a group of people who see themselves, or are seen by others, as a race.

> Human beings are all members of the same species. This means that if any male and female mate they are likely to produce offspring who are themselves human beings. However it is clear that not all human beings look alike and this has led to people being classified into types or 'races' in terms of physical appearance. One of the most commonly used classifications divides the human species into three groups, Mongoloid, Negroid and Caucasoid, as shown in the chart overleaf.
> This is a very broad classification. It is often subdivided – for example the category Caucasoid is sometimes divided into 'whites', 'Asian Indians' and various other groups.

Classification of racial groups

Racial Group	Eyes	Hair	Skin	Face	Main location
Mongoloid	Black 'slanted'	Black straight	Yellow-reddish brown	Flat, high cheekbones, sparse beard	S & E Asia, N & S America Pacific
Negroid	Brown	Black tightly curled	Dark brown-black	Broad nose, wide nostrils, thick lips, sparse beard	Sub-Saharan African
Caucasoid	Light blue to dark brown	Straight, wavy, curly, balding more common	White to dark brown	Narrow nose thin lips, more facial hair	Europe, M. East N. Africa India

The idea of race looked at above is based mainly on physical appearance. Large numbers of people are grouped together and called a race because they are said to look alike. However many biologists reject this view of race as unscientific. On the basis of people's outward appearance, it is possible to divide the human species into any number of races. For example in Britain people with red hair, blue eyes and a pale skin could be classified as a separate race in terms of their physical appearance.

Some biologists now reject the whole idea of different races. They argue that the genetic makeup of all human beings is basically the same. The minor variations that do exist are so small that it makes little sense to talk about different races. Other biologists argue that if the human species is to be divided into types or races, it should be on the basis of genetic characteristics such as blood groups which can be accurately measured. However, there are very few characteristics for which the genetic basis is known and can be measured. We are therefore a long way from a scientific classification of the human species into types or races.

From what has been said so far it can be argued that 'races' are simply social definitions or categories. A race is simply a group of people who see themselves as a race and/or are seen by other people as a race.

At different times and places all sorts of racial classifications have been devised. In Germany in the 1930s and 40s the Nazis divided Europeans into a number of racial groupings from blonde, blue eyed, white Aryans – the 'master race' – to dark haired brown eyed, olive skinned Mediterraneans. In South Africa today the main divisions are seen to be between whites, coloureds ('mixed races') and blacks.

Simply because race is a social definition does not mean it should be dismissed as unimportant. People make race important because, on the basis of supposed racial differences, they reject, discriminate against and kill each other. The idea of race is one of the main factors dividing the human species. This is partly because many people believe that each 'race' has certain inborn characteristics. These characteristics are often seen as undesirable. Thus Western 'whites' sometimes see themselves as superior to, as more intelligent than other 'races'. Few, if any, sociologists would support this view. They point to the evidence of history to dis-prove it. Thus in Africa the Songhai, Ashanti and Zimbabwe civilizations flourished when Europe was in the Dark Ages. John Goldthorpe has argued that if we look at the world in the year 1600, China was probably the most advanced nation with India and Arabia close behind. This type of evidence strongly suggests that there is no basis to the claim that one so-called 'race' is superior to another.

(adapted in part from **The Sociology of Race** by John Richardson and John Lambert, Causeway Press, Ormskirk, 1985)

1. Classifications of races based on physical appearance are un-scientific. Why? (3)
2. a Why do some biologists reject the idea of different races? (2)
   b What do other biologists see as the only scientific way of classifying human types or races? (2)
   c Why are they a long way from this classification? (2)
3. Race is simply a social definition.
   a What does this mean? (2)
   b Why is the idea of race important even though it may simply be a social definition. (3)
4. a What is the physical difference between the two figures shown in the cartoon overleaf. (1)
   b Captain Kirk and the crew of the Starship 'Enterprise' were

Two 'racial' groups engaged in bitter conflict on a distant planet in the galaxy.
(Taken from an episode of the TV programme 'Star Trek'.)

amazed that this physical difference should be the basis for
'racial' conflict.
i) Why might they have been amazed?   (2)
ii) With examples suggest why someone from another
planet might be amazed at 'racial' conflict on our own
planet.   (3)

2 The idea of ethnicity

The term race suggests that a group is in some way biologically
different from the rest of the human species. The term ethnic
group suggests that people are culturally different. Usually the
term is used to refer to a group within a larger society – an ethnic
minority group. The following passage looks at the idea of
ethnicity.

An ethnic group can be defined as a group within a larger society whose members share a common origin, have a sense of belonging to the group, have a distinctive subculture and who mix or interact regularly with each other. This view of ethnicity can be illustrated by looking at blacks in the USA.

1) They are a minority group in society – they make up around 12% of the population.
2) They share a common origin – they were transported as slaves from West Africa.
3) They have a sense of belonging to the group – phrases like 'I'm Black and I'm Proud' and 'Black is Beautiful' suggest a common identity; support for the Black Power Movement (at least in the late 1960s and 1970s) suggests a common goal.
4) They have certain distinctive aspects of culture, for example soul music and black dialect.
5) Many interact regularly with other blacks as they often live in ghettoes which are largely separate from the wider society.

Turning to the United Kingdom, it is possible to identify a number of ethnic groups – Afro-Caribbeans (or West Indians), Chinese, Pakistanis, Cypriots, Punjabi Sikhs and so on. There has been considerable argument however about whether or not these groups have distinctive subcultures. This point will be examined later in the section.

(adapted in part from **Right On: From Blues to Soul in Black America** by Michael Haralambos, Eddison, London, 1974)

1. What is a minority group? (2)
2. What is meant by the following aspects of an ethnic group?
   a a common origin (2)
   b a sense of belonging to the group (2)
   c a distinctive subculture (2)
   d members interact regularly with each other (2)
3. Briefly outline the difference between a racial group and an ethnic group. (4)
4. Select one minority group in the United Kingdom and show with examples how they can be seen as an ethnic group. (6)

3 Ethnicity and life chances

In general, members of ethnic minority groups do not share the same life chances as the rest of the population. They do not have the same opportunity of obtaining those things defined as desirable by the society in which they live, e.g. high status occupations and high quality housing, or of avoiding those things defined as undesirable e.g. illness and unemployment. The following passage examines some of the life chances of Afro-Caribbeans and Asians in the United Kingdom compared to those of the white population.

> Occupation is probably the most important influence on a person's life chances. With a low status job, or no job at all, people's life chances will be limited. In all probability their income will be low, their housing below the standard of the population as a whole, their children will have less chance of obtaining high educational qualifications, they may well have a shorter life and suffer from more ill health than people in higher status jobs.
>
> The following tables compare the occupations and levels of unemployment of whites, Asians and Afro-Caribbeans in the UK. They are based on information from a survey conducted in 1982 by the Policy Studies Institute.

Table 1 Ethnicity and occupation

| | men | | | women | | |
	white %	Asian %	Afro-Caribbean %	white %	Asian %	Afro-Caribbean %
professional, employer, manager	19	13	5	7	6	1
other non-manual	23	13	10	55	42	52
skilled manual/foreman	42	33	48	5	6	4
semi-skilled manual	13	34	26	21	44	36
unskilled manual	3	6	9	11	2	7

Table 2 Ethnicity and unemployment

	men %	women %
white	13	10
Asian	20	20
Afro-Caribbean	25	16

The above tables show that, compared to whites, a significantly higher proportion of Asians and Afro-Caribbeans are 1) manual workers 2) unemployed. The 1982 survey and a number of studies conducted during the 1970s clearly reveal the disadvantaged position of ethnic minorities in the labour market. Here are some of the findings of this research. The earnings of ethnic minorities in non-manual and skilled manual jobs are significantly lower than those of whites in similar occupations. Those employed in semi-skilled and un-skilled manual jobs have slightly higher wages than whites in similar jobs. But this is largely due to working shifts and longer hours in less pleasant conditions. Over three-quarters of whites with degree level qualifications have non-manual occupations but less than one third of ethnic minorities with similar qualifications.

Is the position of ethnic minorities in the labour market improving? Comparing the results of the 1974 Policy Studies Institute survey with those of 1982, the answer is no. At first their position looks better. Compared to whites a higher proportion of blacks has moved from manual to non-manual jobs. But more young blacks than whites are unemployed. Many who in the past would have been doing manual work are now on the dole. Taking this into account, the overall position of ethnic minorities in the labour market has changed little from the 1970s to the 1980s.

Some sociologists believe that many employers are operating a 'dual market' jobs policy. A dual labour market, as its name suggests, has two parts. 1) The primary market made up of jobs with high pay, secure employment, good training and promotion prospects. 2) The secondary market made up of jobs with low pay, insecurity of employment and few opportunities for training and promotion. The secondary market provides relatively cheap labour which can be quickly trained and easily disposed of and replaced. In practice the primary market is largely filled by white male employees. Members of ethnic minority groups and women tend to be concentrated in the secondary market.

(adapted from **Race Relations in Britain** by Andrew Pilkington, University Tutorial Press, Slough, 1984 and 'The Jobs Bias Against Blacks' by David Thomas in **New Society**, 1 November, 1984, pp. 167–169)

1. From Table 1 what percentage of white, Asian and Afro-Caribbean men are employed in
   a working class occupations   (2)
   b middle class occupations   (2)
2. From Table 2 which group has the highest level of
   a male unemployment   (1)
   b female unemployment   (1)
3. Why is occupation probably the most important influence on life chances?
   (Use information from Section 4 to answer this question.)   (4)
4. Even when they have similar jobs to whites, members of ethnic minority groups are often disadvantaged. What evidence in the passage supports this statement?   (3)
5. Has the position of ethnic minorities in the labour market improved from the early 1970s to the early 1980s? Give evidence to support your answer.   (3)
6. Members of ethnic minority groups tend to be concentrated in the secondary labour market. Why should this reduce their chances of improving their position?   (4)

4 Racism and ethnic stratification

The previous passage shows clearly that members of ethnic minority groups are disproportionately represented in the lower levels of the class system. This means that a higher proportion of ethnic minority group members are working class than whites. Because of this it can be argued that ethnicity is an important aspect of social stratification – that there is an ethnic stratification system.

There are two main explanations for ethnic stratification in the UK. The first, known as the host-immigrant model, is the more optimistic. It begins with the observation that many members of ethnic minority groups are immigrants. Among other things, it argues that once migrants adapt to their new home, learn the British way of life and their children travel through the British educational system, they will become a part of the population as a whole. Ethnic stratification and ethnic disadvantage will disappear. The 'immigrants' will become like the 'hosts'.

The host-immigrant model has been strongly criticised. Evidence about the position of blacks in American society does not support

it. Despite being resident in the United States for many generations, blacks as a group have still not entered the mainstream of
American life and the majority remain in the lower levels of the US
class system. In the UK more than 40% of the black population is
British born yet black youth unemployment is significantly higher
than that of white youth. This does not indicate progess towards
the removal of ethnic disadvantage. In fact in 1974 black and
white unemployment had been the same.

The second explanation for ethnic stratification argues that it is
largely the result of racism. The idea of racism and some of its
possible effects are considered in the following passage.

> Racism is a general term used by sociologists to cover all the
> negative attitudes and practices directed towards groups
> seen as racially different. Racism can be divided into three
> main aspects 1) Cultural racism 2) Racialism 3) Institutional
> racism. These will now be examined along with some of the
> evidence for racism in Britain.
>
> **Cultural racism**
> This is a set of beliefs and ideas which provides a false and
> mistaken picture of a so-called 'racial group'. Thus, simply
> because a person is black, whites may believe him or her to be
> 'ignorant', 'primitive' and 'inferior'. Cultural racism is a form
> of prejudice whereby people are pre-judged to be a certain
> way simply because of their physical appearance.
>
> Researchers have identified cultural racism in many areas
> of British life – in storybooks where 'Little Black Sambo' is
> still alive and well; in the media where blacks are presented as
> 'outsiders' and portrayed as a problem with the spotlight on
> black crime; in history courses where the 'civilising' influence
> and conquests of the British over 'backward' peoples are
> recounted daily in classrooms across the nation. It is difficult
> to judge the extent of cultural racism in the UK, partly
> because attitudes are constantly changing. However a
> number of surveys reveal its existence. When it is found in
> groups who work directly with ethnic minorities, it may well
> cause serious problems. Thus a report by the Policy Studies
> Institute in 1983 found that racial prejudice was widespread
> on the Metropolitan (London) Police Force and that terms of
> abuse such as 'nigger', 'coon' and 'wog' were widely used.

Racialism

Racialism refers to racial discrimination – discrimination against people simply because they are seen as belonging to a particular racial group. It refers to actual behaviour rather than attitudes and beliefs. Examples of racialism include an employer refusing a job to someone simply because they are black, or a landlord refusing to rent a house to someone simply because of the colour of their skin.

Surveys from the 1960s to the 1980s show that racialism is widespread in the UK. It is found in employment, housing and services such as insurance, banking and building societies. Even with similar qualifications, occupations and income to whites, members of ethnic minority groups are less successful in applications for jobs, bank loans, mortgages, renting property and obtaining council houses where they were usually given inferior accommodation.

Institutional racism

This view sees racism as a basic part of the structure of society, as built into the institutions which form the foundations of the social system. Thus racism is seen to be entrenched in the political, legal and educational systems, in the labour market and the stratification system.

The following quotation makes clear the difference between racialism and institutional racism. Written by American authors, it refers to the city of Birmingham, Alabama in the Deep South of the USA.

> When white terrorists bomb a black church and kill five black children, that is an act of individual racism, widely deplored by most segments of the society. But when in that same city – Birmingham, Alabama — five hundred black babies die each year because of the lack of proper food, shelter and medical facilities, and thousands more are destroyed and maimed physically, emotionally and intellectually because of conditions of poverty and discrimination in the black community, that is a function of institutional racism. When a black family moves into a home in a white neighbourhood and is stoned, burned or routed out, they are victims of an overt act of individual racism which many people will condemn – at least in words. But it is institutional racism that keeps black people in dilapidated slum tenements, subject to the daily prey of exploitative

slumlords, merchants, loan sharks and discriminatory real estate agents.

(from **Black Power** by S. Carmichael and C. Hamilton, Penguin, Harmondsworth, 1969)

Evidence from the UK provides support for the existence of institutional racism. As the previous passage shows, the operation of the labour market results in ethnic disadvantage. Evidence from a range of life chances suggest that the structure of UK society denies opportunities to ethnic minorities. There are however some signs of improvement. For example, a comparison of the 1974 and 1982 Policy Institute Studies shows that the housing standards of ethnic minorities have risen, though the 1982 report concluded, 'the quality of housing of black people is much worse than the quality of housing in general in this country'. Despite some improvements, the 1982 survey found little change in the overall position of ethnic minorities in the UK – the disadvantaged position of the original migrants had continued into the second generation.

The evidence of racism does not necessarily lead to a rejection of the host-immigrant model outlined in the introduction to this passage. Many blacks arrived in the UK with few paper qualifications or none at all. They were employed in low pay, low status jobs. Their children often started at the bottom of the class system. Even without racism it would have taken time for them to work their way up. However, whatever these disadvantages, they would be considerably less without the barriers erected by racism.

(adapted from **The Sociology of Race** by John Richardson and John Lambert, Causeway Press, Ormskirk, 1985)

1. Why is the host-immigrant model relatively optimistic from the point of view of ethnic minority groups?   (3)
2. a Briefly summarize the evidence which does not support the host-immigrant model.   (2)
   b Despite this evidence it can be argued that the model should not be completely rejected. Why not?   (3)
3. Which of the following are examples of 1) cultural racism 2) racialism 3) institutional racism.
   a A higher infant mortality rate for blacks compared to whites.
                    (1)

   b Blacks have a natural sense of rhythm.　　　　　　　　(1)
   c Refusing a person a mortgage because of the colour of his
      skin.　　　　　　　　　　　　　　　　　　　　　(1)
   d Whites have civilised the 'coloured races'.　　　　　(1)
4. Ethnic stratification will remain as long as racism is widespread
   in the UK. Briefly discuss this statement.　　　　　　(4)
5. There is no such thing as a black problem, only a white problem.
   Discuss in the light of evidence from the passage.　　　(4)

5 Ethnic subcultures

The term ethnic group was defined earlier in this section (see p. 101). Part of this definition stated that it is a group within a larger society whose members have certain beliefs, attitudes and behaviour patterns which are different from those of the wider society – in other words a group with a distinctive subculture. Thus some researchers have claimed that many Pakistanis in Britain have an ethnic subculture. This includes Islamic religion, arranged marriages and three generation extended families with the eldest male as the family head. The claim that ethnic sub-cultures exist has produced a number of questions. These questions are examined in the following passage.

> 1) Do ethnic subcultures really exist? Are the differences in behaviour and attitudes which some researchers identify really important? Or are they simply superficial, surface differences in which case members of ethnic minority groups are, for all intents and purposes, no different from the rest of society? For example, if many Afro-Caribbeans listen to reggae music does this make them much different from mainstream white society? Are there just as many differences within white society as there are between whites and blacks?

> 2) If ethnic subcultures do exist, where do they come from? To answer this question it is necessary to look at a) the country from which the immigrants came e.g. India and Jamaica b) the subculture that each group of migrants brought with them e.g. Sikh Punjabis and Hindu Punjabis each from the same part of India but with different religious beliefs and c) the subcultures which develop from adaptation to a new society e.g. the second generation youth cultures

developed by the sons and daughters of the original migrants to the UK. All the above will probably have some input into ethnic subcultures.

3) How important are ethnic subcultures? Do they help to explain the position of ethnic minorities in society? Many sociologists would argue that racism is the main reason for ethnic disadvantage. Others would see ethnic subcultures as at least part of the explanation. From this viewpoint ethnic subcultures may lead to minority groups living apart from the wider society jealously guarding their own customs, beliefs and cultural identity. This may well prevent them from moving into the mainstream of society.

Asian children at Drummond Middle School, Bradford.

4) Do ethnic minorities choose to remain distinct from the wider society, choose to maintain separate subcultures? Or are they forced by hostility and racism to retreat into their own communities where they develop their own way of life? If this is the case then ethnic subcultures are not freely chosen, they are a response, a reaction to a racist society.

(adapted in part from **The Sociology of Race** by John Richardson and John Lambert, Causeway Press, Ormskirk, 1985)

1. The fact that many members of ethnic minority groups had their origins outside the UK may result in ethnic subcultures. Why? (3)
2. Racism may help to create ethnic subcultures. Why? (3)
3. People may take steps to preserve their ethnic subcultures. Why? (3)
4. Ethnic subcultures may prevent the integration of minority group members into the wider society. Why? (3)
5. In Bradford there are some 40,000 Moslems of Asian origin. The Moslem Parents' Association has demanded separate schools for its children.
   a In view of the history of religious schools in Britain, have they the right to make this demand? Give evidence to support your answer. (2)
   b What does this demand suggest about their attitude towards their subculture? (3)
   c Would you support their demand? Give reasons for your answer. (3)

6 Afro-Caribbean subculture

Some of the questions raised in the previous passage will now be considered in terms of Afro-Caribbean subculture in Britain.

The sociologist Stuart Hall offers the following picture of the development of an Afro-Caribbean subculture. Many Afro-Caribbeans in the UK found themselves trapped in ghettoes and locked into the lower levels of the class structure. They shared experiences of disadvantage and discrimination. Being thrown together in similar circumstances provided the basis

Rastafarian sound system, Notting Hill Carnival.

for a 'cultural revival', for the creation of 'an alternative black social life' based in part on Afro-Caribbean culture. It can be seen in the rise of 'Afro-Caribbean consciousness' which defines blackness in a positive way. It can be seen in the development of 'black' streets, neighbourhoods, cafés and pubs, in the growth of revivalist churches, gospel singing and mass baptisms in the local swimming baths. It can be seen in Caribbean fruit and vegetable stalls, in the shebeen and Saturday night blues party, in sound systems and black record shops selling ska and reggae.

Within this subculture there is diversity. Apart from Afro-Caribbean versions of Christianity the Rastafarian religion, which developed in the 1930s among the Jamaican poor, became increasingly popular amongst young Afro-Caribbeans. Rastafarians are immediately visible with their rolled, uncut hair – dreadlocks – and their Ethiopian colours of red, gold and green and often heard with the Rastafarian inspired reggae of Bob Marley and others. Rastafarians see themselves as living in Babylon – the corrupt and evil white society which oppresses them but which will eventually crumble from its own corruption. They must find their 'true selves' and cleanse their minds of racist ideas of black inferiority imposed by white society. They are joined in brotherhood by the belief that Jah (God) is present in each of them and by the view that blacks are united in a common struggle. Rastafarians rejoice in blackness, they have a pride and self-respect based on their definition of what it means to be black.

On the one hand it is possible to paint a picture of an Afro-Caribbean subculture which appears different and distinctive. On the other hand a number of studies suggest that Afro-Caribbeans are little different from members of the wider society. What appears to be distinctive may simply be surface differences, a matter of style rather than anything basic. In the winter of 1979–80 Gaskell and Smith interviewed 240 blacks aged 16–25 living in London asking them to describe the way of life they most wanted. The answers stressed everyday ambitions – a good job, a decent home, a car, marriage and a happy family life. These results give no indications of a distinctive Afro-Caribbean subculture. What Gaskell and Smith did find however were feelings of hopelessness and despair – many blacks felt that their hopes had little chance of becoming reality.

(adapted from **Policing the Crisis** by Stuart Hall et al, Macmillan, London, 1978 and 'Riot Britain, **The Observer**, 12 July 1981, p. 16)

1. If a group has a subculture then some of its norms and values are distinctive, some are shared with the mainstream culture. In terms of this definition do Afro-Caribbeans have a subculture? Provide evidence in your answer.   (4)
2. In terms of their major values Afro-Caribbeans share the culture of the wider society. Assess this view with reference to the passage.   (4)
3. Suggest why some young blacks are attracted towards the Rastafarian religion.   (4)
4. Some observers argue that Rastafarianism prevents its followers from seeking political solutions to their problems. Suggest why this might be so.   (4)
5. Some Afro-Caribbeans see themselves as black rather than British. Why?   (4)

7 Ethnicity and urban riots

Beginning with disturbances in the St Paul's district of Bristol in 1980, exploding in Brixton and Southall (London), Toxteth (Liverpool), Moss Side (Manchester), St Paul's (Bristol) and other English cities in 1981 and breaking out in Handsworth (Birmingham), Brixton and Tottenham (London) in 1985, urban riots have become a feature of the inner cities in the 1980s. There is nothing new about riots in the UK. In 1919 there were 'race riots' in which black sailors were attacked by mobs of whites in many of the major sea-ports. In the same year crowds in Luton burned the town hall with petrol and troops were called in. Again in 1919, after a police strike in Liverpool, rioting and looting broke out and tanks were used to restore order. Throughout the summer of 1919 crowds of young people fought with the police in various parts of London. There were unemployment riots in 1921 and much larger outbreaks in 1931 when the army was called out in Manchester to support the police.

So in one sense there is nothing new about the 1980s riots. Some things are new, however. 1) The media coverage – via television the riots were brought into living rooms across the country. 2) The fact that Afro-Caribbean youths were the main participants. Some whites also took part, for example in Toxteth, but they were usually in the minority. Asian youths were rarely involved in any numbers except in Southall (1981) which saw a pitched battle between Asian youths and white skinheads with the police caught in the middle. The Asians saw themselves as defending their community against racist attacks. 3) A further new element in the 1980s riots was the first use of petrol bombs on the UK mainland.

The riots took place in deprived, low-income, inner city areas with large ethnic populations and against a background of high unemployment, bad housing and poor police/community relations. Many riots were triggered or sparked off by what the participants saw as 'police injustice', though it is generally agreed that the basic causes go far deeper. The following extracts look at various aspects of the riots. However, all the passages in this section have something to contribute to an explanation of the 1980s' riots.

Many young blacks place the blame for the riots on the police who are sometimes seen as the 'enemy', as an army of occupation, as a racist force who harass and oppress them. Many riots were triggered by an incident seen by the participants as 'police injustice'. The Brixton riot of 1981 was preceded by 'Operation Swamp' in which the area was saturated with plain-clothes police in an attempt to control street crime. In the words of the Scarman Report (the official report on the Brixton riot of 1981) – 'the violence erupted from the spontaneous reaction of the crowds to what they believed to be police harassment . . . the riots were essentially an outburst of anger and resentment by young black people against the police'. Again in Brixton, in 1985, a new police strategy using armed raids to capture suspects led to heightened tension which sparked off a riot after the accidental police shooting of a black woman during a raid on her home.

Some researchers claim that the attitudes, policies and practices of the police are racist. There is some evidence to support this claim. The 1983 Policy Studies Institute report found that racial prejudice was widespread in the Metropolitan (London) Police Force. There is also evidence which may support black claims of harassment by the police. For example, blacks were over ten times more likely to be arrested by the Metropolitan police for 'sus'. (The 'sus' laws, abolished in 1981, gave police the right to arrest someone 'on suspicion of loitering with intent to commit an arrestable offence'. However the police still have stop and search powers.)

Other researchers take a rather different view. They admit that there are instances of police injustice against blacks but in general they believe there is equal treatment under the law. The reason that blacks are more likely to be stopped and arrested is, they argue, that blacks are more likely to be involved in street crime.

Many police forces responded to the 1981 riots with programmes of 'community policing'. Local 'bobbies', were put on the beat in ethnic minority areas. They were instructed to adopt a sensitive approach and to get to know the community. Despite such efforts – for example Handsworth in Birmingham was held up as a model of community policing – riots still broke out in 1985.

(adapted in part from **Race Relations in Britain** by Andrew Pilkington, University Tutorial Press, Slough, 1984, pp. 168–171)

Brixton, 1985

The Police do not create social deprivation though unimaginative, inflexible policing can make the tensions which deprivation engenders greatly worse. Conversely, while good policing can help diminish tension and avoid disorder, it cannot remove the causes of social stress where these are to be found as those in Brixton and elsewhere are deeply embedded in fundamental economic and social conditions.

(from Scarman Report, **The Brixton Disorders 10–12 April 1981**, HMSO, London, 1981, p. 100)

Commander Alex Marnoch, head of the Brixton police force: 'What can we, the police, offer? We can talk to them, we can play cricket with them, we can go to their youth clubs. But we can't give them money and jobs.'

(quoted in **The Observer**, 6 October 1985, p. 7)

The statistics tell the story:
● Since the 1981 riots, unemployment has doubled in the borough of Lambeth, of which Brixton is a part, and now stands at 22 per cent. In Brixton it is 33 per cent.
● The rate of house-building has fallen. In 1981, 1,022 new homes were completed. Last year, it was only 552. In 1981, the council spent £51 million on housing. This year it is spending £34 million.
● Central Government's contribution has fallen dramatically. Although Lambeth's spending on services has risen – from £91.6 million in 1980 to £114.3 million in 1984 – the central contribution has fallen from £56.4 million to only £39 million. Last year, central Government gave the council £13 million aid from the urban programme – and took away £19 million in penalties for overspending.

A group of nine Brixton Anglican priests condemned the situation: 'We deplore the conditions of life which have persisted and worsened in Brixton since the 1981 riots. We deplore the fact that no effective steps have been taken by the Government in the past four years to alleviate unemployment.'

(from **The Observer**, 6 October 1985, p. 7)

Many blacks have been pushed into the margins of society. They are on the outside looking in. They have few organizations to represent their interests and through which to channel their grievances. Traditionally the white working class has been represented by trade unions and the Labour Party. Blacks as a group lack such organizations and political representation.

Riots can be seen in many different ways. One way is to see them as a political activity by those who are largely unrepresented in the wider society. In terms of this view, Jerry White states, 'Riot has classically been a collective weapon of the politically powerless – to get those with power and wealth to share a little more or to take notice...'

(adapted from 'Urban violence and political marginalisation' by J. Young and J. Lea, **Critical Social Policy**, Spring 1982 and 'The summer riots of 1919' by Jerry White, **New Society**, 13 August 1981, pp. 260–261)

1. What do researchers mean when they distinguish between the trigger and the causes of a riot? (3)
2. What evidence suggests that community policing is no solution to urban unrest? (4)
3. How can riots be seen as political activity? (3)
4. Using evidence from the above extracts and from the section as a whole briefly outline your view of the causes of the 1980s riots. (10)

Section 6 Poverty

This section is concerned with four main questions: (1) What is poverty? (2) How is it measured? (3) What is the extent of poverty? and (4) What are the causes of poverty? These questions are closely related. For example, if two researchers use widely differing concepts or definitions of poverty they will produce very different figures on the extent of poverty. Just how different views on poverty can be is shown in the following extract.

1 Two views of poverty

During the early years of this century a group of workers are having their lunch break. The conversation moves around to poverty.

'Poverty', continued Jack after a short silence, 'consists in a shortage of the necessities of life. When things are so scarce or so dear that people are unable to obtain sufficient of them to satisfy their basic needs. Linden is poor. His family are actually starving. There is no food in the house and the children are crying for something to eat. All last week they have been going to school hungry for they had nothing but dry bread and tea every day and this week they don't even have that.'

For Owen, poverty was more than this. 'Yes Linden is poor,' he replied, 'but poverty should not be counted only as those who are starving. People are poor when they are not able to secure for themselves all the benefits of civilisation – not just the necessities but the comforts, pleasures and refinements of life, leisure, books, theatres, pictures, music, holidays, travel, good and beautiful homes, good clothes, good and pleasant food.'

Everyone laughed. It was so ridiculous. The idea of the likes of them wanting or having such things. Any doubts many of

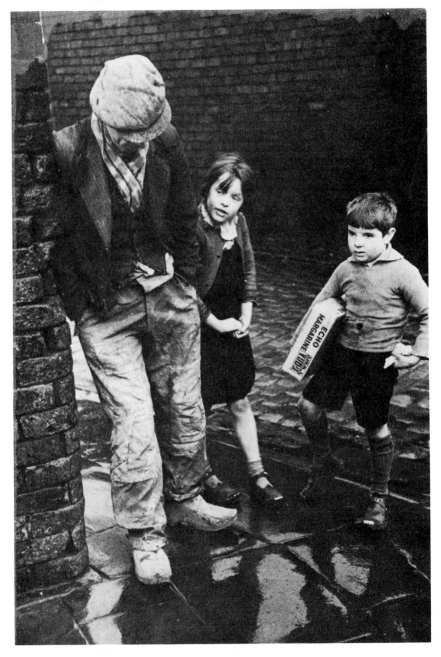

Unemployed miner in Wigan

them had entertained as to Owen's sanity disappeared. The man was clearly as mad as a March hare.

(adapted from **The Ragged Trousered Philanthropists** by Robert Tressall, Grant Richards Press, 1914)

1. What does Jack mean by the 'necessities of life'? (2)
2. How does Jack decide whether or not a person is living in poverty? (2)
3. In terms of Jack's definition of poverty, has the extent of poverty a) increased b) stayed much the same or c) decreased in Britain during this century? Briefly give reasons for your answer. (4)
4. How does Owen's definition of poverty differ from Jack's? (5)
5. Name three 'comforts' or 'pleasures' from modern society without which people would be poor in terms of Owen's view of poverty. (3)
6. a Why did the workmen doubt Owen's sanity? (2)
   b Why would people be less likely to do so today? (2)

2 Poverty in York 1899

One of the earliest systematic studies of poverty was conducted by Seebohm Rowntree in 1899 in the city of York. His view of poverty is similar to the one given by Jack in the previous extract. Rowntree calculated a minimum weekly sum of money which, in his opinion, was 'necessary to enable families to secure the necessities of a healthy life'. Those whose income fell below this sum were defined as poor. This concept of poverty is known as absolute or subsistence poverty. Rowntree admitted that it was 'on the side of stringency rather than extravagance' being 'the lowest standards which responsible experts can justify'. These experts included members of the British Medical Association who drew up a diet sheet which contained food with adequate nutritional value at the lowest possible cost. Presumably Rowntree expected the poor to be able to select and purchase cheap but highly nutritious food.

Early in 1899, with the aid of an interviewer and a secretary, Rowntree began a house-to-house inquiry, extending to the whole working-class population of York. This involved 46,754 people, two-thirds of the total population. The keeping of servants was taken as the dividing line between the working classes and those of a higher social rank.

Rowntree found 20,302 people living in a state of poverty. In other words, almost 28%, or two people in every seven, did not have enough food, fuel and clothing to keep them in good health. Since this was almost half of York's entire working class population, there could be no question but that the Victorian reformers had left a great deal of problems unsolved. Of those in poverty, about a third did not have enough money coming in each week to live a normal, healthy life even if they spent every penny wisely (Rowntree called this 'primary poverty'). All the traditional Victorian 'remedies' like thrift were no use to these people. You could not be expected to save money when you did not have enough for basic essentials. The remaining two-thirds had enough income to give them the bare necessities, but they spent some portion of it unwisely. As a result, they were forced to go short on food or clothing, or both (Rowntree called this 'secondary poverty').

These figures were very close to those arrived at by Charles Booth. He found just over 30% in poverty in East London, working on roughly the same definition of poverty as Rowntree. Therefore it certainly seemed likely that almost a third of Britain's town dwellers were forced to go without some of the necessities of a civilised life. The terrible effect of this on the health and well-being of the people can be seen from the fact that a third of the men applying to join the army at this time were rejected as unfit. These conditions were not confined to the towns. A few years later, Rowntree found that agricultural labourers were even worse off.

What was it like living in poverty? Rowntree found that most of the families in this situation could afford nothing better than a damp, dark slum. Often one water tap supplied several houses and, in many cases, this was fixed to the wall of the W.C.! 'Midden privvies' were the general rule in the slums. In these the functions of lavatory and dustbin were combined in a brick-lined pit. Rowntree said: 'A large number of them are found inches deep in liquid filth, or so full of refuse as to reach above the cemented portions of the walls.' To make matters worse, they were often shared by several families.

Broken window panes were stuffed with rags or pasted over with brown paper. In the neighbourhood of these houses, the smell from dirt and bad air could be almost unbearable. This is a typical example of living conditions taken from a Sanitary Inspector's notebook: '2 rooms. In the lower one a brick floor is in holes. Fireplace without grate in bottom. Wooden floor of upper room has large holes admitting numbers of mice. Roof very defective, rain falling through on to the bed in wet weather.'

In these conditions, it was not surprising that one child out of every four born died before it was a year old and many of those that lived were stunted and deformed.

The diet of the poverty-stricken slum dwellers was often seriously deficient. Many families could afford no butcher's meat at all. Although it may have contained enough bulk to fight off the feeling of hunger, it did not contain sufficient nourishment to keep the family in good health. Extras like clothing often had to be paid for by going short of food. One woman said: 'If there's anything extra to buy, such as a pair of boots for one of the children, me and the children goes without dinner.'

Taking those whose basic incomes were insufficient, i.e. those in primary poverty Rowntree found two main reasons for their plight. In a quarter of these cases, the chief wage-earner of the family was out of action or dead. He might be ill or disabled, too old to work or unemployed. However, in over half the families in this category, the breadwinner was in regular work. His wages were simply too low to meet his family's needs. Unskilled labourers earned roughly 18 to 21 shillings a week in York at this time, yet Rowntree estimated that at least 21s 8d was needed to keep a family with three children out of poverty. The belief that a man could always provide for his family if he was thrifty and willing to work hard was shown to be false. However hard he tried, he could not keep out of poverty if he was seriously underpaid.

In the case of those whose incomes were sufficient but who failed to spend every penny wisely, i.e. those in secondary poverty, it was more difficult to give definite reasons for their poverty. Drink and gambling – in that order – were almost certainly the main causes. When father drank, the children often went supperless to bed. Rowntree deplored these vices, but suggested that men often took to drink and gambling not from weakness of character but because of the terrible conditions under which they lived. Extravagant housekeeping was another cause of unnecessary poverty. Housewives often spent unwisely through ignorance of what was the best value for money. ·

(from **The Making of the Welfare State** by R. J. Cootes, Longmans, London, 1966, pp. 28–33)

1. What does Rowntree consider to be the 'necessities of a healthy life'? (2)
2. How does Rowntree define a) primary poverty and b) secondary poverty? (4)
3. Is it realistic to expect the poor to spend 'every penny wisely'? Give reasons for your answer. (3)
4. What was the extent of poverty in a) London and b) York? (2)
5. What evidence is provided in the extract to explain the high death rate amongst the poor? (3)
6. Why did Rowntree see a national minimum wage as one of the main solutions to poverty? (3)
7. Why doesn't Rowntree blame those in secondary poverty for their situation? (3)

3 Absolute vs relative poverty

Rowntree conducted two further studies of York, one in 1936 and one in 1950. They revealed a steady reduction in the extent of poverty. By 1950 only 1½% of the population of York lived in poverty. It appeared that the days of the poor were numbered. However, Rowntree's research was based on a concept of absolute or subsistence poverty. A very different picture of the extent of poverty will result from research based on the idea of relative poverty. In terms of this view people are poor if they lack the resources to afford what is generally considered to be an acceptable standard of living and a reasonable style of life. The following extract begins with a definition of relative poverty by Peter Townsend. It then compares the results of Rowntree's 1950 study with those of a study by Abel-Smith and Townsend entitled **The Poor and the Poorest**. This was the first major study of poverty in the UK based on a concept of relative poverty. It claimed that in 1960, 7½ million people, that is 14.2% of the population lived in poverty.

> Individuals, families and groups in the population can be said to be in poverty when they lack the resources to obtain the types of diets, participate in the activities and have the living conditions and amenities which are customary, or at least widely encouraged or approved, in the societies to which they belong. Their resources are so seriously below those commanded by the average individual or family that they are, in effect, excluded from ordinary living patterns, customs and activities.

(from 'Poverty as relative deprivation: resources and style of living' by Peter Townsend in **Poverty, Inequality and Class Structure** edited by D. Wedderburn, Cambridge University Press, Cambridge, 1974, p. 15)

Percentage of those in poverty Rowntree 1950	Cause of poverty	Percentage of those in poverty Abel-Smith and Townsend 1960
	Inadequate wages and/or	
4.2	large families	40
68.1	Old age	33
6.4	Fatherless families	10
21.3	Sickness	10
Nil	Unemployment	7
	Percent of sample	
1.5	population in poverty	14.2

(Wages are adequate or not depending on the number of dependent family members who require support)
(adapted from **Poverty: The Forgotten Englishmen** by K. Coates and R. Silburn, Penguin Books, Harmondsworth, 1970, p. 47)

1. In terms of a relative concept, poverty in 1900 is very different from poverty today. Explain this statement. (4)
2. Why might people who cannot afford a refrigerator, washing machine and vacuum cleaner be defined as poor in terms of relative poverty but not in terms of absolute poverty? (3)

3. Briefly explain why the 1950 and 1960 estimates of poverty are so different. (3)
4. Give two reasons for the decline in absolute poverty from 1899 to 1950. (4)
5. Which is the largest group in poverty in a) 1950 and b) 1960? (2)
6. Suggest two measures the government might take to reduce the level of poverty among low wage earners. (4)

4 The culture of poverty

There is a tendency for people who share similar circumstances and problems to develop a way of life which differs to some extent from that of the rest of society. In sociological terms they develop a subculture, that is certain norms, attitudes and values which are distinctive to them as a social group. A number of researchers have argued that the circumstances of poverty tend to produce a 'culture of poverty', that is a subculture shared by the poor. This idea was first introduced in the 1950s by the American anthropologist Oscar Lewis. It proved very influential forming the basis for the US government's 'war on poverty' during the 1960s. The following passage examines Lewis's ideas and their influence on the war on poverty.

Lewis developed the idea of a culture of poverty from his research among the urban poor in Mexico and Puerto Rico. He sees the culture of poverty as a 'design for living' which is transmitted from one generation to the next: 'By the time slum children are age six or seven, they have usually absorbed the basic values and attitudes of their subculture.'

The culture of poverty includes 'a strong present-time orientation with relatively little ability to defer gratification and a sense of resignation and fatalism'. As a result people tend to accept the situation believing that there is little or nothing they can do to change it. They tend to live from day to day, taking their pleasures when they find them with little thought for tomorrow. The culture of poverty also includes a feeling of helplessness and a 'strong feeling of marginality' – the poor feel they are on the outskirts of society, on the outside looking in. They rarely participate in the wider society and are unlikely to belong to trade unions or political parties.

According to Lewis the culture of poverty tends to perpetuate poverty, largely preventing the poor from escaping from their situation. In his words, they are 'not geared to take full advantage of changing conditions or increased opportunities which may occur in their lifetime'.

The idea of a culture of poverty formed the basis for government policy in the fight against poverty in the USA. In 1964 President Lyndon B. Johnson declared a 'war on poverty'. Its main strategy was to rid the poor of the culture of poverty. They would then be able to pull themselves up by their own bootstraps and seize the many opportunities which were supposed to be available.

The government set up a nationwide programme of pre-school education in low income areas known as 'Operation Headstart'. The idea was to nip the culture of poverty in the bud by teaching children middle class norms and values. Programmes were also developed for older age groups. Unemployed youngsters were sent to residential camps in the wilderness with the aim of 'building character' and encouraging initiative and determination. Many work experience programmes were started to develop 'work habits'. The poor were encouraged to help themselves. Government money was provided to finance community self-help groups and small businesses.

By the late 1960s it was clear that the war on poverty had been lost. As one man on welfare put it, 'It's great stuff this war on poverty! Where do I surrender?' The poor, despite the billions of dollars expended on poverty programmes, remained stubbornly poor.

Ideas about the causes of poverty were beginning to change. Various studies of the poor in the United States and other societies found little evidence of a culture of poverty. Even if such a culture did exist, many now argued that it was not the major cause of poverty. The American sociologist Herbert J. Gans writing in the early 1970s reflects this change of viewpoint: 'The prime obstacles to the elimination of poverty lie in an economic system which is dedicated to the maintenance and increase of wealth among the already affluent.' But a war on poverty based on this view would be far harder to win since victory would require considerable sacrifice by the rich and powerful.

(adapted from **Sociology: Themes and Perspectives** by Michael Haralambos with Robin Heald, University Tutorial Press, Slough, 1980 pp. 154–5, 166–9)

1. How is the culture of poverty transmitted from generation to generation? (3)
2. How might 'a sense of resignation and fatalism' help to keep the poor in poverty? (3)
3. How might lack of membership of trade unions, political parties and other organizations help to keep the poor in poverty? (3)
4. 'Work habits' are of little use without jobs. Explain this statement with reference to the situation of the unemployed. (3)
5. Briefly outline the two reasons suggested for the failure of the war on poverty. (4)
6. Why do many people argue that the war on poverty suggested by Gans's ideas is doomed to failure? (4)

5 Poverty and class (1)

From a Marxist point of view poverty is the result of the so-called 'free-enterprise' capitalist system found in Western industrial society. From this viewpoint the poor are poor because the rich are rich. This state of affairs is due to the economic system which operates in the West and the class system which it produces (see Section 3, p. 64 for an outline of a Marxist view of social class). The rich and powerful owe their position to ownership of the forces of production. They own capital which they invest in private industry and, if the company is successful, are rewarded with much of the profit.

The following extract continues the conversation between Owen and his workmates which began this section. It is set in the early years of this century.

Owen continued, 'The theory that drunkenness, laziness and inefficiency are the causes of poverty are so many devices fostered by those who are selfishly interested in maintaining the present state of affairs for the purpose of preventing us from discovering the real causes of our present condition.'

'Well what do you reckon is the cause of poverty,' demanded Easton.

'The present system of Capitalism,' retorted Owen. 'It is not the poor themselves who are at fault but the way that wealth is divided. All the people in the working class are suffering and starving and fighting in order that the rich people, the capitalist class, can live in luxury and do nothing. These are the wretches that cause poverty. They produce nothing but exist on the work done by the people.'

'It can't never be altered,' interrupted old Linden. 'I don't see no sense in all this 'ere talk. There's always been rich and poor in the world and there always will be.'

'But that's where you're wrong,' shouted Owen. 'We can change all that. The rich are only rich because they rob the poor. They have got control of the land, the machinery, the tools and use that control to exploit us. We work all our lives and instead of being paid the real value of our work we are paid a pittance. The Capitalist class keeps the rest as their profit and try to persuade us that it is rightfully theirs. But they have not worked for it – they have just sat and watched us. But we can change all that. If all the working men were to unite we would be too strong for them and they would be forced to give us what is rightfully ours. No one would own the land, the mines, the factories, they would belong to the whole community. We would **all** work and in return receive a just wage which would permit everyone to live a civilised life. Then there would be no poverty.'

The men started to shift uncomfortably and one or two of them on the edge of the group started to collect up their tools ready for the afternoon's labour.

(adapted from **The Ragged Trousered Philanthropists** by Robert Tressall, Grant Richards Press, 1914)

1. What does Owen see as the main cause of poverty?   (6)
2. Why does Owen argue that the view that drunkenness and laziness is the cause of poverty is beneficial to the Capitalist class?   (4)

3. Owen sees a communist system as the solution to poverty.
    a What is communism?   (3)
    b How might it lead to the abolition of poverty?   (3)
4. Why did the men 'shift uncomfortably' after listening to Owen?
                                                              (4)

6 Poverty and class (2)

It is not necessary to take a Marxist position in order to argue that the class system is the main cause of poverty. This is clear from the following extract which summarises the findings of an extensive survey conducted by Peter Townsend and published in 1979 under the title of **Poverty in the United Kingdom**.

'The chief conclusion of this report is that poverty is more extensive than is generally or officially believed, and has to be understood not only as an inevitable feature of severe social inequality but also as a particular consequence of actions by the rich to preserve and enhance their wealth and so deny it to others...The extremely unequal distribution of wealth is perhaps the single most notable feature of social conditions in the United Kingdom.'

Rejecting conventional definitions of poverty as being too imprecise to give a comprehensive picture, Professor Townsend defines poverty in terms of the concept of 'relative deprivation', and this is one of the book's main themes: 'Poverty, I will argue, is the lack of the resources necessary to permit participation in the activities, customs and diets commonly approved by society. Different kinds of resources, and not just earnings or even cash incomes, have to be examined.'

By adopting a more realistic relative deprivation standard, he shows that 14 million people (26% of the population) are living in poverty. This figure contrasts sharply with the state's estimate of five million (9%) in poverty. The difference is explained in terms of under-representation of the poor in Government surveys such as the Family Expenditure Survey, imprecision in the measurement of net income, and the state's meagre standard of income needs, especially for children.

Children and the elderly are by far the largest groups affected by poverty, closely followed by the disabled. A strong correlation (relationship) is shown between social class, poverty and disability at all ages, but to a very marked degree among the elderly.

About one-third of those in poverty by the state's standard live in families where one member is substantially employed. Among the low-paid those with children are most likely to be in poverty.

About one-third of those in poverty are members of families in which someone is disabled or chronically ill. A strong correlation (relationship) is shown between disablement, poverty and social class. Unskilled manual workers and their families are far more likely to be disabled or severely incapacitated than middle-class people.

The elderly poor make up 36% of all the poor in the UK. Nearly 20% of people of pensionable age (1,700,000) live in poverty, while a further 44% (3,700,000) live on the margin of poverty as defined by the state. Townsend states that, 'Those who had held jobs of low occupational status, and whose fathers' status was correspondingly low, were more likely than others to be poor in old age. Conversely, those of high status whose fathers' status was also high were least likely to be poor in old age.'

One of the least recognised forms of deprivation, deprivation at work, affects 12% of the working population and more men than women. None of those in professional or managerial groups were found to be deprived, but 43% of male manual workers were very deprived in this context.

Among the main characteristics of deprivation at work are poor working conditions, neglect of health and safety standards, working at night or before 8 a.m., jobs where the worker has to stand or walk about all day; no entitlement to holidays, to sickness pay or occupational pension; insecure employment subject to one week's notice or less. Those with lower earnings are likely to have poor working conditions.

A sharp difference in command over resources was found between people in manual and non-manual occupations. 'Through the medium of class membership therefore, the maldistribution of resources is created, perpetuated and legitimated,' he says.

Detailed information collected about wealth shows that even on a wide definition of wealth, 5% of the population own 45% of net assets. When income was combined with wealth in a measure of resources, the top 10% were shown to have an advantage nearly 10 times that of the poorest 10%. Wealth was found to be highly correlated with (linked to) occupational class, with members of the professional class accounting for the majority of the rich.

(from 'Townsend's 14 million poor' by Mary Manning, **Community Care**, October 25, 1979, pp. 14–16)

1. Which concept of poverty does Townsend use? Briefly explain your answer. (3)
2. Explain the relationship (connection) between old age, poverty and social class. (4)
3. Explain the relationship between disablement, poverty and social class. (4)
4. Deprivation at work is closely linked to social class. What evidence for this is provided in the extract? (3)
5. Outline the conclusion of Townsend's report. (3)
6. What solutions to poverty are suggested by the evidence contained in the extract? (3)

7 Poverty and the mass media

As a general rule the poor do not have a very good press. There is a tendency for the media to reinforce popular prejudices about the poor. This may well have important consequences as the following extract suggests.

In the last six months of 1976, we analysed all welfare and social security news stories on television news, in the national press, and in the local press and radio in two cities. No fewer than 30.8% of all stories dealt in some way with social security abuse, and 12.6% with legal proceedings. In other words, one in eight of all stories in all media in this period which were about social services, welfare or social security, dealt with the criminal proceedings consequent on social security abuse.

Newspaper articles often picture the poor as undeserving. We are frequently invited to share in righteous indignation over the excesses of the feckless poor, their laziness, dependency or reckless fertility. The **Daily Telegraph** (29 July 1976) in a story headed, 'How to be a failure and get paid for doing nothing' describes how the idle go to great pains to make themselves unemployable ('scruffy dress, surly rudeness...feigned infirmities'). A surprising number of the families featured in the 'scrounger of the week' style stories have several children, notwithstanding the fact that some 70% of families on supplementary benefit have two or fewer children.

The good life provided by welfare benefits is a target whenever benefits are uprated. Lynda Lee Potter complained in the **Daily Mail** about 'Scroungers by the Sea' (13 July 1977). 'The seaside social security offices,' Lynda indignantly assured us, 'are thick with subsidised cigarette smoke, the smell of alcohol paid for by the state, and the smugly tanned faces of the leeches feeding off the hardworking, ordinary, silent majority.'

The focussing of moral outrage in news items like these does as much to create concern as to reflect it. News about social security is never extensive in our media, and when it does appear is framed by political dispute or crime, the only two contexts in which it is likely to surface to the attention of journalism. The news media provide news, after all, and not documentation of social policy. There are many crime reporters sniffing round courtrooms, or general reporters ready to pick up stories like 'Mr Quick's Top-Speed Sex Snoop on Doreen' (**Sun**, 18 August 1976), richly combining sex, crime and welfare abuse into a sub-editor's dream. There are few specialist correspondents dealing with social security, although it now commands 20% of public expenditure: a rather strange neglect found most often in those very papers given to frequently claiming their concern with watching over public expenditure. There is therefore little resistance in the media image machine to the dominant definition of our over-indulgent welfare system grown too open to abuse.

The consequences are real. In 1975, the last year for which detailed figures are available, 930,000 eligible claimants, two thirds of them pensioners, failed to claim £240 million of

From **The Sun**, 15 July 1976

supplementary benefits to which they were entitled. Many other benefits are left unclaimed by people only too wary of the labels they may acquire in the process. The welfare system has increasingly become a mechanism for ensuring that those who are entitled to benefits do not get them.

The number of special investigators employed by the DHSS (Department of Health and Social Security) has increased from 22 in 1955 to 428 in 1978, and has increased by nearly a third since 1974 alone. In 1975 over 46,000 cases of suspected fraud were investigated by the DHSS or the Department of Employment. At local level the number of staff working part-time on fraud-spotting in social security offices was increased by 50% between September 1975 and April 1977.

(from 'Why is the press so obsessed with welfare scroungers?' by Peter Golding and Sue Middleton, **New Society**, 26 October 1978, pp. 195–97, and reproduced with permission)

1. What impression of the poor might be created by the fact that nearly a third of the stories about social security deal with abuse of the system? (4)
2. What prejudices about the poor are reflected in the stories from the **Telegraph** and the **Mail**? (4)
3. What information does the extract contain which clearly shows that many newspaper articles give a false picture of the poor? (4)
4. What are the consequences for the poor of the way they are portrayed by the media? (4)
5. Why is so much media coverage given to 'welfare scroungers'? (4)

Section 7 The Welfare State

A welfare state is a state which provides social services for its citizens. These services are statutory – they are provided by law. This section examines the origins of the welfare state in Britain and its establishment after the Second World War. It looks at the role of voluntary organizations in the provision of social welfare. It then takes a critical view of the welfare state by examining the view that the rich gain more from the state's social policy than the poor. The section closes with a description of the operation of social security in an inner city area. It shows that the welfare state still has a long way to go before it meets the needs of its citizens.

1 The origins of the welfare state

The following passage looks at the origins and development of the welfare state up to 1900. From one point of view this development represents progress towards a more humane and caring society. From another it represents increasing social control made possible by the growing power of the state. In this sense welfare is a means of 'gentling the masses', of controlling the 'dangerous classes'.

In 16th century Elizabethan England the wandering beggar had no security, only hope and desperation. Dragging himself from door to door he could appeal to pity and charity; roving in bands he could threaten and steal. Whipping and branding did little to control desperate people. The Elizabethan Poor Law required men to stay in their own communities where they could be disciplined but this would only be effective if they were provided for. Local parishes were obliged to set the able-bodied poor to work and provide for the sick, disabled and aged, the cost being met by ratepaying householders.

The origins of the welfare state can be traced back to the Elizabethan Poor Laws which provided minimum security for

Female ward in a workhouse, 1843

the destitute. They can be seen as a means of social control concerned with maintaining the Queen's peace and, to some extent, as an act of Christian charity.

The industrial revolution and rapid urbanization in 19th century Britain created a new urban working class. Periodic high levels of unemployment and low wages resulted in widespread absolute poverty. The 1834 Poor Law was based on the idea that unemployment was voluntary, that the unemployed were lazy and idle, that work was available for the able-bodied if they searched hard enough. Workhouses for the destitute poor were established. They were made harsh and degrading, the idea being that any job on the outside would be preferable to life inside. The theory was that relief should be 'less eligible' than the condition of the lowest paid labourer. In practice the sick, disabled and aged often had to endure the same conditions as the able-bodied poor. The workhouse was feared and hated by those who might one day be forced to enter it.

During the last quarter of the 19th century attitudes began to change. Charles Booth's study of London and Seebohm Rowntree's study of York (see Section 6:2) suggested that in many cases poverty was not the fault of the poor. Growing numbers of old people were now receiving poor relief in their own homes, those still in workhouses were provided with little 'luxuries' like tea and tobacco, workhouse hospitals (established during the late 1860s) were improved and ordinary members of the working class began to use them.

Throughout the nineteenth century the state accepted more and more responsibility for the welfare of its citizens. This can be seen from a series of Factory Acts aimed at improving working conditions, limiting hours of work and ending child labour. One result of these acts was that large numbers of children, excluded from the factories, were left to roam the streets. For example in Manchester in 1865, 6% of children between the ages of three and twelve were at work, 40% at school and 54% at neither work nor school. In 1870 a state system of primary education was introduced and made compulsory up to the age of ten in 1880. It was aimed mainly at working class children who were unable to find places in church schools and unable to afford places in fee-paying schools. State schools provided a minimal education based on the 3 Rs and strict classroom discipline.

Slowly the state was moving from providing relief for the poorest to a wider range of provisions for larger sections of the population.

(adapted from 'Social Security: A System Emerges' by E. P. Hennock, **New Society**, March 7, 1968; **Society and Education in England since 1800** by P. W. Musgrave, Methuen, London, 1968 and **Introduction to the Social Services** by W. E. Baugh [3rd edition], Macmillan, London, 1977)

1. The welfare state began as a means of controlling the poor rather than helping them. Briefly discuss this statement.   (3)
2. The 1834 Act has been described as a deterrent poor law.
   a What does this mean?   (3)
   b Why does a deterrent poor law fail to meet the needs of the sick and the elderly?   (3)
3. How can present day attitudes towards 'welfare scroungers' be seen as reflected in the 1834 Poor Law?   (4)
4. How can state education be seen as a means of social control? (4)

5. It would be wrong to assume that a desire to help the poor had no influence on social policy in the nineteenth century. Briefly discuss this view. (3)

2 The foundations of the welfare state

Before the establishment of the modern welfare state, social services were 'selective' – they were available only to those selected as being in the greatest need, in particular the poor. They were often subject to a 'means test' – a person's means (income and resources) were assessed and if they were below a certain level payments or services were provided. Throughout this century more and more services have become 'universal' – available to everyone no matter what their income group or social class. Today, for example, state education and health services are provided for all members of society, not just those defined as being in special need. The slow move towards universal provision can be seen in the following passage which looks at the development of the welfare state during the first forty years of this century.

> The foundations of the modern welfare state were laid by the Liberal governments of 1905–1915. The 1908 Old Age Pensions Act provided pensions for people over 70. Whether or not they received a pension and its size was decided by a means test. They would be refused a pension if they had been convicted of drunkenness or any other crime in the previous 20 years, if they had recently claimed poor relief or if they had a record of 'habitual failure to work'. The 1911 National Insurance Act provided sickness benefit and payment of medical expenses for all manual workers and other workers below a certain income level. It also provided unemployment payments for workers in seven occupations which were subject to high levels of unemployment. Both schemes were paid for by contributions from workers, employers and government. Not everybody welcomed these reforms. Writing in 1916, the Russian communist leader Lenin called them 'sops for the obedient workers'.
>
> In the 1920s these provisions were widened and extended to larger sections of the population. For example in 1920

unemployment insurance was extended to nearly all workers. However, it was not designed for the long term unemployment brought about by the economic recession of the late 1920s and early 1930s. Unemployment benefit was only paid for a limited period and often ran out leaving workers destitute. Realising this and fearing working class unrest, the government introduced a series of 'transitional benefits' – often known as 'the dole' to take over where unemployment payments left off. Sydney Wood gives the following description of how the dole operated.

The dole was only given after families had been checked to see if they had money of their own or other sources of income. Whether this was done by local authorities before 1934 or the Unemployment Assistance Board after 1934, it was strongly disliked. Children who earned a few shillings found that this amount would be knocked off their father's dole: a war-widow's pension or an old age pension could be reasons for cutting a family's payments. Until 1934 the dole might be cut off if officials found that a family had any savings; after that date they were allowed up to £200 of savings. The means test encouraged the break-up of families where one of the younger members had a job that led officials to cut the dole paid the father of the household. Investigators working for the Carnegie Trust thought that 'weakening of family solidarity and disintegration of home life is perhaps the most serious and challenging aspect of the means test. The realisation that every cigarette smoked is paid for by the sacrifice of a brother or sister arouses bitterness, not against the regulations, but rather against the brother or sister who is fortunate enough to be able to help.'

Investigators found that people living in areas of high unemployment were more likely to be ill than those in better-off regions. Some ailments sprang from a poor diet, some from the mental depression of years of struggling to live on the dole. For people who were ill, the inter-war years saw little improvement. The 1911 health insurance scheme did not give the dependants of the insured worker any right to free treatment; it still applied. Fees for dentists and opticians were too high for the poor. Thus people in the depressed areas were more likely to be ill and less likely to get proper treatment.

The government had done enough to prevent people

living on the dole from starving to death. It did not believe it should spend more money partly because the country could not afford it and partly because it thought people would be deterred from genuinely seeking work if their dole were generous.

(adapted from 'The history of social welfare' by Pat Thane, **New Society**, August 29, 1974 and **Introduction to the Social Services** by W. E. Baugh (3rd edition), Macmillan, London, 1977. Quotation from **The British Welfare State 1900–1950** by Sydney Wood, Cambridge University Press, Cambridge, 1982, pp. 33–34)

1. What is the difference between 'selective' and 'universal' benefits? (3)
2. What is a 'means test'? (3)
3. Why did Lenin describe the Liberal Party reforms as 'sops for the obedient workers'? (5)
4. How might the dole undermine the traditional role of the father and threaten family solidarity? (4)
5. The dole failed to meet the needs of the unemployed. Outline the evidence which supports this statement. (5)

3 The establishment of the welfare state

The aftermath of a war often brings changes. People have made great sacrifices, their lives have been disrupted and they are often not prepared to accept their old status – they want something better. This can be seen in the expansion of social services in the early years after the First World War (1914–18) when the then Prime Minister, Lloyd George promised the troops 'homes fit for heroes'. During the Second World War (1939–45) a committee chaired by Sir William Beveridge produced the famous **Beveridge Report on Social Insurance and Allied Services**. Published in 1942 it became an immediate bestseller. Popular support for its principles was widespread both at home and among the troops abroad. Its recommendations appeared to embody the very things being fought for – democracy, freedom and equality.

Before Beveridge social security provisions were largely selective – they were provided for certain occupational and income groups and directed towards the needs of particular individuals.

A **Punch** cartoon from December 1942 shows the high hopes raised by the Beveridge Report.

With Beveridge the idea of universality was established – services should be provided for everyone as a matter of right. Thus the 1945 Family Allowance Act provided weekly cash payments for each child after the first. Every family in the land was entitled to those payments. This was very different from the idea of doling out money to selected individuals on the basis of a means test.

The following passage examines the Beveridge Report and the legislation that followed.

> The Beveridge Report aimed to provide for people's needs 'from the cradle to the grave'. It identified 'five giants on the road to social reconstruction and progress' – want, disease, ignorance, squalor and idleness – which had to be conquered. The Report's recommendations were put into effect by a series of Acts from 1944–1948. Together they created the modern welfare state in the UK.
>
> **Want**. The 1946 National Insurance Act extended, amongst other things, unemployment and sickness benefit and old age pensions. The 1948 National Assistance Act aimed to create a safety net for those who remained poor even with the benefits provided by the 1946 Act. It was based on a 'needs test' to make sure that claims were genuine. This was not as harsh as the old means test since it did not include a check on the earnings of members of the claimant's family.
>
> **Disease**. The 1946 National Health Service Act established a virtually free health service for all to be paid for out of

"Just spots before the eyes. . . . Don't worry, we'll soon cure that!"

Aneurin Bevan 'taking care' of a doctor. The British Medical Association campaigned against the state control of medicine. A cartoon from the **Daily Mirror**.

taxation. The old health insurance scheme only covered employees who had paid contributions – neither their families nor the self-employed were covered. In 1946 Aneurin Bevan, the Minister of Health introduced the new Bill with the words, 'This Bill provides a universal health service with no insurance qualifications of any sort. It is intended that there shall be no limitations on the kind of assistance given – general practitioners' service, specialists, hospitals, eye treatment, dental treatment, hearing facilities.'

Ignorance. The 1944 Education Act established the tripartite (three part) system of secondary education – grammar, technical and secondary modern schools. Education was free and in theory all children were given an equal chance to develop their talents in the type of school for which they were best suited (see Section 10 : 13).

Squalor. The post-war Labour government assumed responsibility for providing decent homes. Restrictions were put on private building and a large scale programme of building council houses for rent was undertaken.

Idleness. The government committed itself to full employment basing its economic policy on the theories of the British economist John Maynard Keynes (1883–1946).

There have been many changes in the welfare state since the 1940s. However, the basic framework created by the post war Labour government remains

(adapted from **Introduction to the Social Services** by W. E. Baugh (3rd edition), Macmillan, London, 1977 and **The British Welfare State 1900–1950** by Sydney Wood, Cambridge University Press, Cambridge, 1982)

1. Why does social change often follow a war? (3)
2. Identify three universal provisions established after 1945. (3)
3. Universality removes the stigma of means tested benefits. Explain this statement. (4)
4. The Beveridge reforms did not remove the means test. What evidence in the passage shows this? (2)
5. Why was the Beveridge Report met with public enthusiasm. Refer to the previous passage in your answer. (4)
6. Beveridge's 'five giants' have proved a lot harder to conquer than he hoped. Briefly discuss in terms of present day British society. (4)

4 Voluntary organizations and self-help

Voluntary welfare organizations are bodies outside the welfare state that provide social services. Their role is examined in the following passage.

During the 19th century voluntary organizations provided many of the services now administered by the state. They were the chief means of collective action for welfare outside the Poor Law. Many were based on ideas of Christian charity and duty. The church provided schools for those who otherwise could not afford them and homes for orphans, the disabled and the elderly. The Salvation Army (founded in 1865) provided for the poor and destitute combining board and lodging with a good dose of religion. Other voluntary groups were organized on a self-help basis. The Friendly Societies were formed by groups of workers who contributed to a common fund from which members could draw in times

Evening service in a Salvation army Shelter, 1908.

of hardship. In 1861 the Friendly Societies had around three million members and some £12 million capital.

The rise of the welfare state produced some changes in the voluntary welfare sector but by no means ended it. After the Second World War much of the work of the Friendly Societies and voluntary hospitals was taken over by the state. But charity and self-help are still vital parts of national welfare. Many 19th century organizations such as Dr. Barnado's homes and the Salvation Army are alive and well. Self-help groups continue to thrive – housing associations build homes for joint ownership, squatters' groups organize their members to take over empty property for homes, mothers join together to form preschool playgroups, widows, one-parent families, alcoholics and drug addicts form associations to help themselves. One of the more recent developments in the voluntary sector is the formation of groups to put pressure on government to improve state services. Such groups include Shelter (the National Campaign for the Homeless) and the Child Poverty Action Group (see Section 8:2).

Supporters of voluntary organizations make the following points in their favour. They offer choice and specialist services so supplementing, supporting and filling gaps in state provision while at the same time saving public money. In some ways they may be better suited meeting certain needs. Groups such as Gingerbread for one-parent families and Cruse for widows are run by people in the same position as those they serve. They can often provide a more sensitive service because they share the problems and experiences of their members. It is important that some groups remain outside the state sector. Organizations such as Shelter and the Child Poverty Action Group can point to the failings in government policy and provide specialist advice for improving state welfare.

Critics of voluntary welfare argue that it is hit-and-miss, that it depends on the whims of private individuals. Services should be provided by the state, not left to chance. In addition, charity provided by voluntary groups is patronizing, it can degrade those who receive it. Needs should not be met by charitable gifts doled out by 'do-gooders'. They should be met by the state – welfare should be the right of every citizen.

(adapted from **The Future of Voluntary Organizations**, Report of the Wolfenden Committee, Croom Helm, London, 1978 and 'A National Perspective' by John Dearlove in **Voluntary Action** edited by David Dickinson, BBC Publications, London, 1973)

1. a Why were the Friendly Societies so important in the 19th century? (3)
   b Why did their importance decline? (2)
2. What are the advantages of self-help groups staffed by people in the same position as those they serve? (4)
3. Why is it important that groups such as Shelter remain outside the state sector? (3)
4. How can charity be seen as degrading for those who receive it? (3)
5. If the welfare state did its job properly there would be no need for voluntary welfare organizations. Briefly assess this view. (5)

5 A critical view of welfare

Rising unemployment and growing numbers of pensioners and one-parent families have resulted in more and more people being dependent on state welfare. In 1984 the Family Policy Studies Centre estimated that a third of all pensioners, over half the unemployed and over half of all one-parent families lived on supplementary benefit. In the eyes of many critics the payments provided by the state are meagre and mean, the services it offers are inadequate and often inefficient. As the section on poverty showed, the welfare state has not removed relative poverty. Figures for the first half of the 1980s, based on various definitions of poverty, all indicate a steady rise in the numbers of poor.

The welfare state has often been seen 1) as mainly benefiting the poor 2) as a means of redistributing income from the better to the worse off. The following passage based on an article by Peter Townsend rejects this view.

What is the value of the welfare state for the rich and the poor. If we look at housing, the more affluent section of the population receives a 'housing subsidy' in the form of tax relief on mortgage payments. If we look at education, the sons and daughters of those at the top are more likely to stay on at school beyond the minimum leaving age and continue into higher education. The cost of education steadily rises from primary to secondary school to university. One study of the value of state social services and tax relief estimates that the richest 20% of the population gain nearly four times as much as the poorest 20%. This is just the opposite of the idea of a welfare state largely designed to help the less well off.

A government's economic policy cannot be separated from its welfare policy. Decisions on investment, taxation and public expenditure will affect all members of society – some will be favoured, others will not. Townsend claims that government policy in the early 1980s favoured the rich. The higher levels of income tax were reduced and between 1979 and 1981 the proportion of income after tax received by the richest 10% increased (from 23.4% to 25.6%) whereas the share of the poorest 10% declined (from 2.9% to 2.4%). In 1979 restrictions on overseas investment were ended. UK investment overseas was £4.6 billion in 1978, £10.8 billion in 1982. This takes jobs abroad at a time of high unemployment and starves British industry of investment. Townsend believes that government priorities are clear – it has mounted a campaign against supplementary benefit fraud by those at the bottom but has done little to clamp down on tax evasion by those at the top.

The economic policies discussed in the above paragraph affect the welfare – for better or for worse – of everybody. For this reason Townsend argues, 'It is impossible to have an economic policy . . . which is not a social policy'. In view of this he makes a number of recommendations. They include an economic policy aimed at creating full employment and a tax system designed to redistribute income from top to bottom. There is little point in tinkering with the existing welfare state, in making 'piecemeal improvements to existing benefits'. Instead government policy in general should be concerned with the welfare of everybody.

(adapted from 'Society' by Peter Townsend in **New Socialist**, Sept/Oct 1981, pp. 26–31)

1. a What is the 'housing subsidy' to which Townsend refers?   (2)
   b Is there any justification for this 'subsidy'?   (2)
2. How can it be argued that the rich gain more from state education than the poor?   (3)
3. Give one reason why
   a The richest 10% increased their share of income between 1979 and 1981.   (2)
   b The share of the poorest 10% declined during those years.   (2)
4. Why might the ending of restrictions on overseas investments increase unemployment?   (2)
5. What evidence does the passage contain to suggest that government policy during the late 1970s and early 1980s favoured the rich?   (3)
6. What does Townsend mean when he states, 'It is impossible to have an economic policy ... which is not a social policy'.   (4)

6 Welfare in the inner city

Inner city areas contain the highest concentrations of people living in poverty (see Section 14:4). The following passage taken from a study of Hackney in London describes the operation of social security in an inner city area.

> The Department of Health and Social Security (DHSS) in Hackney is a key institution. It caters for the unemployed, single mothers, the sick and disabled and pensioners. It determines the incomes of between two-fifths and half the residents of the inner city. The three DHSS offices in Hackney have a number of things in common:
>
>> ... the queue, long suffering, joking to pass the time away, occasionally breaking out into loud, embittered complaint ...
>> Many people arrive at these offices without a penny to their name, because of lost, stolen or delayed giro cheques or benefit books. They sit there for hours, fighting down their children, wondering where the next meal will come from. When they finally reach the front of the queue, their patience is exhausted, their blood sugar low. Then, all too often, they meet with bland excuses, fob-offs, interrogations and insinuations. Abusive and often violent outbursts are

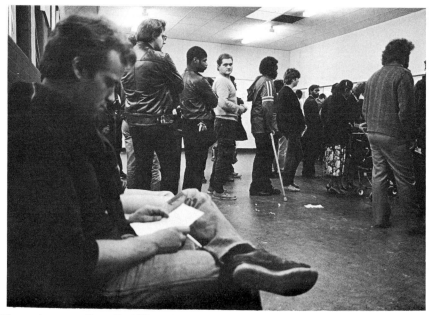

Unemployment Benefit Office, Hackney.

> commonplace. People try to smash the Perspex screens and assault the staff. In September 1981 one man, whose giro was two days late and who hadn't eaten in that time, pulled a replica Magnum gun when he was refused an emergency payment. (p. 138)

Many poor people in Hackney don't get the benefits for which they qualify – they simply don't know about them. The system is complex and confusing. Surveys indicate that no less than half of those eligible for family income supplement and free milk were not claiming them, along with two out of five people entitled to one-parent benefit and a quarter of those who qualify for supplementary benefit. DHSS officers do not make a thorough check of the benefits to which applicants might be entitled.

Social security payments provide a bare survival income. From the point of view of the claimants insult is added to injury by the checks to make sure their claims are genuine. They feel humiliated and degraded by the cross-questioning and prying into their private lives. 'The claimant's credentials, willingness to work, sexual arrangements and honesty are subjected to scrutiny in a way that most claimants I met found deeply offensive and provocative.' (p. 142)

The system is hopelessly inefficient. Despite the rapid rise in claimants, due mainly to unemployment, there was a reduction in the early 1980s in the numbers of DHSS staff dealing with social security claims.

> Social workers in Hackney, approaching the DHSS on behalf of clients, spoke of 'administrative lunacy' and of 'drastically deteriorated efficiency'. Callers were having to hang on the phone for anything from twenty to forty-five minutes before being put through. People in desperate need were having to wait for several months for home visits to assess special needs and single payments. Giros were arriving unsealed through the post, more prone to loss or theft. Claimants reporting losses often found themselves being treated as the prime suspect, and having to wait up to two months for refunds. More common than losses were delays, due to staff shortages again, but also to temperamental computers, deteriorating postal services, or industrial action. Giros were arriving two or three days late. New books of milk tokens or child-benefit books sometimes took months to arrive. For people already on the breadline, such delays could often mean going into debt for rent and fuel bills, and facing eviction or cut-off. (pp. 144–145)

Even when people are aware of the benefits to which they are entitled they often have to fight for their rights and prise money out of the DHSS.

> Perhaps the most telling indicator that something is seriously wrong with the social-security and supplementary-benefits system is the difference that is made when a poor person secures the help of an articulate person, usually middle class by occupation and education, who knows the rules and regulations. Paddy Digney, the coordinator of the Family Centre, an advice agency in Rectory Road, often helps people with social-security problems: 'The people on the counters are often immature and inexperienced, and they're so arrogant, even over the smallest and pettiest of claims. But they pay a lot more attention when people have advocates who sound as if they know what they're talking about.' One of her clients had a part-time job helping in a play group during school term, but when she claimed supplementary benefit for the

holiday weeks, for which she was not paid, she was refused. Her husband was admitted into Bart's Hospital: the fares for herself and her children amounted to £8 per week. That claim, too, was turned down. When her husband came out, he had to go on a special diet, but his claim for the £1.20 a week diet allowance also got the thumbs down. Yet in each of these instances the claim was conceded when Paddy Digney pressed it. (p. 156)

(adapted from **Inside the Inner City** [revised edition] by Paul Harrison, Penguin, Harmondsworth, 1985)

1. The means test is alive and well. What evidence does the passage provide to support this statement? (4)
2. Why would the needs of welfare applicants be met more effectively if DHSS officers checked the benefits to which they might be entitled? (4)
3. Welfare applicants sometimes have to fight for their rights.
   a What evidence from the passage supports this statement. (3)
   b Should they have to fight for benefits to which they are entitled? (3)
4. The operation of social security in Hackney insults and degrades those receiving benefits. Discuss with reference to the passage. (6)

Section 8 Power and Politics

Politics is about power. Power is the ability of an individual or group to realize their aims even if others resist. This section focusses on Britain and asks who holds power, how is power distributed in society and how is it used. It begins with the view that power is widely distributed in Western democracies and rests ultimately with the electorate, those who have the right to vote. The role of pressure groups – groups which represent sectional interests in society – is then examined using the example of the Child Poverty Action Group. This is followed by a Marxist view of power in Britain which presents a very different perspective arguing that power is concentrated in the hands of a small minority, the ruling class. The study of politics does not simply involve such obvious 'political' factors as Parliament and political parties. The mass media, for example, may play an important part in the political process as the extract on television and political bias indicates. A large body of research has been concerned with the people's political attitudes and behaviour. This research is examined in terms of the idea of political socialization and the relationship between the way people vote and their class, age and gender. This is followed with a consideration of the effects of public opinion polls on voting patterns. The influence of social class on political behaviour is again considered in the final extract which looks at the social background of MPs and raises the question of its effect on their policies.

1 Democracy in Britain

Western industrial societies are known as democracies. A democracy is a political system which is based on government by the people. It has been argued that it is not practical or even possible for people in large complex societies to be directly involved in every decision which affects their lives. In practice the only way government by the people can work is in the form of representative democracy whereby a few represent the wishes and interests of the many. The two main institutions of a representative democracy are political parties and pressure or interest groups. In theory political parties represent the nation as a whole. To be elected in the first place, they must reflect public opinion in their election promises. To gain re-election they must reflect the wishes of the people during their term of office.

Pressure or interest groups represent sectional interests, that is the wishes and concerns of sections of society. Thus trade unions represent the interests of workers, the Confederation of British Industry (CBI) represents large, privately owned manufacturing industries, the RAC and AA represent motorists and Friends of the Earth represent those concerned with ·conservation. Pressure groups aim to put pressure on governments to further their members' interests. In a democracy governments do not consistently favour any one pressure group but take account of the wishes and demands of all pressure groups when passing legislation.

By means of political parties and pressure groups both the public in general and particular sectional interests in society are represented. This is the way, at least in theory, that a representative democracy works. The following extract from a study by Christopher J. Hewitt examines a representative democracy in action.

Hewitt's study examines 24 policy issues that arose in the British Parliament between 1944 and 1964. Such issues include Britain's bid to enter the Common Market, air pollution and the debate leading to the 1944 Education Act. Hewitt looked at the various organisations and pressure groups that attempted to influence the government on these issues. Thus stricter controls on pollution were supported by the National Smoke Abatement Society backed by some business interests but opposed by the cotton and chemical industries and the Federation of British Industries (later the CBI) which wanted less stringent controls. Hewitt then looked at the outcome of these policy issues, that is the decisions taken by government, and examined which interest groups were favoured by the government. Thus in the case of air pollution, the wishes of the National Smoke Abatement Society were reflected in the Clean Air Act of 1956. Hewitt found that no one pressure group consistently got its own way. Often government decisions took account of all the pressure groups involved and the final decision was a compromise between their demands. Hewitt also looked at available public opinion polls on the various issues to see whether or not governments reflected the wishes of the public.

The following table looks at some of the findings of Hewitt's research. It lists one, the issue, two, the policy outcome, i.e. the decision taken by the government, and three, whether or not the decision reflected the views of business interests,

| Issue | Policy outcome | Government reflects views of | | |
		a) Business	b) Unions	c) Public
India	Independence for India	–	–	Yes
Russia	Hard-line policy to Russia	–	Yes	–
Abadan	Sanctions against Iran	Yes	–	–
Suez	Military intervention	–	No	Divided
Nuclear deterrent	Independent deterrent policy	No	Divided	–
Central Africa	Federation	–	–	–
US loan	Loan negotiated	–	–	–
Road Haulage	Nationalization	No	Yes	–
Steel	No effective nationalization	Yes	No	Yes
Resale price maintenance	Abolition of RPM	No	–	Yes
Common Market	No entry	No	Yes	–
Railways	Beeching's rationalization policy	Yes	No	Divided
Education	1944 Education Act	Yes	Yes	Yes
National Health	National Health Service	–	–	Yes
National Insurance	National Insurance Act	No	Yes	Yes
Rent Act	Rent decontrol	Yes	No	–
Comprehensives	No support for comprehensives	–	–	–
Motorways	Motorway programme	Yes	Yes	Yes
Town and country	Town and Country Planning Act	No	Yes	Yes
Divorce	No change in divorce laws	–	–	–
Capital punishment	Abolition of capital punishment	–	–	No
Television	Commercial Television	Divided	No	Divided
Immigration	Immigration control	–	–	Yes
Clean air	Clean Air Act	Divided	–	Yes

(from 'Elites and the distribution of power in British society' by Christopher J. Hewitt in **Elites and Power in British Society** edited by P. Stanworth and A. Giddens, Cambridge University Press, Cambridge, 1974, p. 59) trade unions and the public. A dash indicates that business interests or unions were not involved in the issue or that information on public opinion was unavailable. Divided means that the group involved was divided over the issue.

1. From the above evidence, do governments reflect the wishes of the people?   (4)
2. Is there any evidence in the extract to support or reject the view that there is a ruling class made up of business interests in Britain?   (5)
3. Some people claim that the country is run by the unions? Is there any evidence in the extract in favour of or against this view?   (5)
4. On the basis of Hewitt's study, is Britain a democratic society?
                                                                         (6)

2 Pressure groups

The Child Poverty Action Group (CPAG) is a pressure group whose primary aim is to reduce and if possible abolish child poverty. It was formed in 1965. Its main objective has been to raise child benefit payments. The following extract describes how the group attempted to gain support for its views and influence government policy.

From 1965 onwards, CPAG had reasonably good coverage in **The Guardian**, but achieving equally good exposure in **The Times** was important as polls showed that this paper was more commonly read by Tory MPs and senior civil servants. Slowly, coverage was also extended to the **Financial Times**, and from there to the popular papers. For a considerable period of time both the **Daily Mirror** and the **Sun** gave more than fair coverage to CPAG's news stories. Where the Group's coverage was poor, and remained weak, was amongst the **Daily Mail/Daily Express** readership.

The up-market programmes like Panorama would occasionally give the Group's campaigns consideration. There was similarly good coverage on the early-morning breakfast programmes and, most important of all, the Jimmy Young

Show. A working relationship was quickly established with what was known as 'The JY Prog'.

The media coverage had a number of important dynamic consequences. As Professor Mackenzie suggests, politicians' response to the Group was increased because of the coverage it was able to obtain, which MPs took as a sign of the Group's importance. The coverage had a more immediate impact on ministers. Early on, it became very clear that while detailed and often prolonged correspondence with a department was important in trying to corner a minister, because of the size of his post not all letters were read as carefully as they should be. One way of getting the Group's correspondence onto the top of the pile and read by ministers was to ensure publicity for the letters in the media. Partly through natural interest, but also the need for protection when facing the Commons or the media itself, ministers would then request an internal briefing (further information on the subject from civil servants in their department), thereby getting the department's attention onto the issue being raised by the Group.

One key group of people the Group wanted on its side were trade union leaders. On my first visit to Jack Jones I observed that his secretary's desk in the outer office was literally covered by what must have been huge post bags, so much so that the desk took on the appearance of a paper mountain. While Jack Jones, and his successor, always replied carefully to the Group, it was important to find other ways of communicating quickly with the boss of the T & G (Transport and General Workers' Union) and other major unions which would by-pass the normal correspondence process.

Whenever the opportunity arose therefore, trade union leaders were asked which newspaper they read, and particularly the one they read first thing in the morning. The vast majority said that they read **The Guardian**, often at home over breakfast. From then on occasional news stories were placed specifically with **The Guardian**, which, while good news stories in their own right, were aimed at making immediate contact with trade union leaders. This served to good effect in 1976 when the main way of telling trade union leaders on the TUC/Labour Party Liaison Committee of the Government's counter moves against child benefit was for the group to leak to **The Guardian** details of what surprise the Government was planning at that day's meeting.

Access to a Prime Minister is understandably limited. Approaches to those who the Prime Minister likes seeing, and obviously trusts, are much more easily arranged. A careful reading of the court page produced a list of those who had access to the then PM Ted Heath, and who, one then learned from other sources, were respected by him. Three women fell into this category: Dame Peggy Sheppard, Baroness Young and Baroness Elles. The Group made contact with Diana Elles, who was also a powerful figure in the Conservative Women's Advisory Committee. Committed to family allowances, and later to child benefit, Lady Elles has played a major part in shaping the Conservative Party's universal approach to family support. I believe she was also influential in representing CPAG as a serious non-party group in Conservative circles. Members of the CPAG constantly lobbied MPs (met them and tried to gain their support) asking them to raise questions in the House of Commons about poverty. As a result, the Government was continually under a barrage of questions about its policy to, and what was happening to, the living standards of the poor. It also played a part in informally educating MPs on questions which the group judged to be of crucial concern to the poor.

One of the Group's strengths centred on providing 'the best' information. Both politicians and the media accepted that CPAG's case was well argued. This had two important results. Firstly, the greater the public recognition of a pressure group's expertise, the better its chances of influencing MPs. Secondly, much of the information provided by the CPAG was not available from other sources. It often formed the basis of government decisions and directly influenced legislation on social security, education and employment.

During the 1970s the Group tried to enlist the trade unions' active support for changes favourable to the poor. One way of doing this was to build up contact with research officers. Given the pressure under which trade union leaders work, the research officers play a key role both as a means of direct access to the union boss himself and in the preparation of his speeches. From time to time the Group informally met trade union research officers to discuss those issues about which it was most concerned and for which it wanted trade union support. This support was cemented by inviting major trade unions to appear on public platforms with the Group, and the tabling of relevant resolutions in local branches of the trade unions both for their own union's annual meetings and the TUC Conference itself. Fringe meetings were arranged at the TUC Conference and similar briefings to those for the political parties were prepared for the Conference.

(from **Poverty and Politics: The Inside Story of the Child Poverty Action Group's Campaign in the 1970s** by Frank Field, Heinemann Educational Books, London, 1982, pp. 52-7, 61-2)

1. Why was coverage by the mass media important to the Child Poverty Action Group?   (8)
2. Apart from using the media, how did the Child Poverty Action Group attempt to influence MPs?   (4)
3. Apart from using the media, how did the Child Poverty Action Group enlist the support of trade union leaders?   (4)
4. A number of researchers have argued that governments could not operate without the specialized knowledge and expertise provided by pressure groups. How did the information made available to Members of Parliament by the Child Poverty Action Group help its cause?   (4)

3 Power in Britain – A Marxist view

The previous extracts have presented a picture of a democratic society in which governments represent the interests of the people. However, this is only one point of view. Karl Marx, writing in the nineteenth century, saw the state as 'but a committee for managing the common affairs of the whole bourgeoise'. He believed that the state represented the interests of a ruling class made up of those who own and control industry. The Marxist view therefore rejects the idea that governments are democratic and represent the people. It is examined in the following passage.

The private ownership of industry in Britain is concentrated in a very few hands. In 1970 people owning shares of £20,000 or more numbered about one half of one per cent of the entire adult population yet they held nearly 70% of the company shares in private hands. If the government is concerned primarily with supporting private industry then it represents only a tiny minority of the population and can hardly claim to be democratic.

Ownership of a successful company can bring high rewards – those profits which are not re-invested in the business are received by the owners. There are sometimes spin-offs for the workers – these may include higher wages, improved fringe benefits, better working conditions and more secure employment. However such spin-offs are small in cash terms compared with the large sums of money often received by the owners.

Governments support private industry and particularly big business in a number of ways. Firstly they take the position that the success of the nation depends in large part on the success of private industry. If ICI, GEC, BICC and the Big Five banks make big profits, this is good for Britain. It means, say successive government spokesmen, higher employment, higher wages, higher living standards and money from taxes paid by private industry to pay for schools, hospitals and the whole range of public services. Governments do not support and advocate the alternative view – the workers have produced the profits by their labour and should therefore receive them. From a Marxist viewpoint, governments should support this policy if they claim to represent the majority of the population.

Next, governments attempt to provide a framework in which private industry can grow and prosper. This is the main stated objective of the Thatcher government. Its monetary policy aims to produce a fitter and leaner British industry and an end to what it sees as overmanning, restrictive practices, and the abuse of union power. The result it hopes will be a more dynamic and competitive private sector which will once again make Britain great. In the area of foreign policy governments have always borne in mind the need to protect and secure markets abroad for British goods. They provide assistance to firms wishing to export their products. They also make direct financial contributions to private industry. For example, in Britain during the early 1970s, nearly 40% of

A Marxist view of power – political control in the hands of the ruling class

private industry's expenditure on research and development was met from funds provided by the government. If these efforts to help private industry succeed, the owners rather than the workforce stand to gain most.

During this century, however, the state has introduced a wide range of reforms which appear to benefit the mass of the population. These include legislation to improve health and safety in the workplace, social security benefits such as old age pensions and unemployment benefit, a national health service and free education for all. People as a whole have probably benefited considerably from these measures. But it is the people who have paid for them. The Welfare State is largely paid for from taxes on the wages of those who use it. Governments have not acted like Robin Hood, taking from the rich to pay the poor.

Marx believed that workers were exploited and oppressed

because a large part of the wealth they produced was taken from them. If this is the case then there is always a danger of conflict and rebellion. One way of keeping people in their place is to give them the impression that those in power represent their interests and act on their demands. This is what the state in modern western societies has done. It has provided a range of benefits for workers so giving them the impression that their interests are being represented. These measures can be seen as 'sops' to keep the masses happy or at least quiet and to damp down their frustration and resentment. This in turn produces a fairly quiet and passive workforce to earn profits for the owners of private industry. Thus governments help the poor a little and in doing so help the rich a lot.

(based in part on **Class in a Capitalist Society** by John Westergaard and Henrietta Resler, Penguin, Harmondsworth, 1975)

1. If private industry prospers, who gains most? Give reasons for your answer. (4)
2. a Why do workers present a threat to the owners of private industry? (4)
   b How do governments reduce this threat? (5)
3. The view of Britain as a democracy is rejected from a Marxist viewpoint. Why? Use evidence from the passage in your answer. (7)

4 Television and political bias

Television broadcasts have often been accused of political bias, that is of favouring one political viewpoint at the expense of others. In the following extract, Tony Benn MP argues that television supports the established power structure at the expense of the working class and of groups in society which oppose establishment views.

The characteristic of a democracy is that people have the ultimate power to destroy their governments without bloodshed ... Since ultimate power rests with the voters, it greatly matters what information they receive about what is going on and, clearly, the media's information role is of very great importance.

The first comment I would like to make about the television coverage of current affairs is that almost everything that we see and hear is presented from a central Establishment viewpoint. I'll give you a few examples. Take the treatment of trade unionism and industrial disputes which has been brilliantly documented by the Glasgow University Media Group. They have established that by the use of language, all industrial disputes are presented in a particular way. Unions always 'demand' and 'threaten', management always 'offers' and 'pleads'. Pause for a moment to consider the impact of that language.

Or, put it the other way round: take any dispute. You could say that the trade unions are 'offering' to work for 8% when inflation is 10%, and 'pleading' with their management not to cut their real wages, and management are 'demanding' they work for 5%, and 'threatening' to sack them if they don't. Now, it does make quite a difference how you use the language, but we take this so naturally: that all disruption is caused by trade unions. I haven't seen any programme discussing whether it is right for the Government to cut the real wages of health service workers, or to cut the real wages of railwaymen. It just isn't put on the agenda by the media.

If you compare this with the coverage of other interests – for example the endless programmes that are in the interests of investors – you will find tremendous coverage of the problems of those who are deciding where to invest their money. I doubt frankly whether the lower-paid watch that programme along with pensioners, and sell their Yen and buy their Deutchmarks in response to the best advice that the BBC may offer.

CND (Campaign for Nuclear Disarmament) is probably the fastest growing political organisation in the country. There are about 60,000 members of the SDP (Social Democratic Party) and nearly 400,000 members of CND. Yet you compare the coverage of the SDP during the period of its birth with the coverage of the CND, and you will see that the coverage of the CND has probably been about 1% of that of the coverage of the SDP. Even at the height of the Falklands war, when 83

Members of Parliament – of whom I was one – signed a resolution calling for a ceasefire and the transfer of responsibilities to the United Nations, which was a number of MPs four times as great as the SDP in terms of parliamentary strength, what sort of coverage did it get? Coverage of the peace movement was minimalised.

(from 'Agenda Extra' by Tony Benn in **The Guardian** July 28, 1982, p. 14)

1. Why is it important in a democracy that the general public should be accurately informed? (4)
2. Explain how media treatment of trade unions can be seen as biased against the interests of workers. (4)
3. What evidence does Tony Benn provide to support his claim that the peace movement received inadequate coverage on television? (4)
4. From a Marxist viewpoint, the major institutions in Western society (which include the mass media) will support ruling class interests. What evidence for this view is contained in the extract? (8)

5 Political socialization

The previous extract looked at one view of how the mass media might influence opinion. The media are one of the main agencies of socialization in modern industrial society. The following passage considers the effects of various agencies of socialization on political attitudes and behaviour. In other words, it is concerned with political socialization.

If everybody accepted what they read in the newspapers then the Labour Party and the SDP/Liberal Alliance may as well give up all hope of ever winning an election. Nearly all the national daily newspapers in Britain support the Conservative Party – particularly during election campaigns. **The Mirror** is the only major daily newspaper to support Labour. **The Guardian** claims not to side with any party though it is seen as more sympathetic to the Alliance parties than to others. The

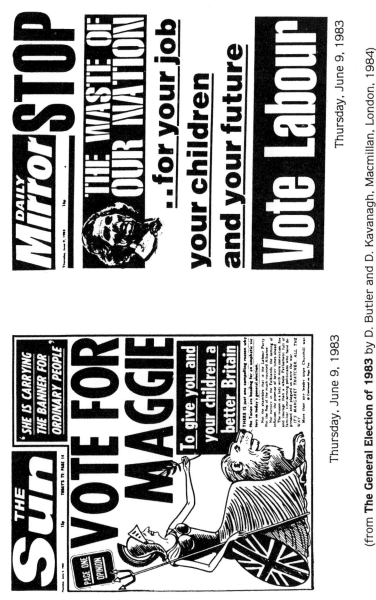

Thursday, June 9, 1983

Thursday, June 9, 1983

(from **The General Election of 1983** by D. Butler and D. Kavanagh. Macmillan, London, 1984) following table shows the party preferences and circulation of national daily newspapers in 1983.

Party preferences and circulations of daily newspapers 1983

Paper	Average daily sales (millions)	General party preference
Sun	4.2	Conservative
Mirror	3.3	Labour
Daily Express	1.8	Conservative
Daily Mail	1.8	Conservative
Daily Star	1.3	Conservative
Daily Telegraph	1.3	Conservative
Guardian	0.4	Alliance (?)
The Times	0.3	Conservative
Financial Times	0.2	Conservative

At least in terms of voting, people clearly do not automatically follow the party preferences of the newspapers they read – Labour has won six elections since 1945.

Do newspapers and the media in general have any influence on people's political attitudes and behaviour? From one point of view the media create opinion in more subtle and hidden ways than simply by telling people how to vote. This is the view taken by Tony Benn in the previous extract. He argues that the media support the status quo, the established order of things, by slanting their reporting in ways which discourage and undermine opposition to the existing power structure. However, a second viewpoint argues that the media **reinforce** rather than **create** opinion. Thus if people wanted to change society they would read papers like the **Morning Star**, a communist newspaper. But they don't – the **Morning Star** has a very low circulation. From this viewpoint people read, listen and watch things that support what they already believe. The media therefore do not create or change opinion, they simply reinforce existing opinion.

In Section 1 it was argued that the family is the main agency of socialization. There is evidence that the family plays an important part in political socialization. People tend to share the political attitudes and party preferences of their parents. For example a high proportion of people whose parents regularly vote for the Conservative Party will themselves vote Conservative. Family influence may well be important in encouraging (or discouraging) people to play an active role in politics.

In the Conservative Party the Churchills and MacMillans are both well-known 'political' families. Michael Foot and Tony Benn of the Labour Party both have fathers who were MPs as does Roy Jenkins of the SDP. The fact that so few women are MPs may be due to socialization practices within the family where girls are less likely to be socialized for leadership roles. To some extent, therefore, people's attitudes to the political system and the roles they see themselves playing within it are influenced by socialization within the family.

The workplace and the neighbourhood may also be important agencies of political socialization. For example, the Labour Party draws its strongest support from manual workers in traditional industries such as mining, shipbuilding and dock work. Trade union membership in these industries is high and workers often live in close-knit 'occupational communities', where a high proportion of people have the same job (this is particularly true of mining villages). Working and living together and sharing their leisure it is to be expected that people will tend to hold similar political views to those of their workmates and friends.

The various agencies of political socialization encourage people to adopt certain political attitudes. But they do not necessarily shape those attitudes. Some **Sun** readers vote Labour, some miners vote Conservative, some Labour voters have parents who support the Conservative Party. People are able to choose for themselves.

(adapted from **Politics: A New Approach** by David Roberts, Causeway Press, Ormskirk, 1986)

1. a Which of the newspapers in the table had the highest and lowest circulations in 1983? (1)
   b People's political behaviour is not necessarily shaped by what they read in the newspapers. What evidence in the passage supports this statement? (3)
3. a The media create opinion. The media reinforce opinion. Briefly explain what these two statements mean. (2)
   b Using evidence from the passage and the previous extract show which view you support. (5)
4. The family influences political attitudes and behaviour but does not necessarily shape them completely. Discuss with reference to the passage. (4)

5. How and why are people influenced by their friends and work-mates in terms of their political views. (4)

6 Voting behaviour and social class (1)

'It's a large, late Victorian terraced house in a fashionable part of town. In the dingy, two-room basement live a retired hospital porter, his wife and their grown-up son. They read the **Daily Express** and vote Conservative. Above them, their landlords, a university lecturer and his wife, a schoolteacher, occupy the other three floors. They have a joint income of £19,000 and part-own a cottage in the Dordogne. They read the **Morning Star** – and **Socialist Worker** when they can get it – and vote Labour.'

Neither family in this house described by Tom Forester is typical of their social class though they do represent sizeable minorities. Roughly a third of manual workers vote for the Conservative Party and a fifth of non-manual workers vote Labour. Most of the research on the relationship between voting behaviour and social class has concentrated on the 'working class Tory'. The Labour Party is usually seen to represent the interests of the working class with its concern for a more equal distribution of wealth and its support for social welfare policies. It has been regarded as the party of change, of changes that will lead to the betterment of the working class. By comparison the Conservative Party is usually seen as more concerned with maintaining the status quo (the way things are). It is regarded by many as the party of the middle and upper classes. With most of its Parliamentary candidates drawn from the ranks of the well-to-do it is often seen as the defender of wealth and privilege. Partly because of these party images, sociologists have been interested to discover why a large minority of manual workers have traditionally turned their backs on the 'party of the working man' and voted Conservative. The following passage examines some of the research which seeks to answer this question.

A study of working class Conservatives by McKenzie and Silver found that 'deference' largely accounted for the voting behaviour of about half their sample. Deference means accepting the direction of those seen as superior in wisdom or position. As one working class Tory told the researchers, 'Breeding counts every time. I like to be set an example and have someone to look up to.' The other half of the sample, called 'secular voters' by McKenzie and Silver, supported the Conservative Party on more practical grounds. They judged it by its policies and hoped to gain a higher standard of living by voting Conservative.

A number of studies have indicated that manual workers who see themselves as middle class are more likely to vote Conservative than those who define themselves as working class. Their middle-class 'self-image' appears to influence their political views.

A study by Eric Nordlinger found that working class Tories earned on average slightly less than manual workers who supported Labour. However income as such did not seem to be the important factor. Whether or not people were satisfied with their income appeared to influence their voting behaviour. Working class Tories were much more satisfied with their level of income than their Labour counterparts.

Working class affluence does not seem to lead to support for the Conservative Party. Goldthorpe and Lockwood's study of affluent workers in Luton showed that 80% voted Labour. They found that 'white collar affiliations' (connections) appear to largely explain why the 20% of affluent workers in the sample voted Conservative. Either their parents, brothers or sisters or wives had white collar jobs or they themselves previously had a white collar job.

The above studies were conducted during the 1960s. In more recent years research has shown that increasing numbers of manual workers are deserting the Labour Party. In the 1979 election 52% of manual workers and their wives voted for non-Labour candidates. Many of these voters believed that Conservative policies reflected their interests. At the same time there appeared to be a rapid decline in working class support for traditional Labour policies such as public ownership, social welfare and the link with the trade unions. The rise of the SDP (Social Democratic Party) may further reduce working class support for Labour. In the Warrington by-election, July 1981, 46% of skilled manual workers, 32% of unskilled workers and 43% of trade union members voted for the SDP's candidate, Roy Jenkins.

(adapted from 'The tale of the working class Tory' by Tom Forester, **New Society**, 15 October 1981 and **Sociology: Themes and Perspectives** by Michael Haralambos with Robin Heald, University Tutorial Press, Slough, 1980)

1. Why should voters with 'deferential' attitudes tend to support the Conservative rather than the Labour Party? (4)
2. Why should manual workers who see themselves as middle rather than working class be more likely to vote Conservative? (4)
3. Why might satisfaction with income partly explain working class support for the Conservative Party? (4)
4. How can 'white collar affiliations' help to explain working class support for the Conservative party? (4)
5. What evidence is there for a decline in the link between social class and Party support? (4)

7 Voting behaviour and social class (2)

Evidence from the 1983 election suggests that the link between social class and the way people vote is weakening. The election produced a landslide victory of 144 seats for the Conservative Party. It differed from previous elections with the appearance of the Liberal/Social Democratic Party Alliance which offered a third alternative for government. The Conservatives received 42.4% of the vote, Labour 27.6% and the Alliance 25.4%. The following passage is based on a survey of a representative sample of the British population commissioned by the BBC, conducted by Gallup and designed by Ivor Crewe. It consisted of 4,141 interviews conducted shortly after the 1983 election.

The Labour Party suffered a humiliating defeat in the 1983 general election. Compared to the 1979 election it was deserted by 37% of its supporters. Many went to the Alliance but for every three switching to the Alliance, one went to the Conservatives and one stayed at home. The main explanation for the Conservative victory in 1983 is Labour desertions.

The following table shows voting by social class in the 1983 election.

Vote by social class – % of three-party vote in 1983

	Professional & managerial	Office & clerical	Skilled manual	Semi-skilled & unskilled manual
Conservative	62	55	39	29
Labour	12	21	35	44
Liberal/SDP	27	24	27	28

Support for the Alliance is spread evenly across all social classes. The Labour vote remains largely working class but the working class as a whole has ceased to be largely Labour. Only a minority of manual workers voted for 'the party of the working man'. The Conservative Party continued to gain the majority of non-manual votes though its support in the middle class was reduced from the 1979 election. Working class support for Labour has been steadily declining over the past 25 years. In 1959 when the Conservatives had an overall majority of 100, 69% of manual workers voted Labour. In 1983 the figure was 38%.

What has happened to Labour's working class support? The survey shows that a segment of the working class remained loyal to Labour in 1983. This was the 'traditional working class' living on council estates, working in the public sector (employed by the government, local authorities and in nationalized industries) and located in Scotland and the North of England. But Labour lost considerable support in the 'new working class' whose members work for private industry, live in the South and own their own houses. Among manual workers who were house owners or lived in the South the Conservatives had a commanding lead over Labour who came third after the Alliance.

Ivor Crewe concludes by saying,

> By 1983 twice as many manual workers were employed in the private than public sector. Almost as many were home-owners as council tenants; almost as many lived in the South as in the North and Scotland combined. The division of Britain into two nations is no longer between the classes but within the working class; and the more secure, more affluent of these nations is increasingly preponderant. To regain its old electoral strength Labour will have to find ways of appealing to both.

(adapted from 'The disturbing truth behind Labour's rout' by Ivor Crewe, **The Guardian**, 13 June 1983, p. 5).

1. Provide figures from the table to support the following statements.
   a The Conservative Party draws its strongest support from the middle class.   (2)
   b The Labour Party draws its strongest support from the working class.   (2)
   c The Alliance vote is spread evenly across all social classes.   (2)
2. Judging from the 1983 election results, can Labour still be seen as the party of the working class?   (4)
3. The Alliance claims to be an alternative to the old 'class-based' parties. What support does the passage provide for this claim?
                                                                      (4)
4. In 1983, for the first election in history, over half (52%) of the electorate was non-manual workers. If this trend continues what effect might it have on election results?   (3)
5. According to the passage what must the Labour Party do in order to regain political power?   (3)

8 Age, gender and voting behaviour

Apart from class a number of other social factors have been linked to voting behaviour. These include gender and age. There has been a tendency for more women than men to vote Conservative. Older people have tended to vote Conservative, younger voters, especially new voters (those entitled to vote for the first time), to support Labour. The reasons for these differences are far from clear. Those given in the following passage are little more than suggestions.

> Traditionally the Labour Party has been seen as the party of change. Certainly in the past its policies on the welfare state and nationalization have produced major changes in British society. Its stated aim of redistributing wealth and income from top to bottom could result in significant changes in the class structure. By comparison the Conservative Party has been seen as the party which conserves the status quo, maintains things the way they are.
>
> These traditional views of the parties have been used to explain the link between gender, age and voting behaviour.

Women, at least in the past, tended to be less radical than men, more cautious in their outlook, less open to ideas for social change. Their domestic roles and responsibilities meant that 1) they were less exposed to change in the wider society and 2) they were more concerned with security and less prepared to accept the risk to their families that change might involve. If this reasoning is correct it may explain gender differences in party support and voting behaviour.

The young have less commitment to the status quo, less of a stake in the existing social order. They are more likely to support policies which offer change and a new direction. They are therefore more likely to vote Labour. By comparison the elderly tend to be more cautious and less likely to take the risks that policies for change might involve. They are therefore more likely to vote Conservative. In addition the elderly are more likely to be female – women tend to live longer than men.

The following table from Ivor Crewe's survey of the 1983 election shows a change in traditional voting patterns.

Vote by age and sex – 1983

	Men	Women	18–22	23–34	35–44	45–64	65+
Conservative	46	43	41	45	47	46	48
Labour	30	28	29	32	27	27	33
Liberal/SDP	24	28	30	23	26	27	19

In 1979, for the first time, new voters divided equally between Labour and Conservative. In 1983 Labour came third among new voters behind the Alliance (in second place) and the Conservatives. This is surprising at a time of severe youth unemployment since Labour presented itself as the party which offered most to the unemployed. But among unemployed 18–22 year olds, almost half (47%) did not bother to vote at all. Conservative support increased steadily from young to old but their support in the older age group (65+) dropped compared to previous elections. This may be because the over 65s are the generation of the 1930s and Second World War – many will have first voted in 1945 when Labour won a landslide victory. Research by Butler and Stokes indicates that people tend to stick to the party they choose when they first vote – and to become more firmly attached to it the older they get. Differences between the way men and women voted in the 1983 election were small. Until 1979 more women voted Conservative than men. In the 1979 election the gap disappeared, in 1983 it went into reverse. For the first time – and under Britain's first woman Prime Minister – more men voted Conservative than women. (A similar reversal of the 'gender gap' occurred in the USA and Scandinavia in the early 1970s.) The Alliance rather than Labour benefited from this change taking 4% more votes among women than men.

(adapted in part from 'The disturbing truth behind Labour's rout' by Ivor Crewe, **The Guardian**, 13 June 1983, p. 5)

1. According to the table from which gender and age groups did
   a the Conservative Party draw its strongest support? (2)
   b the Labour Party draw its strongest support? (2)
   c the Liberal/SDP parties draw their strongest support? (2)
2. a How has the voting behaviour of women changed? (3)
   b What changes in the position of women in society may account for this change? (4)
3. Suggest why support for the Alliance in the 65 + age group was so low. (3)
4. Suggest why so many of the young unemployed failed to vote. (4)

9 Opinion polls

In the run up to a general election the results of opinion polls are presented regularly in the press and on television. The main concern of the pollsters is to preduct the election result. The most common question is therefore, 'How do you intend to vote?' Polls are conducted by professional organizations which specialize in surveys of public opinion. They are usually based on a representative sample or cross-section of the population. The following passage looks at the methods, purposes and problems of opinion polls.

Often the first question people ask about opinion polls is, 'Are they any good?' In other words are they an accurate measure of opinion and intended behaviour. The following table compares the results of the final polls before the 1983 general election with the actual result.

Final Opinion Polls – 1983 General Election (%)

Poll	Conservative	Labour	Alliance
Audience Selection	46	23	29
Harris	47	25	26
Gallup	45.5	26.5	26
Marplan	46	26	26
NOP	47	25	26
MORI	44	28	26
ELECTION RESULT	43	28	26

(from **Politics Pal** [1984 edition] compiled by L. Robins, Great Glen, Leicestershire, pp. 15–16)

All the polls overestimated support for the Conservative Party, all but one underestimated Labour's support, but nearly all were spot on when it came to the Alliance vote.

However the results of different polls have varied much more than those shown in the table. Shortly before the 1982 SDP Conference MORI did a poll which showed that Alliance support had slumped to 14%. A week later two MORI polls put Alliance support at 26–27%. MORI explained the difference by saying that the first poll was a 'top of the mind' result whereas in the later polls the voting intention question was preceded by other questions on party leaders which may have had the effect of prompting a different choice about who to vote for. This suggests that the type, number and order of questions can affect the results of opinion polls.

The methodology of opinion polls has often been criticised. People are suddenly confronted with a list of questions which they often answer rapidly, off the top of their head. According to Conrad James, polls provide 'opinion that chokes off the opportunity to hear arguments pro and con, to consult a neighbour, to read up, to ask a question, to answer back; opinion so half-hearted it is hard to take seriously'. In addition there is the problem of sampling, of obtaining a representative sample. Some polls are conducted by telephone – a method that is unlikely to reach a cross-section of the population.

'I'm a "don't know"! "Don't know" whether to smash your face in or not.'
(adapted from a cartoon by Edward McLachlan in **Private Eye**.

In view of these problems it is difficult to interpret the results of opinion polls. Do they really reflect what people think? Do people actually do what they say they intend to do? One thing is clear – the pollsters make money. In 1982 the going rate for a poll was between £2000 and £5000.

In recent years there has been concern about the possible effects of opinion polls. Do poll results influence people particularly in terms of which party to vote for and whether or not to vote at all? These questions have become more relevant with the growth in support for the Alliance. Polls in one constituency may show Labour in the lead with the Alliance and Conservative candidates neck and neck in second place. This may lead to 'tactical voting' with, for example, Conservatives switching their votes to the Alliance in order to beat Labour, their least favourite candidate. In this case the polls, far from simply reflecting voting intentions will actually influence them. Whether or not polls have this effect has yet to be determined. The head of one polling organization is reported as saying, 'Yes we have influence, but only a little bit.'

(adapted from 'Are opinion polls any real guide' by Adam Raphael, **The Observer**, 28 November 1982, p. 4 and **Politics: A New Approach** by David Roberts, Causeway Press, Ormskirk, 1986)

1. According to the table which poll was a) most successful and b) least successful in predicting the election result? (2)
2. Why should the results of public opinion polls be regarded with caution? (6)
3. a Why do pollsters attempt to obtain a representative sample of the population? (4)
   b Why are telephone polls unlikely to provide a representative sample? (2)
4. It has been argued that opinion polls should be banned throughout election campaigns. Discuss this viewpoint with reference to material in the passage. (6)

10 The social background of MPs

Despite its claim to represent the nation, the membership of the House of Commons is far from representative of the population as a whole. Whether MPs would represent the people more effectively if their backgrounds reflected the social composition of the nation as a whole is a debatable question. The following extract examines the social background of MPs who sat in the House of Commons in 1980.

Although members of parliament are our democratic representatives, they are not, in many ways, representative of British society as a whole. This is particularly true of Conservative MPs, despite the fact that the party gets votes from a wider cross-section than Labour.

In the present parliament, 67% of Conservative MPs went to public school compared with 3% of the population as a whole. Nearly 15% had been to Britain's top public school, Eton. A total of 48% of Conservative MPs went to Oxford or Cambridge, whereas only 5% of the population have been to any university. In contrast, nearly 90% of Labour MPs

Occupations of MPs

	Con	Lab	Lib	other
barristers	54	21	–	1
solicitors	16	10	–	1
journalists	31	19	1	1
publishers	5	–	–	–
public relations	2	–	–	–
teachers	14	53	3	4
medical	3	5	–	–
farmers, landowners	25	2	2	1
company directors	82	1	2	–
accountants	12	4	1	–
brokers	17	–	–	–
managers	52	33	–	2
architects	5	1	1	–
scientists	1	5	–	–
economists	8	9	–	1
banking	12	–	–	–
diplomatic	2	1	–	–
social workers	1	3	–	–
civil servants	–	3	–	–
local government	1	2	–	–
clerical and technical	1	3	–	–
engineers	8	30	1	–
mineworkers	–	16	–	–
rail workers	–	9	–	–
other manual workers	–	7	–	2
trade union officials	1	27	–	–
party officials	12	5	–	–
hoteliers	–	–	–	2
other jobs	10	5	–	–
ministers of religion	–	–	–	2

attended state schools and only 20% went to Oxford or Cambridge. 32% of Labour MPs went to non-Oxbridge universities, compared with 17% of Tory MPs. The vast majority of Conservative MPs come from the middle and upper classes. Many have business, legal or farming backgrounds. Of the 338 Conservative MPs not one is a manual worker: 56 are barristers and some 170 hold directorships in some 475 companies. Although the Labour Party has many more teachers and journalists among its MPs than it used to, about a third of MPs are manual workers – railwaymen, miners, engineers and so on. This is because 132 of Labour's 268 MPs are sponsored by the trade unions. Only six Labour MPs are registered as having business interests.

But the Labour Party is still far from being a true cross-section of society – the middle class is represented among its MPs in greater proportions than among party members or society as a whole. Some researchers have pointed out that if the parliamentary Labour Party becomes increasingly middle class, as it has tended to in recent years, traditional voting patterns could be upset. The Conservatives could lose some of their deference vote to a Labour Party that was seen to be more 'professional', and the Labour Party could lose some of its working class support.

(from **New Society**, 13 March, 1980; reproduced with permission)

1. Which occupational group is most strongly represented a) in the Commons as a whole, b) amongst Conservative MPs, c) amongst Labour MPs? (3)
2. Which party most closely represents the social composition of the nation in terms of the social backgrounds of its MPs? Provide evidence to support your answer. (5)
3. a What change has recently occurred in the social background of Labour MPs? (1)
   b Why might this result in the Labour Party losing some of its support? (4)
4. Some researchers have argued that the social background of MPs, particularly those in the Conservative Party, will lead them to support the interests of the wealthy and powerful. With some reference to the extract suggest why this may be so. (7)

Section 9 The Family

Many sociologists have seen the family as the cornerstone of human society. They find it difficult to imagine how society could operate without it. Part of their argument runs as follows. Without socialization there would be no culture and without culture there would be no society. In every society the family is largely responsible for primary socialization, the first and most important part of the socialization process. Thus the family is essential for society since its major role or function is to transmit culture from one generation to the next.

This section begins with a consideration of the functions of the family, that is the contribution the family makes to the maintenance and wellbeing of society. Sections 1 and 2 examined the family's role in the processes of socialization and social control. This section investigates how the functions of the family have changed by comparing its role in pre-industrial and industrial societies. The section then moves on to examine the changing structure of the family in industrial society. Structure refers to the composition of the family unit – for example does it simply consist of a married couple and their children or is it a three generation unit which includes grandparents. Related to changes in family structure are changes in conjugal roles – the roles of husband and wife. The link between family structure and conjugal roles is examined in several extracts. Conjugal roles are also considered in relation to the rapidly rising divorce rate in Western Society.

There is a tendency to see the family as a 'good thing' or, in sociological terms, as performing essential functions for the maintenance and wellbeing of society. The section ends with two extracts which provide a rather different view. The first suggests that the family in Western society is, on balance, harmful both to its members and to society as a whole. The second considers the possibility of alternatives to the family.

1 The family in pre-industrial society

Many sociologists have argued that the family in industrial society has lost many of its functions. For example in pre-industrial society parents were mainly responsible for the health, welfare and education of their children. Now these functions have been largely taken over by the state in the form of specialized organizations such as hospitals, schools and a widespread system of social security.

The view that the family has lost many of its functions in industrial society is presented in the following extract. It is taken from an interview with a Pomo Indian man well over one hundred years of age. He vividly recalls the role of the family in his society and compares it with what he has seen of the family in white American society. The Pomo Indians live in northern California in the USA. Their traditional way of life came to an end in the nineteenth century after they were herded on to reservations by the white man.

What is a man? A man is nothing. Without his family he is of less importance than that bug crossing the trail. A man must be with his family to amount to anything with us. If he had nobody else to help him, the first trouble he got into he would be killed by his enemies. No woman would marry him because her family would not let her marry a man with no family. He would be poorer than a newborn child; he would be poorer than a worm, and the family would not consider him worth anything. He would not bring renown or glory with him. He would not bring support of other relatives either. The family is important. If a man has a large family and a profession (a specialized occupation such as deer hunter or doctor which requires years of training) and upbringing by a family that is known to produce good children, then he is somebody and every family is willing to have him marry a woman in their group. It is the family that is important. In the white ways of doing things the family is not so important. The police and soldiers take care of protecting you, the courts give you justice, the post office carries messages for you, the school teaches you. Everything is taken care of, even your children, if you die; but with us the family must do all of that.

Without the family we are nothing, and in the old days before the white people came the family was given the first consideration by anyone who was about to do anything. That is why we got along. We had no courts, judges, schools, and the other things you have, but we got along better than you. We were taught that we would suffer from the devil, spirits, ghosts, or other people if we did not support one another. The family was everything, and no man ever forgot that. Each person was nothing, but as a group joined by blood the individual knew that he would get the support of all his relatives if anything happened. He also knew that if he was a bad person the head man of his family would pay another tribe to kill him so that there would be no trouble afterward and so that he would not get the family into trouble all the time.

With us the family was everything. Now it is nothing. We are getting like the white people, and it is bad for the old people. We had no old peoples' homes like you. The old people were important. They were wise. Your old people must be fools.

(from 'An Indian's soliloquy' by Burt W. Aginsky, **American Journal of Sociology**, 46 (1940), pp. 43–44)

1. What evidence does the extract contain which suggests that the social control function of the family in Pomo society was more widespread than that of the family in Western society   (4)
2. Why would a woman in Pomo society not marry a man without a family?   (4)
3. Why does the Pomo Indian state, 'Your old people must be fools'?   (4)
4. What evidence does the passage contain to suggest that the family has fewer functions in modern industrial society compared with small-scale, pre-industrial societies such as the Pomo?   (8)

2 Changing functions of the family

Not all sociologists take the view that the family in modern industrial society has lost many of its functions. For example the

A nineteenth century view of the family's childcare function

British sociologist Ronald Fletcher claims that not only has the family retained its functions but those functions have actually 'increased in detail and importance'. State education, for instance, has assisted parents rather than removed their responsibility for secondary socialization. In Fletcher's words, 'Parents are expected to do their best to guide, encourage and support their children in their educational and occupational choices and careers.' In the same way the state has not removed the family's responsibility for the physical welfare of its members. Fletcher argues that, 'The family is still centrally concerned with maintaining the health of its members, but it is now aided by wider provisions which have been **added** to the family's situation since pre-industrial times.' State health and welfare services have provided additional support for the family and made its members more aware of the importance of health, childcare, proper diet and hygiene in the home.

Although he believes that the functions of the family have not been reduced in industrial society, Fletcher does recognize some important changes. This is particularly true of the family's economic function. In many pre-industrial societies the family was the basic unit of production. Families were the main social groups that produced goods and services. The family therefore had an important economic function in society. This is illustrated in the first of the following extracts which describes a day in the life of a farming family in Manupur, a village in India.

In industrial societies the family is no longer the main production unit. The majority of adults are wage and salary earners. They do not produce goods and services as members of family groups. Athough the family has largely lost its function as a unit of production, some sociologists argue that it has developed an important economic function as a unit of consumption. Goods and services are increasingly bought and consumed in the name of the family – houses, family cars and so on. From this viewpoint, examined in the second extract, the family still has an important economic function in society.

> The day begins early for a farmer in Manupur, around four in the morning. He must first feed the animals (oxen, cows, buffalo) and give them water.
>
> The oxen are tied to the cart at around five o'clock in the morning and the men are ready to go to the fields and work.

Work lasts until seven in the evening, interrupted only for 'fuelling oneself' (as the farmers are fond of saying) – that is, for breakfast in mid-morning (15 minutes around 10:00), lunch (from 12:00 to 1:00), and tea (from 4:00 to 4:15). If it is a hot summer day, lunch might last for two hours instead of one. Meals are brought to the field by the son, or, if necessary, by the daughter. The distance between the house and the farm is sometimes over a mile, and it would be a waste of precious time to go home.

When it begins to get dark – and in the summer this is usually around seven in the evening – oxen are reharnessed to the cart and everybody proceeds home. During sowing and harvest times, work may go on as late as 10:00 p.m. Once home, the animals must be tended. If the farmer has a young son, grass has already been cut; if not, he must employ someone to do it. It remains for him to prepare the fodder, and to feed, wash, and clean the animals.

The farmer's wife has an even greater burden of work. She must prepare the meals (breakfast, lunch, and dinner) and tea (early morning, mid-afternoon, and late night). Meals are made for the husband and the children and, if there are few children, for the labourers who have to be hired. The work is hard. Flour must be mixed with water and made into dough, and dough into wheat or corn cakes – usually six cakes per person per meal. The buffalo must be milked twice a day, morning and evening. The milk is used to make lassi, a yoghurt drink for warm mornings, and to make butter late in the evening. Dishes must be washed after every meal.

There is more. Animal dung must be collected and put in a pit to dry out. She must build a dungcake fire, which provides a slow and gentle heat over which to simmer a lentil curry. While it is cooking, she attends to other tasks. Firewood must also be cut, gathered, and carried to the house. The buffalo must be given drinking water and fed grass if the husband is in the fields at night. Clothes must be washed every day. Cleaning a dirty piece of clothing – and there is a lot of dirt in the fields – means soaking it in soapy water and then beating it with a wooden stick. The use of simple tools requires both time and effort. Younger children have to be tended to, fed, and washed. In the midst of all this, the wife must somehow find time to feed herself.

The farmer's children can be of considerable assistance, even while they are young. A son or daughter can bring grass and water for the cattle before going to school at eight in the morning, can help in the fields in the afternoon if necessary, and can graze the cattle in the evening. In fact, primary responsibility for the cattle can be left to the children and the adult's load lightened a little.

If a farmer's wife has no young children, it would mean intolerable hardship. She would then have to walk to the fields to deliver two meals and one tea every day. The walk over and back, the wait while everybody eats – so the utensils can be taken back, washed, and cleaned for the next meal – can take as much as four hours.

(from 'The myth of population control', **New Internationalist**, No. 15 May 1974 pp. 18–19)

The family (in Britain) remains an important economic unit from the viewpoint of the patterning of consumption, or, as the economist would put it, of the 'consumer's outlay'. The expenditure of family income – whether this is contributed by one or more members, and whether it is to any great extent 'pooled' or not – is still patterned not solely on 'individual preferences' but also on the needs of the family as a whole and the preferences of the family as a group. Advertisers are clearly aware of this, and sometimes play upon it to a rather nauseating extent, as may be seen by watching television advertisements for some foodstuffs, soap powders, holiday arrangements, and the like. Furthermore, although the degree and extent of this throughout the country cannot be said to be known, it is probable that there is still, to some extent, a 'pooling' of proportions of family incomes for the upkeep of the family as a whole, and for the improvement of the home. Indeed, if one is to judge from the present concentration upon schemes of furnishing, schemes of interior decoration, 'do-it-yourself' techniques with appropriate tool-kits, and from the extent to which families devote themselves to improving their 'homes and gardens' along these lines, the present-day concern for the improvement of the family's household must be held to be very considerable indeed.

(from **The Family and Marriage in Britain** by Ronald Fletcher, Penguin Books, Harmondsworth 1966, pp. 183–4)

1. How do members of the Indian farming family combine to form a unit of production? (6)
2. The main unit of production in industrial society is the factory. Briefly explain why the family is **not** an important part of this unit. (5)
3. What does Fletcher mean when he states that family income is not spent 'solely on "individual preferences" but also on the needs of the family as a whole'. (4)
4. Why is the family in industrial society beneficial to the economy? Make reference to the extract from Fletcher in your answer. (5)

3 Family structure in early industrial society

The typical family unit in modern industrial society is known as the nuclear family. It consists of a husband and wife and their children. Most sociologists consider this to be the smallest and most basic form of family structure. In many pre-industrial societies the family contained relatives or kin beyond the nuclear family. This type of family structure is known as the extended family. It may include the parents of the married couple, their brothers and sisters or any kin beyond the nuclear family related by blood or marriage.

It has often been argued that the nuclear family is ideally suited to industrial society. Modern industry needs a geographically mobile workforce – people are required to move to areas where their skills and labour are in demand. The extended family is unsuited to geographical mobility being a large and bulky unit. By comparison the nuclear family is a small, streamlined unit which is not tied down by binding loyalties and obligations to a wide range of kin. It was once argued that industrialization produced a change in family structure from extended to nuclear. This does appear to have happened in some societies but certainly not in Britain.

Research by the historian Peter Laslett suggests that the

nuclear family was the norm in pre-industrial England. He found that from 1564 to 1821 only about 10% of households contained kin (relatives) beyond the nuclear family. This is roughly the same as the figure for England and Wales in 1966. However, research by Michael Anderson suggests that the early years of industrialization encouraged the development of extended families. From a sample of houses listed in the 1851 census for Preston, Lancashire, Anderson found that 23% of households contained kin other than members of the nuclear family. His research is examined in the following passage.

In 1851 between a quarter and a third of the adult male population of Preston worked in factories. Preston was one of the main centres of the cotton industry and women and children were widely employed in the mills. Times were hard for members of the working class. Unemployment was high and families struggled to make ends meet on low wages. Housing conditions were appalling, overcrowding was widespread and rents expensive. Families were large, fertility was high and birth control techniques, if they were used, were largely ineffective. By today's standards, disease was rampant and the death rate unacceptably high. Organized social welfare was woefully inadequate. Social security provision for the old, sick, unemployed, the pregnant mother and the large family was practically non-existent.

Extended families in Preston were found mainly among the poor. They often included old people living with their children. The following table shows the domestic situation of people over 65 in Preston in 1851 and compares it with Britain in 1962.

Household composition of the over sixty-fives

	Married		Widowed, single and separated	
	Britain 1962	Preston 1851	Britain 1962	Preston 1851
Living with:				
Married child(ren)	6	16	27	41
Unmarried child(ren)	26	47	27	29
Spouse only	68	37	–	–
Other kin only	–	–	4	8
No related person	–	–	42	22
All (percentage)	100	100	100	100

Men and boys in Holmes Mill, Clitheroe, near Preston

'Parentless' children formed a major source of additions to the nuclear family. Some were the illegitimate sons and daughters of unmarried women living with their parents. Others were orphans, their parents being part of the high death rate statistics. Apart from the elderly and children, families were extended by the addition of in-laws, siblings (brothers and sisters of the head of the household) uncles, aunts and cousins.

Anderson suggests that extended families will tend to develop if the advantages of this type of social unit outweigh its disadvantages. He argues that in Preston extended families provide an insurance policy for their members against hardship and crisis. They operate as mutual aid organizations, each member providing benefits and gaining support from the others.

(adapted from, 'Family, household and the industrial revolution' by Michael Anderson in **The Comparative History of Family and Household**, edited by P. Laslett, Cambridge University Press, Cambridge, 1971)

1. What percentage of married couples over 65 lived with their children
   a in Preston in 1851?   (1)
   b in Britain in 1962?   (1)
2. How might parents living with their married children benefit all concerned in Preston in 1851?   (4)
3. How might taking in orphaned children provide benefits for all concerned in Preston in 1851?   (4)
4. How might rising living standards discourage the development of extended families?   (4)
5. How might the Welfare State discourage the development of extended families? Give details of the provisions of the Welfare State in your answer.   (6)

4 The working class extended family

The working class extended family has continued well into the present century. This can be seen from the famous study conducted by Michael Young and Peter Willmott from 1953–1955 in the borough of Bethnal Green, a traditional working class community in the East End of London. Young and Willmott define the extended family as 'a combination of families who to some large degree form one domestic unit'. Members of the extended family do not need to share the same dwelling as long as their lives are intertwined sufficiently for the households to be 'to some extent merged'. Young and Willmott see three main reasons for the continued existence of the extended family in Bethnal Green. Firstly, tradition – often families have lived in the same area for three or more generations and a practice begun in the last century has been handed down from one generation to the next. Secondly, proximity of kin – many relatives live near each other and so links can be easily maintained. Thirdly, the common experience of women – the mother-housewife role is shared by female members of the extended family. This provides a common experience which links them together. The extended family is largely organized by women and has sometimes been called 'the trade union of women'.

Most people in Bethnal Green want to live near their parents. Mr. Sykes who lives near his mother-in-law said, 'This is the kind of family where sisters never want to leave their mother's side.' The following table shows the extent to which married couples live near their parents.

Proximity of married children to parents

Parents' residence	Married men	Married women
Bethnal Green	50%	59%
Adjacent borough	18%	16%
Elsewhere	32%	25%
Total %	100%	100%
Number	195	174

The link between mother and daughter in Bethnal Green is often strong. The following example shows how much their lives are sometimes woven together. Mrs Wilkins is in and out of her mother's all day. She shops with her in the morning and goes round there for a cup of tea in the afternoon. 'Then any time during the day, if I want a bit of salt or something like that, I go round to Mum to get it and have a bit of a chat while I'm there.' If the children have anything wrong with them, 'I usually go round to my Mum and have a little chat. If she thinks it's serious enough I'll take him to the doctor.' Her mother looked after Marilyn, the oldest child, for nearly three years. 'She's always had her when I worked; I worked from when she was just a little baby until I was past six months with Billy. Oh, she's all for our Mum. She's got her own mates over there and still plays there all the time. Mum looks after my girl pretty good. When she comes in, I say "Have you had your tea?", and she says as often as not, "I've had it at Nan's." '

Nurse visits a working class family in Bethnal Green in the 1890s. In an era of widespread poverty families such as this looked to their relatives for support.

The following table shows the frequency of contact between married men and women with their parents

Contacts of married men and women with parents

	Fathers		Mothers	
	Number with father alive	Percentage of those with father alive who saw him in previous twenty-four hours	Number with mother alive	Percentage of those with mother alive who saw her in previous twenty-four hours
Men	116	30%	163	31%
Women	100	48%	155	55%

The next table examines the link between the number of contacts between married women and their mothers and the distance between their homes.

Contacts of women according to distance of mothers

Residence of mother	Number of married women	Women who saw their mother in previous twenty-four hours
Same street or block of flats	23	23
Elsewhere in Bethnal Green	49	33
Adjacent borough	25	4
Elsewhere	36	3

The mother is the head and centre of the extended family, her home its meeting place. 'Mum's is the family rendezvous,' as one wife said. Her daughters congregate at the mother's, visiting her more often than she visits any one of them: 68% of married women last saw their mother at her home, and only 27% at their own. When there, they quite often see their other sisters, and brothers too, particularly if they are still living at home, but even if they live elsewhere, the sisters may call there at the usual time in the afternoon for a cup of tea, or just happen to drop in for a chat on their way to the shops. Regular weekly meetings often supplement the day-to-day visiting.

'All my family', said Mrs Shipway, 'gather at Mum's every Saturday afternoon. We sit jawing, and get amused with the children when all of them get together, play cards, and listen to the wireless. No one leaves until tenish at night. It always happens on a Saturday.'

In Bethnal Green the old proverb often applies:

My son's a son till he gets him a wife,
My daughter's a daughter all her life.

The daughter continues to live near her mother. She is a member of her extended family. She receives advice and support from her in the great personal crises and on the small domestic occasions. They share so much and give such help to each other because, in their women's world, they have the same functions of caring for home and bringing up children.

Less than 20 miles away from Bethnal Green, the automatic doors of the tube train open on to the new land of Greenleigh. On one side of the railway are cows at pasture. On the other, the new housing estate. Greenleigh is fairly typical of the council estates to which many Bethnal Greeners have been moved. The changes in frequency of contact with relatives after moving to Greenleigh are outlined in the following table.

Changes in weekly contacts with relatives after moving to Greenleigh

Average number of contacts per week with own
and spouse's parents and siblings

	Before leaving Bethnal Green	Greenleigh 1953	Greenleigh 1955
Husbands	15.0	3.8	3.3
Wives	17.2	3.0	2.4

In summer the most popular time for visiting, is of course, the weekend. On a Sunday morning in the summer dozens of people can be seen coming out of the station, many carrying bags of fruit and flowers, as one person said 'quite like hospital on a visiting day'. 'Last August Bank Holiday,' said Mrs Hall, 'we had fourteen relatives down here.' Visitors do not necessarily stay for only one day. Greenleigh is suitable for holidays as well as day excursions. Sometimes people told us, as Mrs Lowie did, 'Mum comes down to stay two or three times a year.' In Bethnal Green, the kindred are at hand every day of the week. At Greenleigh the family has to wait for summer, for weekends, for holidays, before they appear.

(from **Family and Kinship in East London** by Michael Young and Peter Willmott, Routledge & Kegan Paul, London, 1957)

1. What percentage of a) married men and b) married women in Bethnal Green saw their mothers within the previous twenty-four hours? (2)
2. 'My son's a son till he gets him a wife.
   My daughter's a daughter all her life.'
   What evidence does the extract contain to support this proverb? (4)
3. Members of the extended family provide each other with support and exchange services.
   a Outline the evidence given in the extract which illustrates this point. (3)
   b Suggest two services not mentioned in the extract which members of the extended family might provide for each other. (2)

4. What evidence does the extract contain to show the importance of distance for maintaining contacts with kin beyond the nuclear family?   (5)
5. How might the changing role of women in society serve to weaken the extended family?   (4)

5 The symmetrical family

The Bethnal Green study was conducted from 1953–55. In the early 1970s Young and Willmott conducted a large scale survey of family life in London based on a sample of nearly 2000. They found that the nuclear family was now the typical form of family structure for members of all social classes. The extended family, found in their earlier study of Bethnal Green had all but disappeared. They also found important changes in conjugal roles – the roles of husband and wife. Young and Willmott use the term 'symmetrical family' to describe the type of nuclear family found in their research. The following passage presents an outline of the symmetrical family and the reasons for its development.

> The symmetrical family is a largely self-contained and self-reliant unit. No longer do husband and wife expect and receive the kind of help and support from relatives that was typical of Bethnal Green in the 1950s. Their leisure activities have also changed since the 50s. Husbands are much less likely to be down at the pub with their mates. Typical remarks include, 'My family is my hobby', 'My wife and family are my leisure time.' Compared to the Bethnal Green study, wives are less likely to spend time with their mothers and other female relatives. Leisure for both wives and husbands is centred on the home with watching television, gardening and playing with the children being the main leisure activities.
>   The roles of husband and wife in the symmetrical family have become increasingly similar. In the home, 'They shared their work; they shared their time.' Husbands increasingly help with domestic chores such as washing up and cleaning the house. They also help more with raising children though this still remains the main responsibility of the wife. Decisions about family life are now largely shared. The days of

the Victorian father laying down the law are rapidly disappearing.

Young and Willmott use the term symmetrical family to describe the typical nuclear family unit revealed by their research. Symmetry refers to an arrangement in which the parts are similar. In the symmetrical family, conjugal roles, though not the same, have become increasingly similar.

Young and Willmott give the following reasons for the development of the symmetrical nuclear family. Living standards have steadily improved. The value of wages has risen and many more wives are now working in paid employment. Family allowances, sickness and unemployment benefits and various other provisions of the welfare state have helped to reduce the extent of absolute poverty. There has been a steady reduction in family size from an average of five or six children per family in the nineteenth century to just under two in 1970. People are becoming more geographically mobile moving to new council house developments and new locations when changing jobs. The home has become a more attractive place. Better housing, less overcrowding, improved plumbing and heating facilities, home entertainment in the form of radio and television, fitted carpets and three-piece suites, household technology such as vacuum cleaners and washing machines have produced a more comfortable home environment.

(adapted from **The Symmetrical Family** by Michael Young and Peter Willmott, Penguin, Harmondsworth, 1975)

1. Why do Young and Willmott use the term 'symmetrical family'? Give two examples in your answer of symmetry in the family unit described in their research. (4)
2. a Name the three main leisure activities of husbands and wives. (1)
   b How might these forms of leisure limit contact with kin beyond the nuclear family? (3)
3. What evidence does the extract provide which suggests that husband and wife will be less likely to rely on relatives for assistance and support? (4)
4. How might the fact that growing numbers of wives are working outside the home result in decision making being increasingly

shared between husband and wife?   (3)
5. Why are husbands spending more time at home?   (2)
6. Suggest one connection between the reduction in the numbers
   of children and the development of the symmetrical family.   (3)

6 Conjugal roles

A somewhat different picture of conjugal roles is provided by
research conducted by Ann Oakley in the early 1970s (the same
time as the symmetrical family research). The main aim of her
study was to investigate women's attitudes to housework. The
research was based on a sample of 40 women, with at least one
child under five, who were each given a long, detailed, 'depth'
interview.

> With the emancipation of women has come the virtual
> equality of the sexes – or so many people believe. They also
> believe that one sign of equality is the increasing employment
> of married women, while another is the greater readiness of
> husbands to help in the home.
>   In this small study I tried to find out firstly how much help
> husbands actually give in the home and secondly what was
> thought to be the ideal or proper roles of the sexes.
>   In thinking about the proper roles of the sexes we must ask
> if 'he' actually believes in the domestication of the male? Also
> does his wife? Is there really a change in the old dogma that a
> woman's place is in the home and a man's place is outside it?
>   The women in the sample were asked which household and
> childcare tasks their husbands regularly help with – ranging
> from shopping, general housework and washing up to
> putting children to bed, buying children's clothes and super-
> vising their play. They were also asked about what they
> believed should be the respective roles of husband and wife in
> the home.
>   The most usual pattern was for husbands to share more in
> childcare than in housework. However, the childcare tends to
> involve playing with children rather than doing jobs like
> changing nappies and bathing them.
>   Not one of the housewives questioned their primary duty as

Do husbands make good housewives?

being that of looking after the home and the physical needs of the family. Housework was spoken of as 'my work'. Even where husbands help with childcare, the housewife described this as an activity done 'for' her: 'Sometimes he'll help me to bath them.' Fathers are, therefore, at best, only aids to the mother who retains full responsibility for, and control over, what is done in the home. 'He's a very good father – he plays with the children' was a comment often voiced by both working class and middle class housewives. To play with the children in the evenings and at weekends; to take them off the mother's hands on a Sunday morning; to be interested in their welfare; and to act as a mother substitute in times of illness or childbirth – this defines the father's role for these husbands and wives.

There was little or no support for sex equality. 'I don't agree with men doing housework. I don't think it's a man's job...I certainly wouldn't like to see my husband cleaning a room up.' 'I don't think it's mannish for a man to stay at home. I like a man to be a man.'

Sometimes comments about the women's liberation movement show a real fondness for the man's point of view: 'I think its ridiculous. Well I always think it's a man's place to be head of any family and what they're trying to do is put the woman up above the man – and it'll never work. It's degrading the man, isn't it?' In describing what they think about women's liberation, these women make statements about what they believe the roles of the sexes should be. These beliefs in turn help build up the division of labour between husband and wife.

The women were asked the question: 'What would you think of a marriage in which the wife went out to work and the husband stayed at home to look after the children?' Only a small number of women agreed with the reversed roles marriage as an arrangement which might suit some couples. In general this arrangement still seems to be regarded as 'unnatural'.

Husbands are not regarded as domesticated creatures, nor is domestication set up as ideal. There seems to have been little change in the concept of the male's 'proper' role.

(from 'Are husbands good housewives?' by Ann Oakley, **New Society** 17 February 1972 pp. 337–340; reproduced with permission)

1. What does the term sex roles (or gender roles) mean?   (2)
2. What evidence is there in the extract to show that women still regard housework and childcare as **their** responsibility?   (3)
3. What traditional images of masculinity do the women in the sample hold?   (3)
4. What factors in the wider society reinforce traditional roles in the family?   (4)
5. a What is a reversal of roles?   (2)
   b What difficulties would face a married couple in our society who wished to reverse their roles?   (3)
6. How can the extract help to explain why women are less successful than men in their careers?   (3)

7 Family diversity (1)

From watching the ads on television there appears to be little doubt that the typical British family consists of mum, dad and the two kids. The nuclear family is presented as alive and well, fit and healthy and enjoying life to the full. This picture of the nuclear family as typical is not confined to advertisements. It is the ideal presented to us all, it is the model on which governments usually base their policies and it is accepted by many sociologists. In recent years some sociologists have rejected the view that there is such a thing as the 'typical British family'. They see diversity and variation influenced by social class, ethnicity and region. They recognise an increasing variety of family types, in particular the growth of the one-parent family. This diversity has led the social historian Peter Laslett to argue that we should get rid of the phrase 'the British family' as soon as possible. The following passage provides evidence for and against this view.

Table 1 Households by type in Great Britain 1961–83

	percentages		
	1961	1971	1983
No family			
One person – under retirement age	4	6	8
– over retirement age	7	12	16
Two or more people			
– one over retirement age	3	2	1
– all under retirement age	2	2	2
One family			
Married couple only	26	27	27
Married couple with one or two dependent children	30	26	24
Married couple with three or more dependent children	8	9	6
Married couple with independent child(ren) only	10	8	8
Lone parent with at least one dependent child	2	3	5
Lone parent with independent child(ren) only	4	4	4
Two or more families	3	1	1
Total households	100	100	100

(from **Social Trends 15**, 1985)

The above table shows household types in Britain from 1961–1983. Households consist of people who share a residence or who live on their own. Nearly three quarters of the households in the table are made up of families. However

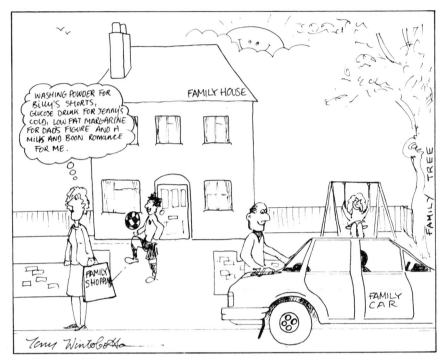

A typical British family?

it is clear that the families are not all of the same type. The table indicates a decline in the proportion of households made up of the so-called 'typical British family' – a married couple with dependent children. As a proportion of all households they declined from 38% in 1961 to 30% in 1983. The number of one parent or single parent families has increased by about 50% from 1961 to 1981, from 1 million to 1.5 million. In 1983 they made up 13% of all families with dependent children. Most of this increase is accounted for by families headed by divorced mothers.

It is possible from the figures given so far to present a picture of growing family diversity. But a rather different view is taken by Robert Chester. He claims that such figures are misleading if taken at face value. He argues that we get a rather different picture if we consider numbers of people rather than just numbers of households. This is shown in Table 2.

Table 2   Households and people in households: 1981

type of household	% of households	% of people
one person	22	8
married couple	26	20
married couple with dependent children	32	49
married couple with independent children	8	10
lone parent with dependent children	4	5
other	9	8

(modified from **Social Trends, 13**, figures for Great Britain)

The table shows that nearly 6 out of 10 people (59%) live in parents-plus-children households. A further 20% of people are married couples who mostly had, or will have, children. At any one time about 80% of people live in households headed by a married couple. Living in a nuclear family with dependent children is a phase of married life which is still experienced by the great majority. Chester concludes that the evidence he presents 'does not mean that the nuclear family has been abandoned as the normal experience'.

(adapted from **Sociology Update 1985** by Martyn Denscombe and 'The rise of the neo-conventional family' by Robert Chester, **New Society**, 9 May 1985, pp. 185–188)

1. From Table 1, what percentage of households consisted of married couples with dependent children in a) 1961 b) 1983?   (2)
2. What evidence does Table 1 provide to support the view that the nuclear family is declining in importance?   (5)
3. From Table 2, what percentage of a) households b) people make up the category 'married couple with dependent children'?   (2)
4. Why does Robert Chester claim that the nuclear family is still the 'normal experience'?   (5)
5. Why do advertisers often link their products to a nuclear family consisting of mum, dad and two kids?   (6)

8 Family diversity (2) Ethnicity

During the 1970s and 80s sociologists began to study the family life of ethnic groups in Britain. These studies support the view that we can no longer talk about 'the typical British family'. They show a wide variety of family structures and relationships. The following passage provides a brief and simplified outline of South Asian families before and after migration to Britain.

The South Asian population of Britain numbers more than a million people about half of whom were born here. Migration began in the 1950s from three main areas – Punjab (about three-quarters came from this region) Gujerat and Bengal. Most migrants came from peasant backgrounds. In Britain they formed communities based on religion, area of origin, caste and, most importantly, kinship.

In South Asia the basic family unit consists of a man, his sons, and grandsons together with their wives and unmarried daughters. At marriage daughters leave the group and become members of their husband's family. Family members hold land or a business or the right to perform a craft (e.g. weaving). They live and work together, sharing domestic, agricultural and other production tasks (see Sections 9:2 and 13:1).

Family membership involves a series of binding obligations and duties. Relationships within the family are hierarchical, with males having more power and status than females, the old having more power and status than the young. Those at the top are expected to support and care for those lower down who in turn are expected to obey and respect them. However few heads of households make important decisions without consulting every member of their family, women as well as men. Males keep close control over the female members of their families. For a woman to challenge her father's or husband's authority in public shames his honour. Parents arrange marriages for both their sons and daughters.

Many migrants found their ideas of honour and family loyalty almost entirely absent in Britain. They made great efforts to maintain the unity of their family and traditional family relationships. Housing proved a problem. The large

Victorian houses where many migrants first settled could accommodate large families but they were often in poor, run-down areas. Moving up-market often meant moving into smaller houses. Some bought adjoining houses and knocked through a connecting door. Others split the family into several nearby dwellings and constant visiting, sharing meals and leisure activities maintained the family unit.

South Asian children born in Britain are exposed to two very different cultures. At home parents expect conformity to the norms of cooperation, respect and family loyalty. Group membership is more important than individual self-interest. At school they are expected to achieve as individuals, they are judged in terms of individual effort rather than as members of a group. Many are multi-cultural – they switch their behaviour to fit the particular cultural setting. Most choose to organize their domestic and personal lives in terms of the ethnic subculture. They value group loyalty and the warm, secure personal relationships which come from traditional family life. However exposure to British culture has brought

Taj Stores, Brick Lane, London.

changes. Young men, though still paying their fathers respect, insist on a greater say 'in decision making. Young people of both sexes are demanding greater consultation in the arrangement of their marriages.

Family loyalty has proved a valuable economic resource in the establishment of small businesses – corner shops, restaurants, market stalls, small clothing workshops. Family members work together as cooperative units producing goods and providing services. Often they work long hours for low wages building up businesses for the group as a whole. Only a minority of South Asian families in Britain own their own businesses. For those that do, the traditional economic function of the family in South Asia has been recreated in Britain.

(adapted from 'South Asian Families' by Roger Ballard in **Families in Britain** edited by R. N. Rapoport, M. P. Fogarty and R. Rapoport, Routledge & Kegan Paul, London, 1982)

1. Outline the main norms and values of traditional South Asian family life. (4)
2. In certain respects the traditional South Asian family was like the British family before the industrial revolution. In which respects? Refer to Section 9 : 2 in your answer. (5)
3. Housing in Britain is often designed for small nuclear families.
   a What problems did this present for some Asian families? (2)
   b How did they solve these problems? (3)
4. British born Asian children are often multi-cultural. Explain with examples what this means. (3)
5. A minority of Asian families in Britain run their own businesses. How has their family organization helped them in this respect? (3)

9 Marital breakdown

The divorce rate is steadily rising in every Western society. Whether or not this means that more marriages are breaking up is not at all clear. Marital breakdown can be divided into three categories: 1) divorce – the legal termination of a marriage 2) separation – the physical separation of husband and wife (they no longer live together) 3) 'empty-shell' marriages – the couple live together, remain legally married, but their marriage exists in name only.

Accurate figures on the extent of divorce are readily obtainable from court records. Some couples who separate apply for a legal separation order and again accurate figures are available from court records. Other couples, however, separate without obtaining a separation order. There are no figures available for people in this category. The same applies to empty-shell marriages. There is little or no information on the extent of this form of marital breakdown.

Simply because the divorce rate is rising does not necessarily mean that marital breakdown is increasing. It may be that people who in previous years separated are now obtaining a divorce. Some researchers believe that the overall rate of marital breakdown is increasing though they admit that this conclusion is based partly on guesswork.

There are probably as many explanations for the increase in divorce as there are people researching the subject. However, all researchers agree that at least part of the increase can be accounted for by changes in the law. The following extract provides figures on the divorce rate and examines some of the more important Acts of Parliament which are related to divorce.

Divorce in England and Wales

Year	Number of divorces (decrees absolute)
1936	6000
1940	7000
1945	16000
1947	47000
1951	29000
1955	27000
1959	26000
1961	25000
1966	39000
1970	58000
1971	74000
1972	119000
1974	114000
1976	127000
1978	144000
1980	148000
1981	146000
1982	147000
1983	148000
1984	145000

(adapted from **Marriage in Britain** by Dr. J. Dominian, Study Commission on the Family, London, 1980, p. 16, **Social Trends 12**, HMSO, London, 1982, p. 37 and **Social Trends 16**, HMSO, London, 1986, p. 38)

Before 1857 a private act of Parliament was required to obtain a divorce in Britain. This was an expensive and complicated procedure beyond the means of all but the most wealthy. In 1857 the Matrimonial Causes Act set up a new court for divorce. The grounds for divorce included adultery, cruelty and desertion. At least one partner had to be proven guilty of one of these 'matrimonial offences'. Although the costs of obtaining a divorce were now reduced, they were still beyond the reach of most people. For the 10 years following the 1857 act an average of nearly 150 divorces a year were granted rising to an annual average of nearly 600 from 1890-1900.

Beginning with the Matrimonial Causes Act of 1878, a series of acts gave Magistrates Courts the power to grant separation and maintenance orders. From 1897-1906 around 8,000 separation orders a year were granted compared to an annual average of 700 divorces for the same period. By 1971, however, only 94 separation orders were granted compared to over 74,000 divorces.

Throughout the first half of this century a series of acts simplified divorce proceedings, reduced the costs involved and widened the grounds for divorce. The financial burden of divorce was eased for the less well-off by the Legal Aid and Advice Act of 1949 which provided free legal advice and paid solicitors' fees for those who could not afford them.

The Divorce Reform Act of 1969 involved a major change in the grounds for divorce. Before this act a 'matrimonial offence' had to be proven, a 'guilty party' had to be found. However many people who wanted a divorce had not committed adultery, been guilty of cruelty and so on. The 1969 Act defined the grounds for divorce as 'the irretrievable breakdown of the marriage'. It was no longer necessary to prove guilt but simply to show that the marriage was beyond repair. The act came into force in January 1971.

(adapted from **When Marriage Ends** by Nicky Hart, Tavistock, London, 1976, pp. 70-71 and **A Textbook of Sociology**, 2nd edition, by Graham Sergeant, Macmillan, London, 1979, pp. 189-200)

1. Describe the trends shown in the above figures for divorce.   (3)
2. a Briefly explain why a rise in the number of divorces does not

necessarily mean an increase in marital breakdown.   (3)
  b What evidence is there in the passage to suggest that the
    extent of marital breakdown may not be as great as the
    figures on divorce make it appear?   (3)
3. How did the 1971 Divorce Reform Act differ from all previous
   legislation?   (3)
4. a Using evidence from the above table suggest the possible
     effect of the 1971 Act on the extent of divorce.   (2)
  b Why might it have had this effect?   (3)
5. How can it be argued that the rise in the number of divorces
   after 1971 does not simply represent a backlog of couples
   waiting for the Act to come into force?   (3)

10 Women and divorce

In 1984 over seven out of every ten divorces were granted to
women. As the following table shows, the proportion of wives
petitioning for divorce has steadily risen. A number of researchers
have argued that the rising divorce rate, particularly over the past
15 years, is related to changes in the position of women in society.
This view is examined in the following extract.

Proportion of petitions for divorce filed by husbands and wives 1946–1984

Year	Husbands' petitions (%)	Wives' petitions (%)
1946	63	37
1948	50	50
1950	46	54
1954	45	55
1961	44	56
1971	40	60
1976	30	70
1980	29	71
1984	27	73

(adapted from **A Textbook of Sociology** by Graham Sergeant, 2nd edition,
Macmillan, London, 1979, p. 196 and **Social Trends 16**, HMSO, London,
1986, p. 38)

In Britain today over half of all married women are
employed compared to one in five in 1951. Some researchers
claim that there is a link between the rise in divorce and the
growth of jobs for women. An American study by Heather

Ross and Isabel Sawhill interviewed a number of families in 1968 and looked at them again four years later. They found that the higher the wife's income in 1968, the more likely the couple were to separate in 1972. Women's employment may not be a basic cause of divorce. It may well be that women who are unhappy with their marriage are more likely to seek employment outside the home.

Nicky Hart has suggested that the increase in female employment 'undermines the traditional division of labour in the home', it threatens the traditional roles of husband and wife. This may cause domestic conflict and in particular undermine the traditional authority of the husband as head of the household.

Some researchers believe that these changes have been accompanied by a change in the way many people view marriage. Increasing importance appears to be given to love and companionship and the satisfaction of emotional needs within the marital relationship. According to Jack Dominian who has spent many years studying marriage and marital breakdown, 'Modern marriage is committed to the goals of independence, freedom and the attainment of the highest standards of personal fulfilment.' Thus if people get divorced they may not be rejecting marriage as such but just one particular marriage which has not lived up to their expectations. Some support for this view is provided by the high remarriage rate for divorcees. In the USA three-quarters of all divorced women and five-sixths of all divorced men eventually remarry.

(adapted from **When Marriage Ends** by Nicky Hart, Tavistock, London, 1976 and **Who Divorces?** by Barbara Thornes and Jean Collard, Routledge & Kegan Paul, London, 1979)

1. What changes might the evidence in the table indicate in women's experience of marriage and attitudes towards divorce? (4)

2. There has been a steady rise in both the rate of divorce and the employment of married women. However the apparent link between them may be simply due to coincidence. Explain what this means. (4)

3. a Why might female employment 'undermine the traditional

division of labour in the home'?   (2)
  b How might this cause conflict between husband and wife? (2)
4. Apart from the reasons given in question 3, suggest two reasons
   why the employment of married women might contribute to the
   rise in divorce.   (4)
5. The rising divorce rate does not reflect a rejection of the
   institution of marriage. Briefly discuss this viewpoint.   (4)

11 A critical view of the nuclear family

The nuclear family in Western society is probably more isolated
today than at any time in its history. Extended family units are
becoming a thing of the past and close knit communities are
tending to break up. This may well place the nuclear family under
considerable pressure. This viewpoint is examined in the following
article by the anthropologist Edmund Leach. He regards the
isolated nuclear family as a major problem in Western society and
suggests that a new form of family structure is long overdue.

> Psychologists, doctors, school-masters and clergymen put
> over so much soppy propaganda about the virtue of a united
> family life that most of you probably have the idea that 'the
> family', in our English sense, is a universal institution, the
> very foundation of organised society. This isn't so. Human
> beings, at one time or another, have managed to invent all
> sorts of different styles of domestic living and we shall have
> to invent still more in the future. Individual families are
> linked up with the outside world in many different ways. The
> external relations of a family can be based on any sort of
> shared interest – politics, sport, leisure time activities of all
> kinds – but as a rule much the strongest bonds are those of
> kinship, neighbourhood and common occupation. It is there-
> fore of the utmost significance that today, in most parts of
> the country, the householders in any one street will not all be
> doing the same job and will not all be related as kin.
>   This discrepancy (difference, inconsistency) reflects a very
> great change in our society which has come about mainly as a
> result of economic developments over the past 50 years. Up

until the First World War a major part of the working population, both in the towns and in the countryside, was residentially immobile. The variety of possible occupations open to working-class people was small, and although there was a steady drift from the villages to the towns, most people had nothing much to gain by moving around from one town to another. In Lancashire, for example, practically everyone worked in the cotton mills, and there was no point in moving from Rochdale to Oldham or from Oldham to Bury. But today the go-ahead young man moves to the place where he thinks he can earn most, quickest, or he may even get shunted around from place to place by his employers. This change has had radical consequences for the basic structure of society. In the old days, bonds of neighbourhood, kinship and occupation tended to coincide; most people spent their whole lives close to the place where they were born, so they were always surrounded by kinsfolk. Moreover, the girl whom a man married was often a near neighbour, and the two families were quite likely to be related already even before the marriage. It is still possible to find places where this state of affairs persists – South Wales mining communities, for example – but the general pattern is fast disappearing.

The effect of this change is as much psychological as social. In the past, kinsfolk and neighbours gave the individual continuous moral support throughout his life. Today the domestic household is isolated. The family looks inward upon itself; there is an intensification of emotional stress between husband and wife, and parents and children. The strain is greater than most of us can bear. Far from being the basis of the good society, the family, with its narrow privacy and tawdry (grubby) secrets, is the source of all our discontents.

We need a change of values here, but it is not at all obvious just what the change should be. History and ethnography (the study of social groups) provide very few examples of societies constructed around a loose assemblage of isolated groups of parents and children. The domestic units are usually much larger and usually based on kinship. But kin groups can only function effectively if most of the members are clustered together in one place, and this requirement conflicts with one of the prime dogmas of capitalist free enterprise: the freedom to move around and sell your labour in the best market.

Our present society is emotionally very uncomfortable. The parents and children huddled together in their loneliness take too much out of each other. The parents fight; the children rebel. Children need to grow up in larger, more relaxed domestic groups centred on the community rather than on mother's kitchen – something like an Israeli kibbutz perhaps or a Chinese commune. Fitting such units into our style of industrial economy could never be easy.

(from 'The inward-looking family' by Edmund Leach, **The Listener**, 30 November, 1971)

1. Give two ways in which families are connected to the outside world. (2)
2. What changes have occurred which have resulted in the family becoming increasingly isolated? (4)
3. What are the consequences of isolation for the nuclear family? (5)
4. a Why does Leach suggest that an extended family unit or some form of commune might solve some of the problems produced by the nuclear family? (5)
   b Why does he go on to say that 'Fitting such units into our style of industrial economy could never be easy'? (4)

12 Alternatives to the family

A number of alternatives to the family have been tried with varying degrees of success. Probably the most famous example is the Israeli kibbutz which is examined in the following passage. A variation on the kibbutz is provided by the 'commune movement' which developed in the West during the 1960s. Communes are self-contained communities which attempt to be self-sufficient – provide for their own needs. They are often formed by people with strongly held political or religious beliefs who wish to create an alternative society and feel they can only do so in the enclosed world of the commune. These beliefs sometimes include the view that the conventional nuclear family is harmful both to adults and children. In some communes marriage is the norm but the rearing of children is seen as the responsibility of the community as a whole. In others there are no marriage ties and all adults are regarded as parents.

Many communes are short-lived. It is difficult to create an alternative society, to avoid the influence of the wider society and to become self-sufficient. In the early 1970s it was estimated that there were one hundred communes in Britain; ten years later the figure was put at fifty.

The following passage looks at the Israeli kibbutz – one of the more successful alternatives to the family.

In Israel about 4% of the population live in about 250 kibbutzim. These settlements vary in size from 100–2000 members. Most are based on agriculture with some light industry. Property such as buildings, machinery and agricultural produce is communally owned by all members of the kibbutz. Commodities such as clothing and shoes and services such as cooking and laundry are provided by the kibbutz.

Many kibbutzim have a system of collective childrearing. Married couples share a single bedroom/living room. Children spend most of the day and all of the night away from their parents in children's houses. Their socialization and education is left to specially trained metapelets (child caretakers and educators) – 'In all the countless ways that a parent educates his children – from how they should spend their time, arrange their day, to how they should eat, sit at the table, talk, play alone or with others, and including such extremely intimate matters as their toilet training – the kibbutz, through its metapelets and the peer group, will educate the child.'

Mothers visit their infants in the communal nursery four or five times a day. These visits continue for six months until breastfeeding stops. Then parents spend about two hours a day, after work, with their children. This is seen as 'fun time' rather than socialization or child training. It is the only time when parents and brothers and sisters come together as a group. As they grow up children move through a series of children's houses, the same age-group staying together until adulthood. The peer group is an important source of security and companionship. Children of the same age-group tend to see each other as brothers and sisters.

Many parents see collective childrearing as protecting their children from 'bad mothering', from family members demanding too much love and attention from each other. However, there remains a strong bond between parents and children. In particular they provide for many of the child's emotional needs. But the kibbutz provides for his or her physical needs – clothing from the communal supply, food from the central kitchen and toys which are shared by all the children. In this respect the community rather than parents provide for children who are 'viewed and cared for as children of the kibbutz'.

In one sense collective childrearing is a rejection of the family and of parental roles. It replaces many of the traditional functions of the family. No longer is the family the unit through which the child passes to become a member of society.

In the early days of the kibbutzim (the 1920s–1940s) all able-bodied adults were needed to work the land and establish the settlements. In recent years these demands have been reduced, standards of living have risen and married couples' quarters have increased in size and often include a kitchenette. In some kibbutzim children now live with their parents, in others parents spend more time with their children. Reasons for these changes include increased exposure to the norms and values of the wider society – many of the early kibbutzim were isolated and had little access to the mass media – and the fact that nowadays parents literally have more time to spend with their children.

(adapted in part from **The Children of the Dream** by Bruno Bettelheim, Thames and Hudson, London, 1969)

1. Why are many communes short-lived? (3)
2. Probably the most important function of the family has been taken over by the metapelets.
   a What is this function? (2)
   b Briefly outline the duties of metapelets. (2)
3. The peer group is more important for children in the kibbutz than it is for children in the West. Why? (4)
4. Even in the early days of the kibbutz, parents were still important to their children. Why? (3)
5. Why do many parents see collective childrearing as protecting their children from 'bad mothering'? (3)
6. Why are many parents demanding to spend more time with their children? (3)

Section 10 Education

Education is one of the major growth industries of the past hundred years. State education began in Britain in 1870 with the Forster Education Act by which the state assumed responsibility for elementary education. In 1880 school attendance up to the age of 10 was made compulsory. In 1918 the state took over responsibility for secondary education which was steadily expanded with the raising of the school leaving age. These developments were accompanied by a rapid growth of higher education with new universities and the polytechnics. From relatively humble beginnings in 1870, the educational system now has its own Minister of State, a clientele of millions and a budget of massive proportions.

This section begins with an examination of the role of education in society. It then considers factors which affect the progress and attainment levels of students with particular emphasis on social class, ethnicity and gender. Social relationships in the classroom are then examined and the section closes with a review of changes in secondary education in Britain since the mid 1940s.

1 Education and society (1)

From one sociological perspective, society has certain requirements or needs which must be met if it is to survive. From this viewpoint the role of education in society can be examined in terms of how it helps to meet these needs. Firstly, society needs a certain degree of social solidarity or social unity. People must feel a sense of belonging to society, a sense of loyalty to the social group. Common norms and values help to provide this. Secondly, every society requires a system for socializing new members. In an industrial society in which occupational status is largely achieved, young people must learn to value individual achievement. Thirdly, every society requires a system for placing people in roles best suited to their talents and abilities. This is particularly true in an industrial society with a highly specialized division of labour. The right people must be matched with the right jobs. Finally, for society to operate effectively its members must possess the necessary skills to perform essential tasks. In an industrial society these skills are highly specialized.

The populations of many societies come from a variety of national and cultural backgrounds. European nations are unusual in this respect since for generations most of their people have been born and bred in a single country. The United States provides an example of a nation with a population drawn from practically every major country in the world. In such societies education has a particularly important role to play. In the United States schools have provided a shared language and a common history for an immigrant population. Students learn about George Washington and Abraham Lincoln, about the War of Independence and the Civil War between North and South. For the immigrant, the history of his new society becomes, in part, his history. He begins each school day with an oath of allegiance to the Stars and Stripes – the national flag and symbol of American society.

Schools in all Western societies emphasize individual achievement. The student achieves his status on the basis of ability, talent, determination and effort. His achievement is measured by his performance in examinations.

Education can be seen as a system for sifting, sorting and grading people in terms of their ability. Students leave school having been thoroughly tested. In theory the most talented will achieve the highest qualifications, the least talented will unfortunately come away with little or nothing to show for their efforts.

State education developed in industrial societies. In Britain at the close of the last century industrial processes were becoming more complex and the demand for technical skills was growing. Industry required a literate and numerate workforce, workers who could read and write and had a basic grounding in mathematics. In 1880 elementary education to the age of 10 was made compulsory. Since then the school leaving age has been steadily increased to the age of 16 in 1973. Throughout this century there has been a growing

Sorting, grading and allocating to roles

demand for clerical, technical, professional and managerial skills. The educational system has steadily expanded offering a widening range of academic and vocational courses at all levels.

(adapted from **Sociology: Themes and Perspectives** by Michael Haralambos with Robin Heald, University Tutorial Press, Slough, 1980)

1. With reference to the United States, suggest how education contributes to social solidarity. (5)
2. Education is an agency of secondary socialization.
   a What does this mean? (2)
   b Which major value is transmitted by schools? (2)
   c How are students encouraged to adopt this value? (3)
3. How does education help to place people in roles best suited to their talents and abilities? (4)
4. What is the relationship between education and the economic system in industrial society? (4)

2 Education and society (2)

A very different view of the role of education in society is provided by a Marxist perspective. From this viewpoint workers in Western industrial societies are exploited and oppressed. Firstly, they produce the wealth but part of this wealth is taken away in the form of profits by the owners of private industry. Secondly, as a subject class, the workers are subordinate to the power of the ruling class, those who own private industry. Thirdly, workers get no real satisfaction or fulfilment from their work since rather than working for themselves and their fellow men, they are mainly working for the benefit of the owners of industry. They must therefore be motivated not by work itself and the satisfaction it should bring but with external rewards connected with work such as pay and job status. Fourthly, in terms of social inequality, there is a large gap between top and bottom – wealth and power are concentrated in the hands of the ruling class. If Western industrial societies are to survive workers must accept this situation and learn to live with it.

The following passage presents a brief summary of the work of Samuel Bowles and Herbert Gintis entitled **Schooling in Capitalist America**. Bowles and Gintis claim that the educational system helps to maintain the structure of Western industrial societies. In particular it helps to produce workers with the kinds of personalities, attitudes and outlooks that will fit them for their exploited status.

In a study based on 237 students in their final year in a New York high school (secondary school) Bowles and Gintis examined the relationship between the students' personality characteristics and the grades (marks) they received. They found that students who were creative, independent and aggressive tended to get low grades. These students were inventive, they thought for themselves and liked to do things their own way. They sometimes step on other people's toes and don't like being told what to do. Such characteristics appear to be penalized and discouraged by the school with low grades. Students who received high grades tended to be punctual, dependable and hardworking. They accepted the authority and direction of the teacher and generally did what they were told. They were unlikely to question what the teacher said. Schools appear to encourage and reward these characteristics with high grades.

Schools are organized on the principle of a hierarchy. The teachers are in charge – they give orders and the students obey. Teaching is based on the 'mug and jug' principle. The teacher fills the empty 'mugs' with knowledge. Students have little say in the matter, they have few opportunities to organize their own work in their own way. As a result they get little real satisfaction from schoolwork. They are motivated not by the work itself but from external rewards connected to work such as examination success and the approval of teachers.

Education is a system of social inequality. Students are graded in the school and in external examinations. Some pass, others fail. The education system promotes the view that the inequality it produces is just and reasonable. In theory it provides fair and open competition for all students. Those who obtain high qualifications deserve them, they have earned them by ability and hard work. The belief is created

Preparation for work: A Marxist view

that the educational system is a meritocracy, that success and failure are based on merit.

(adapted from **Schooling in Capitalist America** by Samuel Bowles and Herbert Gintis, Routledge & Kegan Paul, London, 1976)

1. a Outline the relationship between grades and personality characteristics. (2)

b How does this help to produce the kind of worker required in Western industrial society? (3)
2. a Why do students get little real satisfaction from their work at school? (2)
b How are they motivated to work hard? (2)
c How does this help to produce the kind of workforce required for private industry? (3)
3. a What is a meritocracy? (2)
b How can it be argued that the education system operates on meritocratic principles? (2)
c How does this lead to the acceptance of social inequality? (2)
d Why is this acceptance necessary for the survival of Western industrial societies? (2)

3 Social class and educational attainment

Many people believe in the ideal of equal educational opportunity. This means that everybody should have an equal chance and their educational qualifications should be based on merit, on their ability and effort. Thus if a person is bright and works hard he should do well no matter what his social background. Equality of opportunity for all might be the ideal on which the British educational system is based but it is certainly not the reality. A large body of research has shown that in general, the higher a person's class of origin (the class into which he was born), the greater his chances of achieving high educational qualifications. Social class appears, therefore, to prevent equality of opportunity in education.

The following extract examines the relationship between social class, home background and educational attainment.

Social class, IQ and educational attainment

IQ at age 11	Father's occupation	% obtaining higher education of the following kinds			
		Full-time degree e.g. university	Other full-time e.g. vocational courses	Part-time e.g. day release	Total
130+	Non-manual	37	4	10	51
130+	Manual	18	12	10	40
115–129	Non-manual	17	17	4	38
115–129	Manual	8	7	9	24

(Average IQ is 100)
(from **The Sociology of Education** by Olive Banks, Batsford, London, 1971, p. 55)

Primary socialization, the first and probably the most important part of the socialization process, lays down patterns of behaviour which may last throughout a person's life. Studies by sociologists and psychologists suggest that there are social class differences in childrearing practices which may have important effects on children's educational progress. Compared to the working class, middle class parents place a greater emphasis on high achievement. They expect and demand more from their children and encourage them to continually improve their performance in areas ranging from childhood games to table manners. They give their children greater individual attention and set higher standards for them to attain.

When the child starts school the influence of social class background continues. In general middle class parents place a higher value on education and take a greater interest in their children's progress than working class parents. This is indicated by a large scale study by J. W. B. Douglas which traced the educational careers of 5000 British children from birth to aged 16. Middle class parents were more likely to visit the school to discuss their children's progress. They were also more likely to want their children to stay on at school beyond the minimum leaving age and to encourage them to do so. Douglas believes that the child's pre-school years are important seeing them as a major influence on the early years of schooling. A child's performance at the start of his educational career is often reflected throughout the secondary school. However Douglas argues that the most important factor accounting for educational attainment appeared to be the degree of parents' interest in their children's education. In terms of this, middle class children have a decided advantage over working class children.

(adapted from **The Home and the School** by J. W. B. Douglas, MacGibbon & Kee, London, 1964 and **The Sociology of Education** by Olive Banks, Batsford, London, 1971)

1. What percentage of people from a) non-manual and b) manual backgrounds in the 130 + group are studying full-time for a degree? (2)
2. What evidence does the table provide to support the claim that there is a considerable 'wastage' of working class talent? (4)
3. Why does the table compare manual and non-manual groups with the same IQ in order to examine the influence of social class on educational attainment? (4)
4. How might the primary socialization of middle class children give them an advantage over working class children in the educational system? (4)
5. What evidence does Douglas provide which suggests that the pre-school years directly affect educational attainment? (2)
6. What evidence does Douglas give to support his claim that middle class parents are more interested in their children's education than working class parents? (4)

4 Poverty and educational attainment

In the late 1960s a team led by Ken Coates and Richard Silburn conducted a study of St Ann's, an inner city slum in Nottingham. Their research shows how the disadvantages of poverty are passed on from one generation to the next. This 'cycle of deprivation' tends to transmit the life chances of parents to their children. The following passage illustrates this process in terms of education.

> St Ann's is a depressing area. Many of the houses are damp, draughty and poorly heated. They are often run down and dilapidated and a quarter have one or more rooms which the occupants consider unusable. The people have a sense of hopelessness and powerlessness and many are resigned to their situation believing that there is little they can do to change it. Few show any signs of optimism or self-confidence.
> The children of St Ann's are on average smaller and less hardy than middle class children from the more prosperous suburbs of Nottingham. They have little stamina and are usually on the losing side when their school teams play other schools. Their diet is poor, they have a low resistance to illness

and they are often absent from school. Every epidemic which hits the city flourishes in St Ann's. Some of the children arrive at school without breakfast either because their parents have overslept or have gone out to work before them. Many of the children have emotional problems. Up to two fifths came from broken homes and 16% were defined as educationally subnormal.

When starting school many of the children from St Ann's had little idea about how to play with paints, water, sand or clay. Their vocabulary was small and they had little experience of pencils, pictures or books. As a result they lacked much of the grounding required for learning how to read. They showed little ability to discriminate between shapes and therefore had difficulty solving problems involving different shapes. At home they lacked the jigsaw puzzles and educational toys found in most middle class homes.

The children from St Ann's arrived as 'retarded' pupils in the infant school and all too often continued as such into the junior school. A quarter could not read by the time they were seven and less than a tenth were average readers for their age group. Entry to grammar school in the area was based largely on a verbal reasoning test taken at the age of 11. Reading skills had an important influence on test scores. Not surprisingly only 1.5% of St Ann's school population obtained a grammar school place. This compares with 60% for one middle class suburb in Nottingham.

Coates and Silburn argue it would be wrong to blame the teachers for these results. They give the following quotation from a St Ann's headmistress to illustrate the problems of teaching in the area: 'We begin by setting up what we think is a satisfactory environment: we try to give these children emotional security and establish a contact between teacher and child. Any teacher who can write in her daily report "Today William smiled at me" has probably achieved as much as a teacher somewhere else who could write "Today Johnny did five pages of sums." '

(adapted from **Poverty: The Forgotten Englishmen** by Ken Coates and Richard Silburn, Penguin, Harmondsworth, 1970)

1. a Why are the children of St Ann's more frequently ill than children from middle class suburbs? (2)
   b What effects might frequent illness have on their progress in school? (2)
2. What effects might the feelings of St Ann's residents, as described in the first paragraph, have on their children's performance in school? (3)
3. What evidence does the passage contain which may help to explain why most of the children are poor readers? (3)
4. The effects of poverty continue throughout a child's educational career. What evidence does the passage contain to support this statement? (2)
5. Compared with children raised in poverty, middle class children have a 'head start' when they begin school. Briefly discuss this statement with some reference to the passage. (3)
6. Why does the headmistress believe that a teacher has really achieved something if she can write in her report, 'Today William smiled at me'? (2)
7. Briefly suggest how the idea of a 'cycle of deprivation' can help to explain the low attainment levels of St Ann's children. (3)

5 Speech patterns

Picture the neighbourhoods in which the following statements might be made: 'Me ma learnt me to read'; 'My mother taught me how to read.' A picture of an inner city slum is suggested by the first, a middle class suburb by the second. It is generally recognized that there are social class differences in speech patterns. Some sociologists and psychologists claim that these differences have an important effect on children's educational attainment. They see them as one of the reasons why middle class children are more successful in school than working class children. The following passage examines Basil Bernstein's early work on speech patterns and the work of one of his main critics, William Labov.

Two five year olds, one from a working class background, the other from a middle class background, are given four pictures on which to base a story. In the first picture several boys are playing football. In the second one of the boys kicks the ball

230 Sociology: A New Approach

and it breaks a window in a nearby house. The third picture shows a man and a woman looking out of the window. The man is shaking his fist at the boys. The final picture shows the boys running away in the opposite direction. The middle class child clearly and accurately describes and analyses these events. The listener has no need to see the pictures in order to fully understand what they show. However in order to make sense of the story told by the working class child the listener would need to see the pictures. The child fails to spell out the details of the story, he fails to fully explain the relationship between the boys and the people in the house. Without the pictures his story is unclear and incomplete.

Bernstein uses this example to illustrate some of the differences he believes exist between working and middle class speech patterns. Working class speech is a kind of shorthand speech. In Bernstein's terminology it is a **restricted code**. It uses a smaller vocabulary than middle class speech and makes less use of adjectives and adverbs. As a result it is not well suited for spelling out more subtle, less obvious shades of meaning or for elaborating and developing ideas. Bernstein refers to middle class speech patterns as an **elaborated code**. This type of code spells out many of the meanings taken for granted and left unspoken by the restricted code. It provides the details and background information, the explanations and reasons often left out by a restricted code.

Bernstein claims that speech patterns can affect a child's ability to reason, analyse and think logically. The following example suggests why this might be so. A young child is playing noisily in the kitchen with pots and pans when the telephone rings. A working class mother tells him to 'shut up' or 'be quiet' whereas the middle class mother says 'Would you keep quiet for a minute; I want to talk on the telephone.' The first message is simple requiring little thought. The child is simply told to keep quiet. The second message is more complex. The child is given a reason for the request, asked to consider the wishes of another person and asked to organize his behaviour according to a time dimension – 'a minute'. Such speech patterns repeated daily over a period of years provide greater mental stimulation for the middle class child and result in more complex patterns of speech.

Bernstein claims that class differences in speech patterns

partly explain class differences in educational attainment. Firstly, lessons in school are conducted in an elaborated code. This places the working class child at a disadvantage. Secondly, the restricted code reduces the chances of working class pupils of acquiring some of the skills demanded by the educational system, skills such as describing, analysing and comparing.

A very different view of class differences in speech patterns is provided by the American linguist William Labov. From his research on working class black children in New York, Labov claims that their speech patterns are just as elaborated as those of the middle class. They are just as efficient for describing and analyzing and just as stimulating for the development of reason and logical thought. Why then do they do badly at school? Firstly, they speak a different dialect from the teacher. Secondly, the teacher often criticizes their way of speaking – it is not 'correct' English. Partly as a result of this many young children see the classroom as hostile and threatening. They therefore say little so that as little as possible can be held against them. As a result they appear to have a restricted code.

(adapted from 'Language and social context' by Basil Bernstein in **Language and Social Context**, edited by P. P. Giglioli, Penguin, Harmondsworth, 1972, **The Myth of the Deprived Child** by Herbert Ginsburg, Prentice-Hall, Englewood Cliffs, 1972 and 'The logic of nonstandard English' by William Labov in **Tinker, Tailor . . . The Myth of Cultural Deprivation** edited by N. Keddi' Penguin, Harmondsworth, 1973)

1. Briefly outline the differences between a restricted and ar elaborated code. (3

2. Teachers use an elaborated code. Why might this place the working class child at a disadvantage? (3)

3. How might the restricted code reduce the chances of working class pupils of learning the skills and performing the tasks required in school? Give details of some of these skills and tasks in your answer. (6)

4. If Bernstein is correct the working class child enters school with a handicap that is difficult to remove. Explain this statement with reference to the idea of primary socialization. (3)

5. Why do the boys in Labov's research **appear** to have a restricted code? (2)

6. What effect might constant criticism of speech patterns have on a child's progress in school? (3)

6 Compensatory education

The arguments presented in the three previous passages suggest that working class children, particularly those raised in poverty, are lacking the skills, knowledge and experience necessary to be successful in the educational system. Some researchers who accept this view argue that they must be given a helping hand if they are to compete on equal terms with other children. In particular, what they lack must be compensated for. Many believed the answer lay with 'compensatory education'. Only then would children from low income backgrounds have a real chance of making progress at school. The following passage examines compensatory education in the United States where it formed a major part of educational policy during the 1960s and early 70s.

In the early 1960s in the USA blame was directed at the schools for the widespread failure of children from low income backgrounds. Factors such as school buildings and facilities, teachers' qualifications, pupil-teacher ratios and average expenditure per pupil were held to be responsible. Bring these up to the same high standard for all schools, it was claimed, and social class differences in educational attainment would be reduced or even disappear. In 1966 the publication of the Coleman Report showed that there was no evidence to support these views. The qualifications of teachers, the size of classes, the amount of resources going into the school seemed to make little or no difference to the performance of the pupils.

Attention then shifted from the schools to the pupils. It was they who now required attention. The answer was compensatory education. It was based on the idea of positive discrimination, on discrimination in favour of children from deprived backgrounds. Billions of dollars were poured into a massive programme of pre-school education. The aim of programmes like Operation Headstart was 'planned enrichment', the provision of a rich and stimulating educational environment which would lay the foundation for effective learning in the school system. This would compensate for what was lacking in the backgrounds of low-income children. Since it caught them in their early years, its effects should be lasting.

The results of programmes like Operation Headstart were disappointing. They appeared to produce few long-term beneficial results. One explanation for this failure was that the programmes tried to do too much and could not hope to compensate for all the deprivations of poverty. What they should do is concentrate on those areas which are crucial to progress in the schools. This view was taken by Bereiter and Englemann who state, 'What is lacking is the use of language to explain, to describe, to instruct, to inquire, to hypothesize, to analyse, to compare, to deduce and to test. And these are the uses that are necessary for academic success.' Bereiter and Englemann devised a series of pre-school programmes to teach language skills to three and four year olds. Again the results were disappointing. Many of the children did better during their first few months at school than those not in the programme. However for most this progress was shortlived and they soon dropped back to the level of those who had not had training in language skills.

Various explanations have been given for the failure of compensatory education. The schools have been blamed for not building on the foundations laid by the programmes. The programmes themselves have been blamed for being inadequate. The idea that a few hours a week of pre-school education can in any way compensate for the deprivations of poverty has been dismissed as ridiculous. Many sociologists now believe that as long as social class exists there can never be equality of opportunity in the educational system.

(adapted from **The Myth of the Deprived Child** by Herbert Ginsburg, Prentice Hall, Englewood Cliffs, 1972 and **Educational Differences** by Arthur R. Jensen, Methuen, London, 1973)

1. Why did the Coleman Report lift blame from schools for the failure of children from low income backgrounds? (4)
2. What is 'positive discrimination'? (3)
3. Why did programmes of compensatory education concentrate

on the pre-school years? (4)

4. Why did Bereiter and Englemann see language as a crucial area?
(3)

5. Suggest one reason why children who had experienced compensatory education often made progress during their first few months at school but then dropped back. (3)

6. In the light of the failure of past programmes of compensatory education suggest how equality of opportunity in education might be provided. (3)

7 Streaming

The previous extracts have examined the effects of factors operating outside the school on educational attainment. The following passages look at what goes on inside schools. A number of studies has shown that the internal organization of schools and, in particular, the way pupils are streamed into ability groups, can have a direct influence on educational attainment. This view will now be examined using information from David Hargreaves's study **Social Relations in a Secondary School.**

Lumley Secondary Modern School for Boys is situated in an industrial town in the North of England. Hargreaves's study focusses on the fourth year boys who were divided into four streams, 4A, 4B, 4C and 4D. The boys were placed in streams on the basis of their performance in school examinations and the teachers' assessment of their ability.

In the eyes of both teachers and boys there is a marked difference of behaviour, attitudes and dress between the higher and lower streams. This was confirmed by Hargreaves's observations. 'A' stream boys conform to the standards of dress approved by the teachers. They wear ties, grey trousers and a sports jacket or sweater and have relatively short hair. Long hair and jeans are typical of lower stream boys (the study was conducted in the mid-1960s). Higher stream boys tend to share the values held by the teachers. They approve of pupils who work hard, who do not copy, who pay attention in class, obey teachers and have good manners. Boys who fit this description would be out of place in the lower streams. 'Messing' is the norm there. As one 4C boy observed, 'In this class they're always acting daft just so they can keep up with their mates.' As a general rule, the higher a boy's stream, the less likely he is to be absent from school and the more likely he is to take part in school activities such as playing for a school team.

Boys in the lower streams are given little prestige by those in authority in the school. Many teachers refer to them as 'worthless louts' and 'a waste of time'. The boys' prestige is reduced even further because they attend a second class school, a secondary modern. In Hargreaves's words, 'In the low streams, the boys are deprived of status in that they are **double failures** by their lack of ability or motivation to obtain entry to a Grammar School or to a high stream in the Modern School.'

One solution to being defined as a failure is to reject the system and the people who define you and the values they represent. This solution was adopted by many boys in the lower streams. They reject the values of the school – hard work, high educational attainment, good manners and good behaviour. They reject the people who stand for these values. From the results of a questionnaire, Hargreaves found that only 5% of the boys in 4D have anything favourable to say about their teachers.

Lower stream boys not only reject the values of the school but go one step further and develop values in direct opposition to them. They take the school's values and turn them upside down. Being bad becomes being good. Disrupting lessons, giving cheek to teachers, refusing to do homework, fighting and smoking on school premises is applauded by many boys in the lower streams. By the fourth year two sub-cultures have developed in Lumley Secondary Modern School. One is the subculture of 4A and 4B, the other the subculture of 4C and 4D.

Most boys choose their friends from members of their own stream. Boys in the lower streams tend to form their own groups in whch they can gain status and respect from their friends. In this way the 'anti-school peer group' is formed. Boys are given prestige for being successful in terms of the values of the lower stream subculture. With an audience of their peers they are applauded for what the school terms 'bad behaviour'. As one 4C boy said about a friend, 'I like him 'cos he's always messing about. We get a lot of laughs out of him.' A lower stream boy defined as unsuccessful by the school can be highly regarded in terms of the values of the anti-school peer group. Clint in 4C who was 'cock of the school' is a case in point. His fighting ability brought high status in the eyes of his peer group.

In this way, the boys help to solve their problems of 'status deprivation' (lack of prestige) and 'status frustration' (a sense of frustration and dissatisfaction with their status in the school). They may still be failures in the eyes of the school but by acting in terms of the values of the anti-school peer group they at least have a chance of being successful in somebody's eyes.

(adapted from **Social Relations in a Secondary School** by David H. Hargreaves, Routledge & Kegan Paul, London, 1967)

1. Why are boys in the lower streams 'double failures'? (4)
2. a How did the teachers define the boys in the lower streams? (2)
   b What effect might this definition have on the boys' educational progress? (4)
3. What effect might the lower stream subculture have on the boys' educational progress? (4)
4. a What is an 'anti-school peer group'? (2)
   b How does the anti-school peer group help to solve the lower stream boys' problems of status deprivation and status frustration? (4)

8 The self-fulfilling prophecy

People have a picture of themselves, a self-image or a self-concept. This picture comes in part from the reactions of others towards them. Thus if others respond to a person as if he were bright or dull, he would tend to see himself as such. People can be labelled by others as a certain type of person, as a clown, an idiot, a high achiever and so on. If the label sticks, if everybody sees the person concerned in terms of the label, a self-fulfilling prophecy will tend to develop. The person will be likely to see himself in terms of the label and to act accordingly. Thus if he is defined as a clown, he will tend to behave as a clown. In this way the prophecy is fulfilled – the prediction made about the person comes to pass.

These ideas were applied to education by Robert Rosenthal and Leonora Jacobson. They claim that the way teachers define pupils can have an important effect on the pupils' educational attainment. They outline their research in a Californian school in the following extract. The first paragraph is an introduction to their work for an English readership by E. Stones.

> One of the commonest practices in English education is the categorization of children. In a very large number of schools we have A, B, C and D children. We have children who have been ascertained educationally sub-normal and we have 'high flyers'. In recent years another group has been identified: the 'Disadvantaged'. In England most of these children are from the schools of decaying inner ring urban areas, often including disproportionate numbers of children from non-English backgrounds. It is important to discover whether these labels set up attitudes in teachers which help to produce the results expected. This effect is called a self-fulfilling prophecy. Thus if a teacher thinks a child is an 'A' child he is likely to produce 'A' results for that teacher even if he is really a 'C' child in disguise. We have an old saying 'Give a dog a bad name' which is closely related to this problem.
>
> (from **Readings in Educational Psychology** edited by E. Stones, Methuen, London, 1970, pp. 414–15)

Our research tries to test the operation of the self-fulfilling prophecy. It was conducted in Oak School, a public elementary (primary) school in a lower class community of a medium sized city. About one sixth of the school population is Mexican. Oak School is a streamed school with fast, medium and slow streams. The Mexican children are heavily over-represented in the slow stream.

It was decided to test the proposition that a favourable expectation by teachers could lead to an increase in intellectual competence (i.e. brighter children). In order to do this the first step was to test all the children of Oak School with a standard intelligence test. The teachers were led to believe that from the results of this test one could predict intellectual blooming or spurting.

At the beginning of the year following this school-wide IQ testing, each of the 18 teachers of grades (classes) one to six were given the names of those children in her classroom who, in the academic year ahead, would show dramatic intellectual growth. These predictions were supposedly made on the basis of those 'special' children's score on the IQ test. For each classroom the names of the special children had in fact been chosen at random and bore no relationship to their score on the IQ test. **The difference between the special children and the ordinary children, then, was only in the mind of the teacher.**

All the children of Oak School were retested with the same IQ test after one term, after a full academic year and after two full academic years. After the first year of the experiment, a significant expectancy advantage was found and it was especially great for younger children and Mexican children. The advantage of being expected to bloom was evident in the children's IQ scores. After the second year when these children had a different teacher the younger ones lost the advantage of the expectancy effect but the older children maintained it.

We can only speculate as to how teachers brought about an improvement in intellectual competence simply by expecting it. Perhaps by what she said and how and when she said it, by her facial expressions, postures and perhaps by her touch, the teacher may have communicated to the children of the experimental group that she expected improvement in intellectual performance. Such communications together with possible changes in teaching techniques may have helped the child learn by changing his self-concept, his expectations of his own behaviour and his motivation, as well as his cognitive (thinking) style and skills.

(from **Pygmalion in the Classroom** by R. Rosenthal and L. Jacobson, Holt, Rinehart & Winston, New York, 1968, pp. 174–81)

1. a How might a teacher's expectations of an 'A' stream student differ from those for a 'D' stream student? (2)

b What effect might these expectations have on the progress of the students?   (3)
2. How are the expectations of teachers communicated to students?   (3)
3. Students from low-income and ethnic backgrounds are often defined as 'disadvantaged' or 'underprivileged'.
   a What effect might these labels have on teachers' expectations of students?   (2)
   b How might these labels help to explain the large numbers of Mexican children in the lower streams?   (2)
   c Why did the Mexican children defined as high ability make **particularly** good progress?   (2)
4. If Rosenthal and Jacobson are correct, how might destreaming (mixed ability teaching) help the lower stream student?   (3)
5. How might Rosenthal and Jacobson's findings help to explain the failure of programmes of compensatory education?   (3)

9 Ethnicity and educational attainment (1)

In the 1980s the focus of attention moved from social class differences in educational attainment to those of ethnicity and gender. In terms of ethnicity one of the main questions guiding research is whether membership of an ethnic minority group affects a person's educational attainment. The following passage looks at this question.

School leavers: achievements, destinations and further education

	Asians	Afro-Caribbeans	all other leavers	all maintained school leavers in England
CSE and O level achievements	%	%	%	%
no graded results (include those attempting)	19	17	22	14
at least 1 graded result but less than 5 higher grades	63	81	62	66
5 or more higher grades	18	3	16	21

Destination of school leavers	Asians	Afro-Caribbeans	all other leavers	all leavers in England
university	3	1	3	5
other further education	18	16	9	14
employment	54	65	77	74
unknown	25	18	11	8
Full-time further education courses				
degree	5	1	4	6
A level	6	2	1	2
any other course	11	15	7	11
no course (including unknown destination)	78	83	88	81
total (number)	527	799	4,852	693,840

(from **Rampton Report**, 1981)

The above table is based on information from six local education authorities. It includes about half the school leavers from ethnic minority groups in England in 1978/9.

The results show that the educational attainment of Asian students is broadly similar to that of whites but the attainment level of Afro-Caribbeans is lower. Part of this 'under-achievement' – probably about half – can be explained in terms of social class. Afro-Caribbean pupils are more likely to come from working class backgrounds than Asians or other school leavers. However this still leaves an important part of the difference unexplained.

There are two main explanations of the relatively low attainment of Afro-Caribbeans. The first explains it in terms of Afro-Caribbean subculture, the second in terms of racism and in particular the way many Afro-Caribbeans react to racism. In 1985, the report of the Swann Committee, a government appointed body to study ethnic minority education, was published. It stated that 'the reasons for the very different school performance between Asians and West Indians seem likely to lie deep within their respective cultures'. Thus it has been suggested that Asian family structure and community organisation are stronger, more tightly knit and cohesive, than those of Afro-Caribbeans. As a result, the argument goes, Asian children have a stronger sense of identity, higher levels of self-esteem and self-confidence and a firmer foundation on which to base their educational careers. By comparison many Afro-Caribbean children have low self-esteem, and lack confidence. The result is low motivation and low educational attainment.

Critics have fiercely attacked this type of argument. Although some studies show that Afro-Caribbeans are more likely to have negative self-concepts and low self-esteem than Asians or whites, other studies, particularly the more recent, find no significant differences between these groups. In fact recent evidence suggests that ethnic minorities are increasingly developing a pride in their own ethnic identity. So far there are no firm conclusions about the effect of ethnic subcultures on educational attainment. The Swann Committee states that 'the research evidence is lacking and where it exists it is sketchy or conflicting or both'.

The second explanation of Afro-Caribbean educational attainment is based on racism. Firstly, it is suggested that Afro-Caribbeans experience more racial discrimination than Asians and, secondly, they react to it differently. According to the Swann Committee, Asians are given to 'keeping their heads down and adopting a low profile' thereby making it easier for them to succeed in a hostile environment. Many Afro-Caribbeans react in just the opposite way, protesting against and opposing what they see as discrimination. This makes educational success more difficult. There is also some evidence that teachers are more likely to see Afro-Caribbean students in a negative light. A study conducted in 1972 involving 510 teachers from 25 schools found that two thirds of the teachers saw Afro-Caribbean students as less able and more likely to be disruptive. This view is hardly likely to encourage high educational attainment.

(adapted from **Race Relations in Britain** by Andrew Pilkington, University Tutorial Press, Slough, 1984 and Diane Spencer's report on the Swann Committee findings in **The Times Educational Supplement**, 15 March 1985, pp. 12–13)

1. What percentage of a) Asian and b) Afro-Caribbean students obtained '5 or more higher grades'? (2)
2. Why is it important to look at social class as well as ethnicity for explaining educational attainment? (4)
3. a What is a subcultural explanation of educational attainment? (4)

b Why has this type of explanation been criticised in the case of
   Afro-Caribbean students?   (4)
4. How might the attitudes of teachers discussed in the last paragraph affect Afro-Caribbean attainment?   (6)

10 Ethnicity and educational attainment (2)

The Swann Report said relatively little about the extent of racism
in schools. This was remedied by a second major survey published
later in 1985. It was conducted by a team led by John Eggleston. Of
particular interest is a detailed study of two comprehensive
schools in the Midlands. This study was conducted by Cecile Wright
who carried out some 900 hours of classroom observation in each
school and formal and informal interviews with teachers and
pupils. Although the schools are not said to be typical, there are
many similarities between the findings of this study and the
national survey. Some of these findings are looked at in the
following passage.

> The study set out to establish whether ethnicity was a factor
> influencing the placing of students in streams or sets in two
> comprehensive schools. Afro-Caribbean pupils entered the
> schools with reading scores equal to and in one case superior
> to those of white and Asian students. Yet they were seen as
> less well-behaved and less cooperative and this led to many
> being placed in lower ability streams. In one school (school B)
> nearly 20% of Afro-Caribbeans compared to 7.7% of Asians
> and no whites were placed in remedial groups. In the other
> school (school A) Afro-Caribbean students in the lower ability
> stream had the highest average performance of all the groups
> in the sample. Even when there was a clear case for re-
> allocation to a higher stream, teachers were extremely
> reluctant to make the change. An educational psychologist
> attached to school B tried to have a bright but discontented
> Afro-Caribbean girl transferred to the top stream – 'I went
> into this room where about six teachers who were all hostile (I
> have never picked up such hostility before) because "over

their dead bodies was this child going to be moved into an 'A' stream".'

Afro-Caribbean students encounter, or feel they encounter, racial prejudice and discrimination from teachers. By about the third year in the secondary school they respond with lack of interest in their work and with disruptive behaviour. As a result they are placed in lower streams and put on to lower level examination courses which do not match their ability. They therefore leave school with fewer qualifications and poorer job prospects. This can be seen from tables 1 and 2. Table 1 shows the third year examination marks of 12 pupils (4 Afro-Caribbean, 4 Asian and 4 white) and their allocation to examination sets. It clearly shows that ability, as indicated by internal school exams, is not the basis for placing students on 'O' level or CSE courses. As the report says, 'How is it possible to "confuse" a mark of 82 percent (pupil D, French in table 1) in allocating a child to a CSE set?' Table 2 shows the results of this policy. It shows examination entries for one year in the two schools. As the report says, Afro-Caribbean students 'entered the two schools with reading ages on a par with or higher than those attained by the other two groups; and finish up with only one child each in both schools entered for five or more O levels'.

Table 1 School B: individual pupils and allocation to exam sets

Pupil		Subject marks (out of 100)				Set placement (O = GCE O level)			
		English	maths	French	physics	English	maths	French	physics
Afro-Caribbean	A	73	44	58	–	CSE	CSE	CSE	–
	B	62	63	60	59	CSE	CSE	CSE	CSE
	C	64	45	56	72	CSE	CSE	–	CSE
	D	68	37	82	–	CSE	CSE	CSE	–
Asian	E	51	77	–	55	O	O	–	O
	F	60	56	58	–	O	O	O	–
	G	61	62	55½	–	O	O	O	–
	H	54	55	–	40	O	O	–	O
White	I	61	62	–	62	O	O	–	O
	J	52	57	55	–	O	O	O	–
	K	75	82	77½	72	O	O	O	O
	L	54	75	64	72	O	O	O	O

Table 2

	Asian	Afro-Caribbean	White
School A	(29)	(19)	(155)
	%	%	%
5 or more CSEs	69	78.9	80
1 or more O levels	58.5	26.3	41.9
5 or more O levels	20.5	5.3	24.5
School B	(92)	(36)	(95)
	%	%	%
5 or more CSEs	65.2	78	57.6
1 or more O level	46.7	22.2	34.8
5 or more O levels	16.3	2.7	18.5

(figures in brackets refer to actual numbers of students)

The report finds evidence of racism both in the attitudes and practices of the teachers and the policies of the schools. The following examples are taken from observations and interviews in school A. Some teachers regularly made racist remarks such as sending black students 'back to the chocolate factory'. Some were 'amazed' when they discovered black students were bright. Staffroom gossip sometimes labelled Afro-Caribbean students as troublemakers which meant that teachers jumped to conclusions before even meeting students. Black students objected to teachers using racist terms and jokes – 'The jokes are disrespectful' – and to what they saw as racist harassment – 'The teachers are forever picking on the black boys.' They felt this affected their school work – 'We got no time, as you sit down to work they pin something on you.'

Students reacted to this treatment by forming a 30 strong 'all black' group which was anti-school and to some extent anti-white. As one member said, 'We try to get our own back on them. We behave ignorantly towards them, and when teachers talk to us and tell us to do something we don't do it, because we just think about how they treated us.' The evidence presented in the report provides some justification for this reaction.

(adapted from Biddy Passmore's report on 'The educational and vocational experience of 15–18 year old young people of ethnic minority groups' in **The Times Educational Supplement**, 25 October 1985, p. 8)

1. Why were many Afro-Caribbean pupils placed in lower ability streams? (2)
2. a From information in Table 1 reallocate students (A–L) to CSE and 'O' level groups for English in terms of their subject marks. Place 4 students in CSE groups (those with the lowest marks) and 8 in 'O' level groups. (2)
   b In view of this, was the original placement justified? Give reasons for your answer. (3)
3. How might the idea of a self-fulfilling prophecy explain the attainment of Afro-Caribbean students in external examinations? (4)
4. Explain the reaction of black students to their experience cf school. (4)
5. Schools reflect the wider society. Discuss with reference to material in the passage. (5)

11 Gender and educational attainment

The 1980s have seen a growing number of studies concerned with the question of whether girls have an equal opportunity in the educational system. The following passage looks at statistics on the educational attainment of girls and boys. It goes on to consider why girls, despite doing better than boys at sixteen, do not maintain their lead at 'A' level and degree level.

Table 1 The academic attainment of school leavers

Percentages for England and Wales

	1965/66		1975/76		1982/83*	
	Boys	Girls	Boys	Girls	Boys	Girls
3 or more 'A' level passes	8.9	4.8	9.9	7.0	10.3	8.8
2 'A' level passes	4.0	3.8	4.1	4.5	4.0	4.6
1 'A' level pass	2.8	2.8	2.9	3.3	3.0	3.5
5 or more higher grade 'O' level GCE or CSE	7.1	9.6	5.4	7.4	9.2	11.4
1–4 higher grades GCE or CSE	15.2	16.4	24.6	28.3	25.1	29.7
1 or more grades GCE or CSE			34.2	32.5	37.0	34.2
No GCE or CSE qualifications	62.0	62.5	18.9	17.0	11.3	7.9

(from **Social Trends**, 1977, p. 74 and **DES Statistical Bulletin** 11/84)
* 1982/83 figures refer only to England.

Table 1 shows some interesting differences between the educational attainment of boys and girls. Girls have done consistently better than boys at 'O' level. At 'A' level, in terms of three or more passes, boys have maintained a lead though the gap is steadily closing.

Table 2   Higher education – full-time students

| | United Kingdom | | | | | Thousands |
| | Males | | | Females | | |
	1970/71	1975/76	1982/83	1970/71	1975/76	1982/83
Full-time students						
From the United Kingdom						
Universities – undergraduate	128.3	130.1	142.4	57.0	73.6	100.0
– post-graduate	23.9	23.2	19.3	8.0	10.2	10.9
Other higher education	102.0	109.3	133.4	113.1	120.1	115.4
Total full-time UK students	254.2	262.6	295.1	178.2	203.8	226.3

(from **Social Trends**, 1985, p. 53)

Table 2 shows the numbers of male and female students in higher education. The most dramatic change is the growing numbers of women taking full-time degree courses at university. Between 1970/71 and 1982/83 the number of women undergraduates at university increased by over 75% compared to an increase in male undergraduates during the same period of only 11%. Despite this, men still outnumber women at university and in higher education generally.

Why do girls, who do better than boys at sixteen, not maintain their lead at 'A' level? Why do fewer girls than boys continue into higher education? Some of the answers may come from a study conducted by Sue Sharpe of working class girls in secondary schools in the London Borough of Ealing. What did the girls see as important – 'love, marriage, husbands, children, jobs and careers, more or less in that order'. The girls' attitudes to work reflected the general view of women's occupational roles. Office work was the most popular choice followed by a group of occupations which included teachers, nurses, bank clerks and shop assistants. Many of the chosen jobs did not require 'A' levels. In addition, most girls saw marriage and motherhood as their main roles in life. As a result many saw little point in continuing their education beyond the age of sixteen.

Sue Sharpe's research was conducted in the early 1970s. The figures presented in the above tables suggest that attitudes are changing. It appears that increasing numbers of girls expect or at least hope that there will be more to their lives than marriage and motherhood. However the discrimination against women in the job market (see Section 12) indicates that this generation of women will have to fight extremely hard to translate their hopes for a career into reality.

(adapted in part from **Just Like A Girl** by Sue Sharpe, Penguin, Harmondsworth, 1976)

1. What percentage of a) boys and b) girls obtained 3 or more 'A' level passes in 1982/83?   (2)
2. How many female undergraduates attended university in a) 1970/71 and b) 1982/83?   (2)
3. If present trends continue girls will soon overtake boys in terms of educational attainment. Provide evidence to support this statement.   (4)
4. Primary socialization has tended to discourage girls from continuing to higher education. Discuss.   (4)
5. Sue Sharpe titled her book **Just Like A Girl**. This title is becoming increasingly inappropriate. Briefly suggest why.   (4)
6. Why will women have to fight extremely hard to translate their hopes for careers into reality?   (4)

12 Gender and schooling

In view of the way girls are treated in schools they do remarkably well in terms of educational attainment. A number of studies have shown that sexism is widespread in the classroom, that teachers, boys and even girls themselves discriminate against girls. The following extract reviews some of the findings of one such study, **Gender and Schooling** by Michelle Stanworth.

Teachers – whether men or women – like boys best. More time, attention, affection and concern is given by teachers of mixed classes to boys than to girls. Boys dominate class discussion while girls, often described by teachers and by boys as 'faceless', are allowed to sit silent at the back of the class. Teachers are less likely to know girls' names, and tend to have low expectations of their job prospects. These are the findings of a study of co-educational A-level classes in humanities subjects (at which girls excel) in a further education college.

Interviews with teachers and pupils revealed that both men and women teachers took more interest in their male pupils, asking them more questions in class and giving them more help. Asked which students they were most concerned about, women teachers named boys twice as often as girls. Men named boys 10 times as often as girls. When asked which pupils they were most 'attached' to, teachers named boys three times as often as girls.

Teachers underestimate girls' ambitions. Only one girl was mentioned as likely to get a management job and male teachers could not envisage any occupation other than marriage for two thirds of the girls. One girl, who was getting the top marks in her class in both her main A-level subjects, and who wanted a career in the diplomatic service, was described by her woman teacher as likely to become 'the personal assistant to somebody rather important'. The teachers' views were echoed by pupils. 'I can't really imagine where the girls will end up. You can't really imagine they want to **be** anything. Whereas the boys, they definitely want to get to university and get good jobs', one boy said.

Both boys and girls, asked to list their class in order of ability, tended to exaggerate the capacity of boys and to downgrade girls. 'It's hard to imagine a girl that's better than me,' one boy said. 'I can if I try but it is unusual'. Several of the girls in his class were getting better marks than he was but he could not know since marks were not made public.

The results of this bias, the author claims, is to give both boys and girls an unjustified reverence for male abilities. When asked who in the class they would least like to be, all the students, boys and girls, named girls. The girls named as unpopular by girls were those who did speak out in class, refusing to accept the silent role played by other girls. They were accused by girls of 'hogging the limelight'. The girls most disliked by boys were the ones who 'sit at the back of the class and might as well be sucking lollipops all day'.

The study leads Ms Stanworth to conclude: 'Girls may follow the same curriculum as boys – may sit side by side with boys in classes taught by the same teachers – and yet emerge from school with the implicit understanding that the world is a man's world, in which women can and should take second place.'

(from 'Study finds boys are teachers' pets' by Auriol Stevens in **The Observer**, 13 February 1983, p. 3)

1. Judging from figures in the previous passages, girls often succeed despite their teachers. Briefly discuss this statement.
(4)
2. Sexism is widespread in the classroom. Provide evidence from the passage to support this view. (4)

3. Even girls are prejudiced against girls. Explain with examples. (4)
4. Schools reinforce girls' primary socialization. Discuss.   (4)
5. Sexual inequality in the classroom reflects the position of women in the wider society. Discuss.   (4)

13 The tripartite system

This extract and the one that follows examine the structure of secondary education (the 11–16 age group) in Britain since 1944. The Education Act of 1944 aimed to provide a fair and free system of secondary education for all. It set up the tripartite (three part) system consisting of grammar schools, technical schools and secondary modern schools. The three types of school were supposed to have 'parity of esteem' – their status was intended to be the same. At the age of 11 children were selected for the type of school seen as most appropriate for their particular talents and abilities. Selection was usually on the basis of an intelligence test known as the 11 plus. In theory all students would have an equal opportunity to develop their talents. The following extracts present views on the tripartite system by two well known educationalists – John Vaizey and Rhodes Boyson.

> The biggest changes in education since the war have taken place in the secondary schools. The grammar schools were made free schools entirely for children of high ability whereas previously they combined clever scholarship winners with children of less ability from the middle classes whose parents could afford the subsidised fees.
>
> In England we have always, until very recently, had different types of schools for different types of children. There they were intended to learn different groups of subjects, because it was thought that children came in layers – clever children (17%) who were able to study classics, mathematics, foreign languages, science and other 'difficult' subjects at grammar schools, not-so-clever children who were to do technical subjects at technical schools (5%) and then the great mass who were to be hewers of wood and drawers of water, able to live life fully doubtless, but not with aid of books.

There is still a great deal of hostility to the secondary modern school. Allocation to a secondary modern school is almost universally regarded as a 'failure' in the 11 plus. Despite the fact that selection at 11 is supposed to be by objective tests of ability and attainment, the grammar school still consists to a large degree of children of the middle class to the exclusion of children from the working class. Because of this the reputation of the secondary modern schools has lagged far behind that of the grammar schools.

(from **Education for Tomorrow** by John Vaizey, Revised edition, Penguin, Harmondsworth, 1966, pp. 47–49)

There is no doubt that the 11 + test made considerable mistakes, that very many secondary modern school pupils can undertake academic work and that the arrangements for transfer (from secondary modern to grammar school) within the tripartite system were unsatisfactory. My five years as a secondary modern school class teacher and five as a secondary modern school head convinced me that the view that secondary schools (in the tripartite system) were equal but different was poppycock. The recent Schools Council Enquiry into Young School Leavers shows that parents see schools largely as places which train their sons and daughters for better jobs and in this basic requirement the secondary modern schools were and would remain inferior to the grammar schools.

(from 'The essential conditions for the success of a comprehensive school' by Rhodes Boyson in **Black Paper 2: The Crisis in Education** edited by C. B. Cox and A. E. Dyson, The Critical Quarterly Society, London, 1969, p. 57)

1. Why did those who set up the tripartite system believe it would give equal educational opportunities to all students? (5)
2. The 11 plus was not intended to be an examination to pass or fail. Why not? (3)
3. Why was selection for a secondary modern school seen as a 'failure' in the 11 plus? (4)
4. What effect might the general view of secondary modern schools have on the progress of students who attended them?(3)
5. How can it be argued that the tripartite system helped to maintain and perpetuate the class system? (5)

14 The comprehensive system

From the beginning the tripartite system had its critics. Their numbers grew over the years and the abolition of the system became official Labour Party policy in the early 1950s. Criticism was wide ranging. The 11 plus was said at best to give a rough idea of a student's performance in GCE exams but nothing about his or her creative, artistic and wider intellectual abilities. To decide a child's educational future at the age of eleven was dismissed as ridiculous. To consign a large section of the population to what was regarded as a second rate institution, the secondary modern school, was condemned as both wasteful and immoral. To suggest that the system gave all students an equal opportunity to develop their talents was regarded as laughable. Added to this, the tripartite system was criticised as socially divisive – it divided the student population into two unequal nations.

Many critics believed that equality of opportunity in secondary education could only come from a single common system of secondary schools for all. Their answer was the comprehensive system. This would end selection at the age of 11. It would provide a broad, basic, high quality course for every student. Children from a broad range of backgrounds would attend the same schools and this social mix would hopefully produce tolerance and understanding. In 1950 there were 10 comprehensive schools in England and Wales, in 1965 – 262, by 1969 – 962. By 1977, 80% of all students in secondary education attended comprehensives.

Like the tripartite system before it, the comprehensive system produced a storm of criticism. The major worry of its critics was that bright children would be held back. They needed special schools (i.e. grammar schools) to develop their 'special' talents. Only a small proportion of the population, it was claimed, is suitable for this type of education. The following passages consider these criticisms.

A study was conducted of 1,000 boys who failed the 11 plus but were provided with a public school education paid for by their parents. Three quarters passed the GCE examination at O-level in five or more subjects. This compares with 56% of all grammar school students. About one third of them passed two subjects at A-level and between a fifth and a quarter went on to university.

(adapted from 'The argument for comprehensive schools' by Peter Townsend in **Education in Great Britain and Ireland** edited by R. Bell, G. Fowler and K. Little, Routledge & Kegan Paul, London 1973)

Bright children do just as well in comprehensive as in grammar schools, according to the results of a major and authoritative survey which has been handed to the government. The government-funded study, carried out by the National Children's Bureau, is the first to follow a large, nationally-representative group of children through different types of secondary school.

The research is based on 16,000 children, all born in the same week of 1958, whose progress has been followed by the bureau since birth. They were tested on reading and maths at 11, just before they started secondary school, and again at 16, just before they left.

The results show that children of high ability (their scores were in the top 20% when they were tested at 11) made, on average, the same amount of progress in reading and maths over the five years of secondary education, regardless of whether they went to grammar or comprehensive school.

This was true both for bright working class and for bright middle class children. Children of lower intelligence did slightly better if they went to comprehensives rather than to secondary modern schools.

These results cast doubt on the need for the Conservatives' assisted-places scheme, which would take some bright children out of comprehensives and put them in independent schools.

Equally striking is the survey's evidence that comprehensive schools have not had a fair chance to prove themselves. In many areas, comprehensives have co-existed with grammar and direct-grant schools, which have 'creamed' the brightest children. Further, there are more comprehensives in working class than in middle class areas.

The study also provides new evidence of the injustices of the selective system. Bright children who ended up in secondary moderns – often because of errors in the 11 plus selection made less progress than their peers who went to grammar and comprehensive schools. Children who went to grammar schools, despite coming outside the top 20% on the tests at 11, did better than children of equivalent ability who went to other schools.

(from 'Bright children "do not suffer" in comprehensives' by Peter Wilby, **The Sunday Times**, March 16, 1980; © Times Newspapers Ltd)

1. There was a considerable wastage of talent in the tripartite system. Consider this statement with reference to the first extract. (4)
2. What does the second extract suggest about the claim that bright students will 'suffer' in comprehensives? Assess the evidence in your answer. (4)
3. Why have comprehensives 'not had a fair chance to prove themselves'? Explain the points made in the extract. (4)
4. What points does the second extract make to support the view that selection in secondary education is unjust? (4)
5. Why might the fact that many comprehensives are streamed cast doubt on the claims of some that they provide equality of opportunity? (4)

Section 11 Youth Culture

Since the early 1950s a colourful parade of young people has brightened television screens and adorned the pages of news-papers and magazines. Teddy boys, beatniks, hippies, mods, rockers, skinheads, punks, new romantics, futurists, rude boys and rockabillies have surprised, shocked, infuriated, amused and titillated the older generation.

At first sight some young people appear very different from their elders. This difference may extend beyond clothes and music to attitudes and behaviour. The term youth culture has been used to describe the distinctive lifestyles of young people. Youth sub-culture is a more suitable term since many aspects of the behaviour of youth are similar to those of other members of society.

This section begins by examining the position of young people in various pre-industrial societies. It then considers the changing status of youth in industrial society. It moves on to examine one particular youth subculture – teddy boys in the 1950s. The section closes with a survey of research which suggests that the attitudes and behaviour of young people are much the same as those of their elders.

1 Initiation ceremonies

In all societies some of the important stages in a person's life which involve a change in his or her status are marked by ceremonies. These ceremonies are known as rites of passage. They mark the transition or movement from one social status to another. Marriage and death are two such changes of status which are commonly recognized with a ceremony. Often rites of passage are associated with religion, for example church marriages and funeral services in Western society. In many societies, particularly pre-industrial societies, the transition from childhood to adulthood is marked by an event known as an initiation ceremony. The following passage examines such ceremonies.

In some societies initiation ceremonies are held at the onset of puberty which in boys is marked by the appearance of facial and bodily hair, in girls by bodily hair and the beginning of menstruation. Puberty is a fairly abrupt event and refers to the beginning of sexual maturity. Adolescence is the period from puberty to sexual maturity. It lasts several years and is a gradual process. In some societies initiation ceremonies occur during or at the close of adolescence.

In many societies girls are initiated to adult status at the onset of menstruation. They are often placed in seclusion and given instruction by older women in matters of sex and marriage and the duties of a wife and mother. Girls often experience hardship which results in changes in their appearance. They may have their ears pierced, skin tatooed, hair cut off or teeth filed. A feast or dance usually ends the period of seclusion and the girl appears in public in the clothes of an adult woman. She now adopts the status of an adult.

Initiation ceremonies for boys usually contain similar elements. This is shown in the following description of an initiation ceremony of the Bakaua tribe of New Guinea in south-east Asia. The boys are taken away from the village and led blindfolded to the ceremonial building which is to be their home for the next three to five months. The details of the ceremony have been kept secret from them and they approach it with feelings of anticipation, wonder, awe, fear and pride. Two sentries guard the boys and terrify them with strange noises and threaten them with a sharp adze (axe-like tool). During their stay the boys must observe certain food taboos – they must not eat everyday food such as pork, mice and lizards or drink fresh water. Male elders instruct the boys in the ways of adults and in the ethics and values of the tribe. The boys are circumcised during the ceremony. Just before this event the elders frighten them with the booming of bull-roarers (a flat strip of wood tied to a string which makes a roaring sound when whirled round) and the strange rattling of shells and stones hung from the tops of trees. The bull-roarers have a religious significance – they are believed to contain the souls of dead tribesmen.

After the initiation ceremony the boys return to the village wearing ornaments, their faces daubed with paint and finely carved combs in their hair. They are warmly greeted and after a large feast the ceremony comes to a close. The boys have now been admitted to adult status. They now have the rights, duties and privileges of adult members of the tribe.

(adapted from **Primitive Religion** by Robert H. Lowie, George Routledge and Sons, London, 1936 and 'Development in the individual' by C. S. Ford and F. A. Beach in **Understanding Society** edited by the Social Sciences Foundation Course Team, Macmillan, London, 1970)

1. An initiation ceremony can be seen as an intense, concentrated and very important period of socialization. Explain this statement using evidence from the extract. (4)
2. Why do initiation ceremonies often involve changes in dress and appearance? (3)
3. Why is there often a religious element in initiation ceremonies? (3)
4. Why do initiation ceremonies often end in a dance or feast at which the whole community is gathered to welcome the newly initiated young people? (3)
5. a In the West the status of adolescents is often ambiguous and unclear. Briefly suggest why this is so. (4)
   b Why is it not so in societies which have initiation ceremonies? (3)

2 Youth in industrial society

The following passage examines the changing position of young people in industrial society.

Childhood and adolescence as we know them today can be seen as a creation of modern industrial society. In pre-industrial societies children were like miniature adults following in the footsteps of their mothers and fathers. For example in agricultural societies children often had important duties and responsibilities such as caring for the livestock. In early industrial society child labour was widespread and these 'little adults' often made an important contribution to family finances. From today's viewpoint they were old before their time. During the nineteenth century child labour was banned and compulsory education introduced. The minimum school leaving age has been steadily raised from 10 in 1880 to 16 in 1973. As a result of these changes the length of time between childhood and adulthood has been extended and young people have been increasingly separated from the world of adults.

In pre-industrial societies and during the early years of industrialization, status was largely ascribed. Children usually adopted their parents' occupational roles. Today fewer and fewer children follow in their parents' footsteps when choosing an occupation. Family life therefore fails to present young people with clear role models for the future. As a result they may feel insecure about their status and anxious about their identity. In the family and to some extent in school, a young person's status as a child is ascribed. Yet in the wider society he must achieve his occupational status. In both family and school the young person is part of a group yet in the wider society he must achieve as an individual. Some researchers have argued that the socialization process in the family and school does not adequately prepare young people for their adult roles. Again the result might be insecurity about status, anxiety about identity.

The transition to adult status in industrial society is not helped by the legal situation. For example a 14-year-old is held to be fully responsible for any crime he commits but cannot leave school or join a trade union until aged 16. At 16 a young person can marry and leave home but cannot do so without parental consent until his eighteenth birthday. At 18 he is legally entitled to vote and buy drinks in a public house but he must wait until he is 21 before standing as a candidate in Local or Parliamentary elections. Some researchers have argued that this gradual and piecemeal process of becoming adult results in 'status ambiguity' – confusion and lack of clarity surrounding the status of young people.

The period of time during which young people are financially dependent on the older generation has steadily lengthened in industrial society. As a result the young are subordinated to adult authority well beyond the onset of physical maturity. Some researchers see this development resulting in increasing demands by young people for independence from the adult world and in some cases hostility towards or even an outright rejection of that world.

In industrial society adolescence has been prolonged and adulthood postponed. Young people continue their education for longer and longer periods during which time they are thrown together with their own age group and largely segregated from adults. They share certain experiences, circumstances and problems which separate them from the adult world. As a result the peer group becomes extremely important for many young people providing them with support, security, understanding and a sense of belonging.

(adapted from **From Generation to Generation** by S. N. Eisenstadt, The Free Press, New York, 1956, **Power and Privilege** by G. E. Lenski, McGraw-Hill, New York, 1966 and **School Leavers** by T. Veness, Methuen, London, 1962)

1. How can the transition to adulthood be seen as relatively easy in pre-industrial and early industrial society? (4)
2. Family and school do not adequately prepare young people for adult status in modern industrial society.
   a What evidence does the passage contain to support this statement? (3)
   b Why might this 'failure of socialization' produce anxiety and insecurity for young people? (3)
3. Youth in today's society are in limbo – they are neither one thing nor the other. Briefly discuss this statement with reference to the passage. (3)
4. Why are some young people hostile towards the adult world? (3)
5. How does the peer group assist young people in the transition to adulthood? (4)

3 Youth and social class

Much of the early writing on youth culture saw the behaviour of the young as a reflection of their age and as a response to their status as young people. Little mention was made of the fact that young people belong to different social classes. Thus, apart from his age, the lower-working class boy from an inner city area may have little in common with the upper-middle class boy from a well-to-do suburb. More recently a number of researchers have argued that youth subcultures must be seen as a reflection not just of age but also of social class.

The following passage looks at the lifestyle of teddy boys which developed in Britain during the early 1950s. Teddy boys were drawn largely from the working class, particularly the lower-working class. Many lived in run-down inner city areas scheduled for redevelopment. They had few if any educational qualifications and dead-end jobs offering little or no chance for advancement. The lifestyle developed by teddy boys can be seen as a response both to their position as young people in society and to their position in the class system.

In the summer of 1954 a late night train from Southend to London ground to a halt. Someone had pulled the communication cord. Light bulbs were smashed and carriages vandalized. When the train reached Barking the police arrested a gang of youths dressed in Edwardian suits.

In the same year a 16-year-old youth was convicted at Dartford Magistrates Court of robbing a woman 'by putting her in fear'. The Chairman of Magistrates stated:

There are a lot of things and so-called pleasures of the world which demand a lot of money. You tried to get hold of money to pay for ridiculous things like Edwardian suits. They are ridiculous in the eyes of ordinary people. They are flashy, cheap and nasty, and stamp the wearer as a particularly undesirable type.

Again in 1954, two gangs wearing teddy boy clothes fought with bricks and sand-filled socks at a railway station in Kent. 54 youths were arrested and taken in for questioning.

During August Bank Holiday, 1954, the first 'Best Dressed Ted Contest' was held at Canvey Island, Essex. It was won by a 20-year-old greengrocer's assistant. Teddy boys had arrived and were making their presence felt.

The Edwardian suit based on styles current during the reign of Edward VII (1901–1911) was reintroduced in London around 1950. Originally it was adopted by upper class young men. They soon discarded the style when it was taken up by working class youth who adapted it into the teddy boy uniform. The jacket or 'drape' was long, knee length or below, in pea green, deep purple, shocking pink or bright blue with narrow lapels and velvet collar. The drape owed as much to the frock-coat of the Western gunfighter as it did to the jackets of Edwardian times. Drain-pipe trousers emerged

A style begins – a teddy boy photographed in 1954

below the drape followed by electric pink or green socks and
thick crepe-soled suede shoes known as 'brothel creepers' or
'beetle crushers'. Completing the picture were skinny ties
known as 'slim jims' or bootstring ties reminiscent of the Wild

West held together by medallions featuring death's heads, cross-bones skulls, eagles or cows heads based on the skulls of Texas longhorns.

Hair was worn long with an ample supply of Brylcreem, swept into a large quiff at the front and combed into a DA or 'duck's arse' at the back. Sideboards or sideburns, named after the American General Burnside, were popular. The picture presented by teddy boys in full regalia was dramatic and quite a shock to the straight world of grown-ups.

Teddy boys adopted American rock and roll as their own. They listened and danced to the music of Bill Haley, Elvis Presley, Eddie Cochran, Jerry Lee Lewis, Carl Perkins and Little Richard. When Bill Haley's 'Rock Around the Clock' was shown in British cinemas, teddy boys danced in the aisles and occasionally rioted, slashing seats and ripping them from their mountings.

Dress, music and manner were aggressive. Rival gangs fought for territory, dance halls were wrecked and immigrants attacked. There is evidence that teddy boys started the 1958 'race-riots' in Nottingham and Notting Hill. After the Notting Hill riots nine unskilled working class youths in teddy boy outfits were each sentenced to four years in prison. The violence must not be exaggerated however. Most teddy boys were probably content to strut around in their colourful costumes simply looking tough and aggressive.

(adapted from 'Cultural responses of the Teds' by Tony Jefferson in **Resistance through Rituals** edited by S. Hall and T. Jefferson, Hutchinson, London, 1976, **Working Class Youth Culture** edited by Geoff Mungham and Geoff Pearson, Routledge & Kegan Paul, London, 1976, **The Teds** by Chris Steele-Perkins and Richard Smith, Travelling Light/Exit, London, 1979)

1. How can the lifestyle of teddy boys be seen to
   a Express and symbolize the separation of young people from the adult world? (3)
   b Indicate a desire for independence from adult authority? (3)
   c Express hostility towards or even rejection of the adult world? (3)
   d Strengthen peer group solidarity? (3)
2. How can the behaviour of teddy boys be seen as a response to their position in the class system? (8)

4 Is there a generation gap?

The picture of young people sometimes presented by the mass media suggests that they are very different from the older generation. Hippies were sometimes portrayed as turning their backs on the 'straight' world, living in communes, practicing free love and preaching peace and happiness through a haze of marihuana smoke. Punks have been presented as being totally negative and destructive in their attitudes, living the life suggested by their slogan 'No future!'

Media images of the young often give the impression that many are committed to youth subcultures. However, a number of studies suggests that this is not the case. The first passage looks at some of this evidence. It indicates that many young people who look the part are probably little more than ordinary youngsters in fancy dress. The second passage considers an explanation of the concern of the older generation, often expressed in the media, about the behaviour of the young.

In 1956 a survey of the attitudes and expectations of 702 boys and 600 girls in the west of England was conducted by Thelma Veness. The youngsters were in their final year of school – at that time the school leaving age was fifteen. Veness concluded that, 'these young people do seem to be remarkably like us'. They thought ambition was a good thing and believed that hard work was the key to getting on in life. They placed a high value on property and material possessions and wanted to improve their living standards. They expected to get married, have children and settle down in much the same way as their parents before them.

In the early 1970s Sue Sharpe conducted a study of girls in secondary schools in the London borough of Ealing. There was remarkably little difference between the Ealing girls and those in Veness's survey. Sharpe found that their main concerns were 'love, marriage, husbands, children, jobs and careers, more or less in that order'.

In 1974 the National Children's Bureau conducted a large scale survey of more than 13,000 sixteen-year-olds. The vast majority held traditional attitudes about marriage and the family – only 3% rejected marriage and most wanted children. Four out of five claimed they got on well with both parents. Arguments with parents were mainly over dress and hair styles though in only 11% of cases was this a frequent source of conflict.

(adapted from **School Leavers** by Thelma Veness, Methuen, London, 1962, **Just Like a Girl** by Sue Sharpe, Penguin, Harmondsworth, 1976, **A New Introduction to Sociology** by Mike O'Donnell, Harrap, London, 1981)

The type of evidence presented in the above passage has led some researchers to claim that youth subcultures are little more than a creation of the mass media. They argue that at most only a small minority of young people has distinctive subcultures. If this is the case why does the media give so much attention to this minority and exaggerate the differences between young and old? The British sociologist Stanley Cohen provides the following explanation.

In every society certain individuals and groups are treated as scapegoats. They are forced to bear the blame and suffer the anger of others for something of which they are innocent. In the middle ages certain unfortunate women were said to be witches and burned. In the 1950s in the USA a number of people were tried and convicted as communists and the fear of 'reds under the beds' was widespread. Stanley Cohen argues that these scapegoats or 'folk devils' are created during times of 'moral panic' when many people fear that the major values and institutions of society are under threat. This often occurs during periods of rapid social change, in times of political and economic upheaval. Certain individuals and groups are seen as a threat to society and concern about this threat is whipped up into a storm – a moral panic. Then, in Cohen's words, 'The moral barricades are manned by editors, bishops, politicians and other right-thinking people.'

The 'folk-devils' of the past 30 years have included teddy boys, skinheads, punks and various other groups of young people. They fit the bill as scapegoats. They are relatively powerless, they are easily recognizable and it is possible to exaggerate certain aspects of their behaviour so as to make them appear as a threat to society. They are an easy target for the hate, wrath and fear of many people in the wider society.

(adapted from **Folk Devils and Moral Panics** by Stanley Cohen, Paladin, London, 1973)

1. Name three values of Western society which, on the evidence of the first passage, are held by most young people. (3)
2. The majority of young people do not belong to youth sub-cultures. How does the evidence in the first passage support this statement? (4)
3. What is a 'moral panic' and when does it arise? (4)
4. Why are scapegoats often created during a period of moral panic? (3)
5. a Why do young people fit the bill as scapegoats? (3)
   b Why are 'welfare scroungers' often selected to play a similar role? (3)

Section 12 Women and Society

Women produce children; women are wives and mothers; women do the cooking, sewing, mending and washing; they take care of men and are subject to male authority; they are largely excluded from positions of high status and power. To some degree these generalizations apply to all known human societies. In every society there are men's jobs and women's jobs, in other words there are sex or gender roles. In terms of the rewards of prestige, wealth and power attached to gender roles women nearly always come off worse.

In many societies it is regarded as 'natural' for a woman to raise children and perform domestic tasks. She is seen to be biologically equipped for such jobs and her role is simply an expression of her female nature. Some social scientists have adopted a similar argument claiming that gender roles are linked to the biology of men and women. Thus the American anthropologist George Peter Murdock argues that biological differences such as the greater physical strength of men and the fact that women bear children lead to the sexual division of labour in society. From a survey of 224 societies Murdock finds that tasks such as hunting, lumbering and mining are usually part of the male role while cooking, gathering wild vegetables, water carrying and making and repairing clothes are usually assigned to women. He claims that, 'Man with his superior physical strength can better undertake the more strenuous tasks, such as lumbering, mining, quarrying, land clearance and housebuilding. Not handicapped, as is woman by the physiological burdens of pregnancy and nursing, he can range further afield to hunt, to fish, to herd and to trade. Woman is at no disadvantage, however, in lighter tasks which can be performed in or near the home, e.g. the gathering of vegetable products, the fetching of water, the preparation of food and the manufacture of clothing and utensils.'

Particularly in recent years, with the rise of the Women's Liberation Movement, the view that gender roles are shaped by biology has been strongly criticized. Many sociologists argue that the roles of men and women are determined by culture and therefore learned as part of the socialization process. If this is the case then there is nothing 'natural' about the roles women play. Some support for this viewpoint is provided by the following extracts which give brief descriptions of gender roles in three societies.

1 Women in non-Western societies

The Kgatla Tribe of South Africa

The women and girls till the fields, build and repair the walls of the huts, granaries and courtyards, prepare food and make beer, look after the fowls, fetch water, earth and wood, collect wild plants, and do all the other housework.

The women fill in their time with one or other of the many tasks that village life may entail. A new coating of plaster may be needed on the walls, or there are cracks that must be mended, and for these purposes loads of earth must first be dug, carried in baskets and worked into a suitable mud.

Men, on the other hand, have no regular daily work in the villages. The herding of livestock is done by the boys, who take the animals out in the morning to graze and bring them back again in the afternoon. Specialists like the doctors and thatchers will generally have something to do almost every day, but the rest seem to work spasmodically, and frequently spend days on end merely lounging about.

(from **Married Life in an African Tribe** by Isaac Schapera, Penguin, Harmondsworth, 1971, pp. 141–2)

The Manus Tribe of New Guinea

For a year mother and baby are shut up together in the house. For that year the child still belongs to its mother. But as soon as the child's legs are strong enough to stand upon and its small arms adept at clutching, the father begins to take the child from its mother. Now that the child is in no need of such frequent suckling, he expects his wife to get to work. The plea that her child needs her would not avail. The father is delighted to play with the child, to toss it in the air, tickle it beneath its armpits, softly blow on its bare smooth skin.

On the eve of the birth of a new baby, the child's transfer of dependence to its father is almost complete. While the mother is occupied with the new baby, the older child stays with its father. He feeds it, bathes it, plays with it all day.

(from **Growing Up in New Guinea** by Margaret Mead, Routledge, London, 1931, pp. 57–9)

The Tchambuli Tribe of New Guinea
The women go with shaven heads, unadorned, determinedly busy about their affairs. Adult males in Tchambuli are skittish (highly strung and fickle), wary of each other, interested in art, in the theatre, in a thousand petty bits of insult and gossip. The men wear lovely ornaments, they do the shopping, they carve and paint and dance. Men whose hair is long enough wear curls, and the others make false curls out of rattan rings.

(from **Male and Female** by Margaret Mead, Penguin, Harmondsworth, 1962, pp. 106–7)

1. Because of their superior physical strength men do the heavy work. What evidence do the extracts provide to contradict this view? (4)
2. There are certain 'feminine characteristics' which are a 'natural' part of a woman's makeup. What evidence do the extracts contain to challenge this view? (5)
3. Some psychologists have argued that in order to develop into a normal, well-balanced adult a child needs a close, warm and continuous relationship with its mother. How can this view be questioned given the fact that the children described in the extracts grow into well-balanced adults? (4)
4. How can the evidence in the extracts be used to argue that gender roles are shaped by culture rather than biology? (7)

2 Women and industrialization

As the previous extract indicates the role of women can vary considerably from society to society. It can also change significantly over a period of time within a single society. This is shown in the following passage which summarizes Ann Oakley's analysis of the changing status of women in British society from the eve of the industrial revolution in 1750 to the 1970s.

> In pre-industrial Britain the family was the basic unit of production. Agriculture and textiles were the main industries and women were essential for both. In the production of cloth, the husband did the weaving while his wife spun and dyed the yarn. On the farm women were in charge of dairy produce – they made the butter and cheese. Most of the housework – cooking, cleaning, washing, mending and child-care – was performed by unmarried children.
>
> During the early years of industrialization (1750–1841) the factory steadily replaced the family as the unit of production. Women were employed in factories where they often continued their traditional work in textiles. However a series of factory acts, beginning in 1819 gradually restricted child labour. Someone now had to care for and supervise children, a role which fell to women. The restriction of women to the home had begun.
>
> Women were seen by many men as a threat to their employment. As early as 1841 committees of male workers called for 'the gradual withdrawal of all female labour from the factory'. In 1842 the Mines Act banned the employment of women as miners. Women were excluded from trade unions, men made contracts with their employers to prevent them from hiring women and laws were passed restricting female employment in a number of industries. Tied down by dependent children and increasingly barred from the workplace the restriction of women to the home continued.
>
> Victorian beliefs about a 'woman's place' reinforced this process. No less a figure than Queen Victoria announced, 'Let a woman be what God intended, a helpmate for man, but with totally different duties and vocations.' Articles in the **Saturday Review** illustrate the ideal of womanhood. In 1859 – 'Married life is a woman's profession, and to this life her

CUPID'S HARNESS.

Most women naturally look forward to matrimony as their proper sphere in life, but they should constantly bear in mind that a fair, rosy face, bright eyes, and a healthy, well-developed form, are the best passports to a happy marriage. All those wasting disorders, weaknesses, and functional irregularities peculiar to their sex, destroy beauty and attractiveness and make life miserable. An unfailing specific for these maladies is to be found in Dr. Pierce's Favorite Prescription. It is the only medicine for women, sold by druggists, **under a positive guarantee** from the manufacturers, that it will give satisfaction in every case, or money will be refunded. This guarantee has been printed on the bottle-wrappers, and faithfully carried out for many years. $1.00 per Bottle, or six Bottles for $5.00.

Copyright, 1888, by WORLD'S DISPENSARY MEDICAL ASSOCIATION, Proprietors.

An American advertiser's view of Victorian womanhood

training – that of dependence – is modelled.' And in 1865, 'No woman can or ought to know very much of the mass of mean-ness and wickedness and misery that is loose in the wide world. She could not learn it without losing the bloom and freshness which it is her mission in life to preserve.'

Slowly but surely women were being locked into the mother-housewife role and confined to the home. In 1851, one in four married women were employed, by 1911 this figure was reduced to one in ten. From 1914 to 1950 the employment of married women grew slowly but the mother-housewife role remained their primary responsibility. During these years women received many legal and political rights, for example the vote in 1928, but these had little effect on their main role in life. Even today when about half of all married women are employed, most see their occupational role as secondary to their duties as a wife and mother and their responsibility for the home.

Oakley concludes that industrialization has had the following effects on the role of women. First, the 'separation of men from the daily routines of domestic life'. Second, the 'economic dependence of women and children on men'. Third, the 'isolation of housework and childcare from other work'. The result is that the mother-housewife role has become 'the primary role for all women'.

(adapted from **Housewife** by Ann Oakley, Allen Lane, London, 1974. Quotations in paragraph four from **The Place of Women in Society** by K. Hudson, Ginn, London, 1970)

1. How did industrialization lead to the 'separation of men from the daily routines of domestic life'? (5)
2. How did industrialization lead to the 'economic dependence of women and children on men'? (5)
3. How and why were women increasingly restricted to the home during the last century? (6)
4. Suggest why the mother-housewife role continues as the primary role for women despite the growing numbers of married women entering the workforce? (4)

3 Socialization and the role of women (1)

The previous extracts suggest that gender roles are shaped by culture and society rather than biology. If this is the case then there should be evidence that boys and girls are socialized for their adult roles. The table overleaf presents an analysis of six reading schemes, including the **Janet and John** and the **Ladybird** series. Many children learn how to read from these books. The analysis shows that certain objects, activities and roles are linked to girls, others to boys and some to both sexes.

1. How do the books lend support to the following views?
   a Men are physically stronger than women.   (3)
   b Boys are more adventurous than girls.   (3)
   c Men are more dominant than women.   (3)
   d Women are mothers and housewives, men are breadwinners and wage earners.   (5)
2. What effect might books such as **Janet and John** have on children's adult roles? Use the idea of socialization in your answer.   (6)

4 Socialization and the role of women (2)

As Sections 1 and 2 indicated, behaviour patterns learned during the early years of life may well have a lasting effect. The following extract, taken from an article by Jacqueline Penrose, supports this point of view. It argues that children are prepared from birth for their adult roles as men and women.

In a high street toyshop I picked up a catalogue. It states – and I think rightly – that 'babies are ready to start to learn about the world right from the start... The right toys will provide the stimulation they need...'

And they learn that certain types of toys are suitable only for boys, and others for girls. There's Judy and Velvet, her pony: 'This pretty pair are tipped for the top...' What boy would be caught dead with that? There are 'dolls' for boys:

Sex-roles that occurred in three or more of the six schemes

Sex for which role was allocated	Toys and Pets	Activities	Content of the Children's Roles		Adult roles presented
			Taking the lead in activities that both boys and girls take part in	Learning a new skill	
Girls only	1 Doll 2 Skipping rope 3 Doll's pram	1 Preparing the tea 2 Playing with dolls 3 Taking care of younger siblings	1 Hopping 2 Shopping with parents 3 Skipping	1 Taking care of younger siblings	1 Mother 2 Aunt 3 Grandmother
Boys only	1 Car 2 Train 3 Aeroplane 4 Boat 5 Football	1 Playing with cars 2 Playing with trains 3 Playing football 4 Lifting or pulling heavy objects 5 Playing cricket 6 Watching adult males in occupational roles 7 Heavy gardening	1 Going exploring alone 2 Climbing trees 3 Building things 4 Taking care of pets 5 Sailing boats 6 Flying kites 7 Washing and polishing Dad's car	1 Taking care of pets 2 Making/Building 3 Saving/Rescuing people or pets 4 Playing sports	1 Father 2 Uncle 3 Grandfather 4 Postman 5 Farmer 6 Fisherman 7 Shop or business owner 8 Policeman 9 Builder 10 Bus driver 11 Bus conductor 12 Train driver 13 Railway porter
Both sexes	1 Book 2 Ball 3 Paints 4 Bucket and spade 5 Dog 6 Cat 7 Shop	1 Playing with pets 2 Writing 3 Reading 4 Going to the seaside 5 Going on a family outing	—	—	1 Teacher 2 Shop assistant

(Source: 'Data report on British reading schemes' by G. Lobban, **Times Educational Supplement**, March 1, 1974, p. 12 © Times Newspapers Ltd)

'The Cosmic Command defence forces. These brave heroes...'
And Tommy Gunn, 'a man of many roles. He is trained as a
medic, but can use a gun...'

For the girls: 'Sweet Baby. Advice for young mothers from
Auntie Brenda. Dear Auntie Brenda – I want to be sure to
keep my baby warm this winter, but it is also very important
that she has pretty clothes...' And there's Rachel Ballerina,
'of great beauty and grace but she is also a young lady with a
tremendous interest in fashion'.

Even when children themselves want to experiment with a
wider range of toys, this hard sell makes it very difficult. So
does the packaging. I saw a large chemistry set in the
window, a boy and a girl shown on the box. The boy was eight
inches high, the girl only two. Before the Renaissance artists
would make the most important figure in a picture the
largest; children's own work follows the same principle and
they can recognise it when they meet it on a box. This toy is
for boys.

In another shop I picked up a selection of children's birthday
cards, which will be chosen by adults, presumably to conform
to their notions of what children are like – or ought to be like.

First, for the newborn boy. His cot is trimmed with blue.
Inside it says: 'A baby boy – You must be proud; and very
happy, too...'

The baby girl is dressed in pink, with a ribbon in her hair.
Inside: 'Bet she's even sweeter than you ever dreamed she'd
be...'

Sons one is proud of, daughters are sweet.

For the four-year-olds: the girls' card shows a girl in a
flounced pink dress, flowers in her hat. She pushes a pram
and carries a handbag. The four-year-old boy is dressed in
jeans and trainers, and he is fishing.

At eight the girl is wearing a dress (with a tiny waist) made
entirely of pink roses. There are roses in her long fair hair –
but she does nothing. Inside it says: 'For a sweet young Miss
who is eight today and growing up in such a lovely way...'

The eight-year-old boy is on a racing bike, in a T-shirt, jeans
and trainers.

Such examples abound. They show that girls are still
expected to be sweet, demure, pretty and passive, destined
only for domesticity and motherhood. They are reminded of it

wherever they look. It is not a matter of choice. Hard luck if they are born with a creative, dynamic intelligence. Parents and teachers need to be more aware of the problem if this unjust and arbitrary division of people into active and passive roles is to stop.

(from 'The girl who always says yes' by Jacqueline Penrose, **The Guardian,** April 6 1982, p. 13)

1. Using evidence from the extract suggest how women **learn** to be 'feminine'. (4)
2. What evidence does the extract contain which suggests that girls are socialized for the mother–housewife role? (4)
3. In schools boys are more likely than girls to select science subjects. How does the extract help to explain their choice? (4)
4. The top jobs in society often involve taking decisions and managing and directing the activities of others. They are 'active' roles. Using evidence from the extract suggest why men greatly outnumber women in these occupations. (4)
5. Why does Jacqueline Penrose argue that the ways in which girls and boys are divided and distinguished are unjust? (4)

5 Housebound wives

Hannah Gavron writes, 'The pattern of work for women today is work till marriage, work after marriage, stop when the children are young and return again when they grow older.' Judging from her study of housebound mothers, the hardest work begins when women leave 'work' to raise children. Gavron's study, **The Captive Wife: Conflicts of Housebound Mothers**, is based on a sample of 48 middle class and 48 working class wives with at least one child under five. The following passage examines their reasons for giving up employment and their reactions to being housebound mothers.

10% of the middle class sample had not worked after marriage. This rose to 62% after the birth of the first baby. Yet most of the wives who gave up work would have preferred not to do so. Patterns of employment for the working class wives are similar. 12% had not worked after marriage. This rose to 71% after the birth of the first child with most wishing they were still working. The following table summarizes the reasons the women gave for stopping work.

Social class	No help available	Work not suitable	Wrong to leave children	No desire to work	Husband said stay at home
Middle class	32%	4%	41%	4%	18%
Working class	7%	0%	54%	11%	29%

Comments from mothers include, 'You've got to put your children first when they are young' and 'I feel I must be around at least till the children are three years old.' However for many this involved sacrifice. Most wives would rather have been at work. All the middle class mothers who left work after the birth of their first child said they were often bored at home and a quarter said they were lonely. The experience of most working class wives was similar. A labourer's wife said, 'Some days I'm so fed up I could scream.' 'You've no idea', said the wife of a plumber's mate, 'what it's like to spend all day in one room, trying to keep the children quiet because the landlady can't bear noise. I feel like I'm in a cage.'

Many of the wives found themselves in a curious situation. They sensed their great responsibilities towards their children but at the same time wanted to be at work. They felt they were somehow 'functionless' at home yet still believed it was essential to be with their children. Gavron concludes that most wives 'appear from the discussion of their own views on home and work to be essentially on the horns of a dilemma'.

(adapted from **The Captive Wife: Conflicts of Housebound Mothers** by Hannah Gavron, Routledge & Kegan Paul, London, 1966)

1. What was the most common reason given for stopping work after the birth of the first child?   (1)
2. Given that many women rely on relatives for help with child-care, suggest why a higher percentage of middle class as compared to working class wives gave up work because there was no help available.   (3)

3. Suggest one reason why a higher percentage of working class as compared to middle class wives said they had no desire to work.

(3)

4. Why did most wives wish they were still at work? (4)

5. 'I'm **only** a housewife.' How might this statement help to explain the experience of many housebound mothers? (4)

6. Gavron's study is entitled **The Captive Wife: Conflicts of House-bound Mothers**. Why did she choose the word conflict to describe their situation? (5)

6 Why women go to work

By 1951 approximately one in five married women were employed outside the home, by 1984 the figure had risen to over one in two. A variety of reasons has been given for this increase. They include a shortage of labour particularly during the 1950s and 60s and an expansion of jobs seen as suitable for women, for example clerks, shop assistants, nurses and social workers. There is less disapproval of working wives and less discrimination against them in the labour market – in 1944 the ban on married women teachers was lifted and in 1946 they were allowed to join the London metropolitan police force. More recently the Equal Pay Act (1970) and the Sex Discrimination Act (1975) aimed to give women an equal opportunity in the labour market. In addition there has been an increase in the availability of part time work and special shifts which allow women to continue with their responsibilities as housewives and mothers.

However women could not be entering the labour force in increasing numbers if they did not want to or believed they had to. The following extract examines women's motives for working and looks at some of the consequences of their growing participation in the labour force.

One million women left home for work between 1971 and 1976 – the most massive workforce increase Britain has ever seen.

A Gallup poll commissioned by **Woman's Own** has shown that 80% of present mothers want to work. The Pill has been one reason for the transformation, Elspeth Howe believes; the equal rights movement, another. The industrial recession, too, did a lot to encourage women to work. Simply, they needed more money; and there were incentives in the form of better pay for manual work. But at heart the revolution is not economic, but personal.

The Gallup poll shows that four out of five mothers would work even if they were millionaires. 'There's been a huge change in grassroots attitudes,' says Ann Oakley, a sociologist at Bedford college, London. So-called 'ordinary' women, once shy of 'bra-burning attitudes', now frankly state they believe in equal opportunities and rights. 'Strangely enough, it is now only a handful of middle class women who say they don't want to work – the rich ones surrounded with cleaners, wall-ovens and home-made yoghurt-making equipment, for whom house-keeping is playtime and fun.'

For most other women, unmitigated (continuous) home-making in its present guise is not much fun. Ann Oakley has found a strong correlation (relationship) between being home-bound and mental misery, which is confirmed by a separate Cambridge study, which found that 42% of home-bound mothers are clinically depressed. Those at work are protected from this plight, and the impact on their children is strong. A long-term study for the Home Office by D. J. West of Cambridge shows the children of full-time working mothers are less delinquent and less disturbed.

The Gallup poll indicates that working mothers – without any State help – take great care of their children and their family life. Ann Oakley finds they rely on grandmothers, relatives, husbands, friends: with unexpected social benefits. Isolated, useless-feeling widows are given roles and young company; fathers are getting to know their children properly; a social force is being created which keeps extended families in touch, and creates friendships and social contacts in a world in which families and neighbours are increasingly becoming strangers to one another.

Shorter hours, flexitime, and job-sharing are already possible in a wide range of jobs, from the Civil Service to insurance, House of Commons research to banking. They are popular – and they are effective.

(from 'Revolution and backlash' by Lyn Owen, **The Observer**, February 4, 1979, p. 39)

1. Give three reasons stated in the extract for the increasing employment of women during the 1970s.   (3)
2. What evidence is contained in the extract to support the argument that the main reason why women return to work is 'not economic but personal'?   (3)
3. What are the benefits for children of full-time working mothers?   (4)
4. a How do working mothers take care of their children?   (3)
   b How does this benefit other members of the community?   (3)
5. What changes are taking place in production methods and working practices which may well make it possible for more women to work outside the home?   (4)

7 Women in the labour force (1)

Women are not spread evenly throughout the labour force. They are concentrated in low status, low skilled and low paid jobs. Largely because of their domestic situation they are much more likely than men to take up part-time employment which is usually unskilled and poorly paid. The American sociologist Theodore Caplow argues that the main reason for the position of women in the labour market is the belief of employers that they will leave work to produce and raise children. This means that employers will not normally invest money in expensive training programmes for female workers and will make sure they are easily replaceable. This results in women being placed in low skill jobs which can be learned quickly. These jobs are poorly paid.

The following extract examines the position of women in the labour force in Britain.

> Though women are moving into the world, men are not moving back to home responsibilities, or yielding one inch of their old bread-winner work-pattern, or spheres of work. They watch wives take on jobs, continue all household responsibilities and, increasingly, community care involvements, without assisting. And they moan piteously about 'women stealing men's jobs'. Women, like immigrants, are becoming scapegoats.
>
> But, as recent investigations by the Department of Employ-

ment show, male fears in this connection are completely unfounded. Women, for the most part, still remain in their job ghetto, which men are reluctant to penetrate – the soft heart, scrubbing, and body beautiful jobs. 60% of all women work in 10 almost entirely low-grade, and entirely low-paid, categories of job. The Ten Deadly Cs are – catering, cleaning, clerking, counter-minding, clothes-making, coiffure, child-minding (otherwise known as primary school teaching), clothes-washing, care of the sick, and clicking at typewriters.

To which can be added cashiering, cooked food processing, and cobbling – not the remunerative sort done by chaps in High Streets, which the women never do, but the low-paid tougher job of cutting, piecing together and sewing of shoes in factories.

Women figure rarely or not at all in the areas of high male employment – the motor industry, ship-building, lorry driving, construction, storehouse-keeping and warehouse manning, heavy engineering, middle-line management, accountancy and farm labouring. Their representation in the professions continues at an abysmal level – they provide 4% of architects, 1% of surveyors, 1% of public health inspectors, 6% of solicitors, 7% of barristers, 2% of accountants, less than 1% of engineers, with the trend towards decline rather than advance. Where they have gained ground in management, they have done so in the 'woman's jobs' of personnel management.

Their only large gain has been in medicine, where they now make up 30% of National Health Service doctors. But so few men are rushing for this job here nowadays – and so many are rushing to practice medicine in the United States, having been trained here – that Britain has to import doctors from overseas.

Even when men and women are in the same industries, segregation remains so watertight that women can be found universally in low-grade manual work and men in skilled, high-grade work. Only in education, welfare and nursing, in shops and clerical work, are there actual fights for jobs – and there it is a matter, not of women pinching men's work, but men infiltrating long-established women's areas.

It may come as a shock to most people that a report com-missioned recently by the Employment Department found women worse off in the job market than they were in 1911.

'It is wrong to believe the position of women in the labour force has steadily improved over the century – on the contrary it has deteriorated quite markedly in some respects,' the report says. In 1911, 19.8% of women who worked were in management and administrative posts. By 1931, the level had sunk to 13% and was little higher in 1961. There were more women in the higher ranks of the Civil Service in 1919 than there are today.

Also in 1911, 63% of employed women were in the 'lower professions', as the report puts it, in white-collar jobs but below 'management and executive' levels. The percentage had fallen to 52 by 1971. Among the female work-force in 1911, 24% were skilled. 60 years later, that percentage was down to 13.5.

The percentage of employed women in unskilled 'married women's jobs – no prospects' rose, between 1911 and 1971, from 15.5 to 37.

We think now the legislation to promote equal rights is liberating women further. But, like our beliefs about the condition of working women now and in the past, that idea is false.

(from 'Revolution and backlash' by Lyn Owen, **The Observer**, February 4, 1979, p. 39)

1. Why does the author suggest that, 'Women, like immigrants, are becoming scapegoats'? (5)
2. How can a) catering and b) primary school teaching be seen as extensions of the mother–housewife role? (4)
3. In view of the argument given by Theodore Caplow in the introduction to the extract, suggest why a) counter-minding and b) clothes-washing are jobs for women. (4)
4. Why are men reluctant to enter the female 'job ghetto'? (5)
5. Select two pieces of evidence which challenge the belief that the position of women in the labour force has improved this century. (2)

8 Women in the labour force (2)

The previous extract examined the position of women in the labour force in the first half of the 1970s. The following extract completes the picture for the decade by looking at the years 1975 to 1980.

Jo Richardson, Labour MP for Barking, sums up women's progress in recent years, 'We have definitely gone backwards', she says. Women's earnings, after creeping up towards men's, have dropped and levelled out at around 73%. Women have borne a disproportionate share of unemployment; joblessness among women has risen from 22% to 29% of the registered unemployed in five years, and that does not include an estimated one million unregistered women.

And although women now make up 40% of the work force, 55% of female manual workers are in catering, cleaning, hair-dressing and other personal services, compared with 47% five years ago and 55% of non-manual workers in clerical and related jobs (58% in 1975). Only one in 12 managers are women, compared with one in ten in 1975.

Rising unemployment has also meant a severe curtailment in job opportunities for women because the part-time jobs tend to go first, and these are traditionally filled by women. At the same time, inflation has increased the pressures on women to find work to help the household income.

Again it is the women who are the hardest hit by the public sector cuts. Cuts in social services for the young, old and sick, such as nurseries, home-helps and day care centres, have forced women back into the home once more, to fill the gap left by the scaled-down welfare state.

The biggest stumbling block in all this is still that of attitudes. In any profession or trade, women are still con-centrated in the lowest ranks. Over 90% of primary school teachers are women, but only 43% of women are head teachers. In the Civil Service, there are no women permanent secretaries and only 3% of deputy secretaries are women, while 80% of the clerical assistants are women.

Although things have improved in schools and the tendency

to insist that girls do cookery and boys woodwork has largely gone, traditional attitudes among pupils themselves, parents and teachers ensure that old patterns of training and employment persist.

Boys still outnumber girls at all levels of further and higher education and still predominate in the sciences, while girls predominate in the arts. In 1970, 2.1% of engineering and technology students were girls, but in language, literature and related studies they comprised 57%. In 1978, the figures were 5.5% and 65% respectively.

The same applies on the TOPS training schemes, with women overwhelmingly concentrated in colleges where they follow traditionally 'female' courses such as shorthand and typing, although more are now taking skills and crafts courses.

So the depressing conclusion is that despite some break-throughs – women have got such previously all-male jobs as air pilot, station master, deaconess and coastguard as well as the most obvious of all, Prime Minister – there is still a long way to go.

It is still almost impossible for women to combine a career and run a home. Creches are rare and most employers look askance at the idea of job sharing and flexible hours. If a woman leaves to have children, her career prospects are irredeemably blighted and she never catches up.

(from 'Women at work: the five wasted years' by Frances Gibb, **The Times**, June 11 1981, p. 11; © Times Newspapers Ltd)

1. Except in individual cases, women are increasingly likely to have 'women's jobs'. What evidence does the extract provide to support this statement? (4)
2. What evidence does the extract provide to suggest that women have suffered more than men from the economic recession of the late 1970s? (4)
3. The author claims that attitudes are the biggest stumbling block to female equality in the labour market.
   a What does she mean by this? (3)
   b What evidence does she provide to support this view? (5)
4. How might the measures listed in the final paragraph improve women's job opportunities? (4)

9 Women in the labour force (3)

The two previous extracts looked at women's position in the labour market from 1970 to 1980. They focussed on the kinds of work women did. The following passage continues this survey to 1985 with particular reference to pay.

Labour force participation: estimates and projections

| | Great Britain | | Millions |
	Males	Females	Total
Estimates			
1971	15.6	9.3	24.9
1976	15.6	10.1	25.7
1979	15.6	10.4	26.0
1981	15.6	10.6	26.2
1983	15.3	10.6	25.9
1984	15.5	10.9	26.4
Projections			
1986	15.6	11.2	26.8
1991	15.8	11.5	27.2

(from **Social Trends 16**, HMSO, London, 1986, p. 62)

As the previous table shows, female participation in the labour force continued to increase during the 1980s. The proportion of women has grown from 37% in 1971 to 41% in 1984 accounting for the entire increase in the size of the labour force during this period.

Women's earnings as a percentage of men's 1970–1985

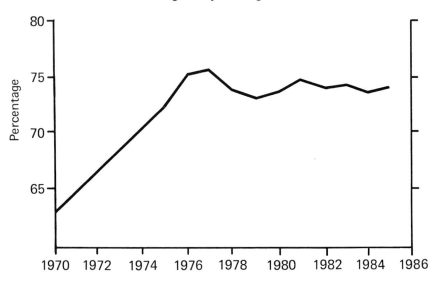

(based on gross hourly earnings of full-time employees aged 18 and over from figures in **Employment Gazette**, October 1985, p. 387)

As the above graph shows, the average earnings of women compared to those of men rose steadily during the early 1970s when the effects of the Equal Pay Act (1970) were seen. Since the mid-1970s there has been little change – in 1976 women's earnings averaged 75.1% of those of men, in 1985, 74%. A report entitled **Cheap Labour** (1984) by the Low Pay Unit shows that women form the majority of the low paid. Defining low pay as two-thirds of average male earnings it finds that women make up 5.7 of the 8.3 million low paid workers.

A number of suggestions have been made to improve the pay (and status) of the low paid and of women in particular. Some favour a statutory minimum wage i.e. a minimum wage established by law. Others would prefer to leave the matter to free collective bargaining arguing that unions should give special priority in pay claims to their low paid members. However some see the only real solution as an end to 'women's jobs' and equal participation in all forms of employment by both sexes.

During the early 1970s the Equal Pay Act made a real contribution to improving women's pay. It largely eliminated differences in pay between women and men doing the same jobs. But about two-thirds of women do work done only by other women. Until 1984 these 'women's only' jobs were outside the scope of the Act. Then an amendment stated that women could claim equal pay if they could show that their work is of equal value (on measures like skill and responsibility) to a man's. However the problem with equal value claims is that they have to be pursued case by case before tribunals. It now requires unions to follow up the victories and press for the upgrading of the masses of low paid (largely female) workers. (For further material on women in the labour force in the 1980s see Section 16.)

(adapted from 'Society at Work' in **New Society**, 2 August 1984, p. 72; 8 November 1984, p. 222; 20/27 December 1984, p. 477).

1. Briefly summarize the trends shown in the graph on women's pay in relation to men's.   (2)
2. What evidence does the graph provide which suggests that the effects of the Equal Pay Act were fairly short-lived?   (3)
3. What percentage of low paid workers is made up of women? (2)
4. Briefly assess the three suggestions to improve women's pay.(6)
5. a Why did many women fall outside the scope of the Equal Pay Act?   (2)

   b How did the 1984 amendment bring them within the scope of the Act?   (2)

   c How effective do you think the amendment will be in raising women's pay?   (3)

Section 13 Population

The study of population is known as demography. It involves the measurement of the size of populations and of births, deaths and migration which account for changes in population size. Demography also involves an examination of the factors which underlie changes in population. If, for example, the number of births in a society rises rapidly, demographers will try to explain this change in terms of the possible influence of social, political and economic factors. They will also be concerned with the consequences of population change. Thus they will consider the effects on society of a rapid rise in births.

This section concentrates on the population of Britain over the past 150 years. It begins however with a brief examination of population in the Third World – the countries of Asia, Africa and Latin America.

World population is growing at what many consider an alarming rate. Much of this growth is occurring in Third World countries due mainly to a dramatic decline in the death rate. This decline in mortality has been largely due to a successful fight against infectious and contagious diseases such as malaria, cholera, smallpox, tuberculosis and dysentery. With little change in the numbers of babies being born but with a rapid decline in the numbers of people dying each year, the size of the population increases. This can be seen from the size of India's population which in 1951 stood at 361 million, in 1960 – 429 million, in 1970 – 539 million, in 1980 – 659 million and in 1984 – 746 million. In an attempt to reduce population growth many Third World countries have introduced programmes of birth control. The following extract considers one such programme in India.

1 Population and the Third World

A project known as the Khanna Study was India's first major programme of birth control. It was conducted in seven villages with a total population of 8,000 people. The programme, financed by the Rockefeller foundation in the USA and the Indian government, lasted six years and cost a million dollars. It was a failure. Some of the reasons why people 'failed' to accept family planning are given in the following extract. It is a summary of some of the main findings of a book by Mahmood Mamdani who conducted research in Manupur, one of the villages in the Khanna Study.

One of the foundation stones of the Khanna Study was the belief that people were having more children than they actually wanted – because they were still working on the assumption (thankfully no longer true) that half their children would die in infancy. But from months of talking to the villagers of Manupur, Mamdani concludes that 'an overwhelming majority of the people in the Khanna Study area have a large number of children not because they overestimate their infant mortality rates (the proportion of infants dying between birth and one year) but because they **want** large families. More important, they want them because they **need** them.'

The majority of people in Manupur need children because they are poor. The work of staying alive is hard work – and they cannot afford to buy labour-saving machines or to pay other people for the help they need.

From a very early age, the children of Manupur make a vital contribution to the family well-being. They look after cattle; they help with sowing crops, weeding and harvesting; they bring in the family's water supply and take the food out to the fields at midday (jobs which can take several hours); they help with household jobs – sewing, cleaning, cooking and washing. For one who labours in the field, the day centres around work. Time for relaxation or for tending to personal needs is usually found between different types of work. Without children to help, the workload can become unbearable and more stress and suffering is often the result.

A man and his wife who pray for many children can hardly be expected to respond enthusiastically to family planning programmes.

What is more, children are often the only 'insurance' for the poor. Without children, there is no help or support in illness or old age – and illness is frequent and old age can begin at 40.

Youngsters in an Indian village collecting cow dung to be used as manure

The land dominates life in Manupur. 95% of the people earn their living directly or indirectly from agriculture. The poor, the majority, are those with the least land. And the less land a farmer has, the more labour per acre he needs – for he cannot afford labour saving machines like tube wells or cutting machines or tractors – which are in any case uneconomical for very small plots.

So the farmers who need labour most are the ones least able to afford it. And children are the only answer. Farmer after farmer in Manupur told Mamdani that the cost of having children was almost negligible compared with the benefits they bring.

(from 'The myth of population control', **New Internationalist**, May 1974, pp. 18–19)

1. What is the connection between farming, poverty and family size? (6)
2. Why are children in Manupur seen as 'insurance' by their parents? (3)
3. How might a Welfare State on the British lines encourage the people of Manupur to have fewer children? (4)
4. What does the reference to religion in the extract suggest about the importance of children to the people of Manupur? (2)
5. Freely available contraceptives and knowledge about their use are not enough, in themselves, to reduce the birth rate. Discuss this statement with reference to the passage. (5)

2 The death rate in England and Wales

The death rate refers to the number of deaths per thousand of the population per year. In England and Wales the death rate fell steadily during the last century. In 1770 it is estimated at 32 per 1000, by 1870 it had fallen to 20 per 1000. The fall continued until 1920 when the rate levelled off and has remained largely unchanged to the present day. Changes in the death rate are shown on the graph. The passage that follows considers some of the possible reasons for the decline in the death rate in England and Wales.

During the last century medical science was primitive compared with today's standards. A vast range of 'cures' was available but few were effective. Some simply relieved pain, such as drugs derived from opium. A variety of purgatives effectively emptied the bowels but didn't cure anything. At best few medicines did anything other than give patients the impression that something was being done for their ailments.

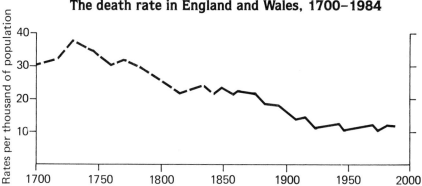

The death rate in England and Wales, 1700–1984

(Registration of births, marriages and deaths began in 1847. Recent historical research suggests that death rates recorded during the early years of registration under-estimate the actual figures) (from **Population Trends 5**, HMSO, London, 1976, and **Social Trends 16**, HMSO, London, 1986, p. 26)

Surgery offered even less hope. Anaesthetics were not available until the close of the last century and deaths following surgery were common. Surgeons sometimes commented that the operation was successful but the patient died.

Sanitation, particularly during the first half of the nine-teenth century, was appalling by today's standards. The following description of a street in Bethnal Green in London's East End given by Dr. Southwood Smith in 1838 provides a flavour of the times: 'Along the centre of the street is an open, sunk gutter, in which filth of every kind is allowed to accum-ulate and putrefy. A mud bank on each side commonly keeps the contents of the gutter in their situation; but sometimes, and especially in wet weather, the gutter overflows; its contents are poured into the neighbouring houses and the street is rendered nearly impassable. The privies are close upon the footpath of the street, being separated from it only by a parting of wood. The street is wholly without drainage of any kind. Fever constantly breaks out in it and extends from house to house.'

Improvements in sanitation dating from the last half of the nineteenth century were probably far more significant in reducing the death rate than the slow advance of medical

Advertisements such as this reflect the growing concern for children's health at the turn of the century science. The provision of piped water and effective sewage disposal systems (in 1865 the new London sewage system was officially opened by the Prince of Wales) plus improvements in hygiene in the home, such as flush toilets, led to a significant decrease in diseases such as typhus and dysentery.

However improved nutrition probably had the greatest effect on the death rate. Recent evidence from developing countries in the Third World shows a close link between diet and death rates. In particular, the more nutritious the food, the lower the infant and child death rates. From 1770 to 1870 infant mortality in England fell from over 200 per 1000 to just over 100 per 1000. During this period the virulence of common infectious diseases such as scarlet fever diminished – they were much less likely to kill. This may well have been due to the fact that people were better fed and so more able to ward off the worst effects of such diseases.

From the late nineteenth century onwards medical science began to reduce the death rate. During the early years of this century increasing attention was given to maternity and child welfare and local authorities began to assume responsibility for the health of children in schools. In later years innoculations were available against many of the common infectious diseases. Their main effect appears to be in the areas of infant and child mortality. However the major fall in infant and child death rates occurred during the first half of this century. The most effective drugs – sulphonamides and antibiotics – and the establishment of widespread immunization date from the 1940s and 50s.

(adapted from **People Populating** by Derek Llewellyn-Jones, Faber, London, 1975, pp. 190–194 and 'Population' by Roger Gomm in **Fundamentals of Sociology** edited by P. McNeill and C. Townley, Hutchinson, London, 1981, p. 327)

1. Briefly summarize the changes in the death rate shown in the graph. (3)
2. Assess the effect of medical science on the death rate in
   a the last century (3)
   b this century (3)
3. There has been a significant decline in absolute poverty during the first half of this century. What effect might this have had on the death rate? (5)

The 'Water King of Southwark' reigning over the polluted River Thames (cartoon by George Cruikshank, 1828).
The inhabitants of Southwark had to boil their water and skim off the scum to make it drinkable.

4. With reference to the information in the passage, suggest why the death rate for members of the working class has been consistently higher than the rate for members of other social classes.   (6)

3 Birth and fertility rates in England and Wales (1)

This passage considers the main trends in birth and fertility rates in England and Wales over the past 100 years. It also examines some of the reasons put forward for changes in these rates. The birth rate refers to the number of live births per thousand of the population per year. The fertility rate refers to the number of live births per thousand women of childbearing age (15–44) per year.

In Britain, as in other Western industrial societies, there has been a steady decline in the birth rate over the past 100 years. This is mainly due to a decline in fertility – women are producing fewer children – and as a result the average size of families has grown smaller.

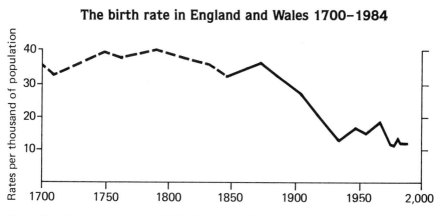

The birth rate in England and Wales 1700–1984

(from **Population Trends 5**, HMSO, London, 1976, and **Social Trends 16**, HMSO, London, 1986, p. 25)

There seems to be a link between the fall in the death rate and the fall in the fertility rate. In pre-industrial Europe there was an extremely high rate of infant and child mortality and only about 50% of children survived to adolescence. This meant that a family which produced six children (the average for the time) could only expect three or four to reach adulthood. Today almost all children survive beyond adolescence. A present day couple therefore needs a fertility rate of only half their pre-industrial counterparts to produce families of the same size. In Britain birth and fertility rates declined significantly between 1870 and 1920, a period when the death rate, especially for infants and children, also fell steadily.

The 1870s mark the beginning of the decline in fertility in Britain. It began in the upper and middle classes, in the families of military and naval officers, lawyers and doctors, with dentists, teachers and clerks not far behind. The years 1850–70 saw a rapid expansion of middle class occupations and a growing demand for the status symbols of a middle class lifestyle – large houses, expensive food and wine, servants, carriages and holidays abroad. The prosperity of these years was followed by the so-called 'Great Depression' of 1870–90. Although it was not particularly serious in economic terms, many people at the time thought it was. Rather than put their standard of living at risk many middle class families decided to cut down on what was becoming an increasingly expensive item – children.

The growing expense of children was partly due to the fact that education was becoming increasingly lengthy and costly. Qualifications were becoming more important for entering professions such as medicine and law and for a career in the army and civil service. Fees for public schools for the rich and private schools for the nearly rich cut deeply into many family budgets.

At the very time when infant and child mortality was steadily falling, children were becoming more expensive. The combination of these factors probably led many parents to decide to limit the size if their families. Developments in contraceptive techniques helped to provide the means for doing this. During the second half of the nineteenth century the discovery of vulcanization (a process which increases the elasticity and strength of rubber) led to the condom (contraceptive sheath) being manufactured in rubber. Around 1880 the vaginal diaphragm and cervical cap appeared. Increasing publicity was given to birth control. In 1877 Charles

Bradlaugh and Annie Besant were prosecuted for encouraging the publication of Charles Knowlton's **Fruits of Philosophy** which described methods of contraception. Within three months 125,000 copies had been sold. This century has seen the development of increasingly effective methods of birth control, such as the coil and the pill, which was intro-duced in the early 1960s. There has also been a more general acceptance of the idea of family planning. The Family Planning Association was started in 1930 and in the same year the Church of England accepted the use of artificial tech-niques of birth control. However it is important not to exag-gerate the effect of advances in birth control techniques. Research has shown that the decline in births in the 1930s in Britain and the Western world was achieved mainly by with-drawal (coitus interruptus), abstinence (refraining from sexual intercourse), late marriage and probably widespread illegal abortion.

Decline in working class fertility was somewhat slower than in the middle classes. The financial benefits of children were steadily reduced throughout the last century. A series of factory acts limited child labour. In 1880 school attendance was made compulsory up to the age of 10, in 1893 up to the age of 11 and in 1899 up to the age of 12. The process has continued during this century with the school leaving age being raised to 16 in 1973. The development of the Welfare State with measures such as old age pensions and unemploy-ment benefits meant that parents had less need to rely on their children for support. As Rowntree's three studies of York (1899, 1936, 1950) indicated, the extent of absolute poverty declined significantly during the first 50 years of this century. Rising working class living standards meant that parents were less likely to look to their children for financial assistance.

Despite the economic advantages of smaller families, old attitudes die hard. Willmott and Young recount the following incident from their study in the early 1950s of Bethnal Green, a traditional working class community in the East End of London. A woman was persuaded by a social worker to have a contraceptive cap fitted. Two months later she was pregnant again. Asked what had happened she said, 'My husband wouldn't have it. He threw it on the fire.' Apparently he saw the device as a threat to his masculinity.

However attitudes do change. During this century working class fertility steadily declined though it remained significantly higher than that of the middle class. By the late 1960s class differences in family size were not significant though working class fertility still remained slightly higher than that of the middle class.

(adapted from **Human Societies** edited by Geoffrey Hurd, Routledge & Kegan Paul, London 1973, 'Population' by Roger Gomm in **Fundamentals of Sociology** edited by P. McNeill and C. Townley, Hutchinson, London, 1981 and **Population** by Roland Pressat, Penguin, Harmondsworth, 1973)

1. Briefly outline the changes in the birth rate shown on the graph.
(4)
2. Infant and child mortality rates for the working class have always been higher than those for the middle class. How might this help to explain social class differences in fertility? (4)
3. What evidence does the extract contain to suggest that advances in contraceptive techniques may have had little effect on the birth rate until recent years? (4)
4. The decline in fertility is due mainly to economic factors. Briefly outline the evidence to support this view with reference to
a the middle class (4)
b the working class (4)

4 Birth and fertility rates in England and Wales (2)

Although the overall trend in birth and fertility rates is downward, there have been a number of fluctuations in the rates. This section examines the ups and downs in the birth rate during this century and looks at some of the reasons suggested for these fluctuations.

The birth rate in England and Wales 1900–1984

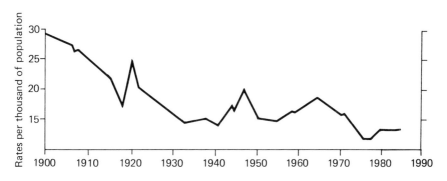

(from **Population Trends 1**, HMSO, London, 1975, p. 6, **Annual Abstract of Statistics 1982**, HMSO, London, 1982, p. 35 and **Social Trends 16**, HMSO, London, 1986, p. 25)

The two World Wars – 1914–18 and 1939–45 – were followed by sharp but shortlived rises in the birthrate. This appears to be mainly due to postponed births. The separation of men from home and families prevented many marriages and births within existing marriages.

The rapid increase in the birth rate shortly after World War 1 was followed by a steady decline. Part of this was due to a return to peace-time conditions, part to the fact that the large number of men killed in World War 1 meant that there were not enough husbands to go around and part to the severe economic depression during the early 1930s. With up to 20% of the working population unemployed, many marriages were postponed, the proportion of people getting married fell and fertility declined. The increase in the birth-rate from the mid-1930s to 1947 was probably due in part to people getting married at an earlier age and a higher proportion of people getting married rather than any change in completed family size.

Since 1947 there has been a number of fluctuations in the birth-rate but family size has remained much the same at between two and three children. The ups and downs in the birth-rate do not appear to reflect decisions to have more or less children. Rather they are due to decisions about **when** to have children. Thus the rise in the birth rate from 1954 to

1964 appears to be due to a change in timing. Previously many women had continued to work for a number of years after marriage before having children. However from 1954 to 1964 many women decided to have their children soon after marriage. This coincided with births by older women who had put off starting a family. The result was a 'baby boom' with births being crammed together in a fairly short time period. As a result of this babies were relatively thin on the ground during the late 1960s and early 70s.

Since 1964 the birth rate declined steadily until 1977 when it began to rise again. Despite this rise the fertility rate is low compared with past rates and is some 10% below that needed for the long-term replacement of the population. The fertility rate (live births per 1000 women aged 15–44) for England and Wales dropped from 93.0 in 1964 to 84.3 in 1970 to an all time low of 58.7 in 1977. It rose to 65.0 in 1980 then dropped to just under 60 from 1982 to 1984. The most dramatic fall was for the youngest age group, those aged under 20, for whom the number of births per thousand women almost halved between 1971 and 1984. This reflects the recent trend for women to delay starting their families perhaps because of economic circumstances or for career reasons. If the pattern of the late 1970s and early 1980s continues, average family size will drop below two children. However, as the evidence in this passage indicates, it is not possible to make firm predictions about future birth and fertility rates on the basis of figures from so short a time period.

Figures from the 1970s and early 1980s may indicate that people want fewer children rather than indicating postponed births. If so the means for achieving this are increasingly available – effective contraception to prevent pregnancies and legal abortion to end unwanted pregnancies. The following graphs provide an indication of the possible effects of these developments.

Live births 1961–1984 (United Kingdom)

Abortions 1969–80 (England and Wales)

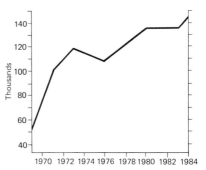

(adapted from **An introduction to Population Geography** by W. F. Hornby and M. Jones, Cambridge University Press, Cambridge, 1980, p. 58 and **Social Trends 16**, HMSO, London, 1986, p. 25)

(adapted from **Social Trends 16**, HMSO, London, 1986, p. 44)

(adapted from **Human Societies** edited by Geoffrey Hurd, Routledge & Kegan Paul, London, 1973, 'Births and family formation patterns' by David Pearce, **Population Trends 1**, HMSO, London, 1975, 'Population' by Roger Gomm in **Fundamentals of Sociology** edited by P. McNeill and C. Townley, Hutchinson, London, 1981 and **Social Trends 12**, HMSO, London, 1982)

1. a Identify the two sharpest rises in the birth rate shown on the graph at the beginning of the passage. (2)
   b What explanation can be provided for these rises? (2)
2. What evidence does the passage contain to suggest that economic factors can affect the birth rate? (2)
3. Fluctuations in the birth rate reflect changes in the timing of births rather than changes in family size. Briefly explain this statement and outline the evidence given in the passage which supports it. (5)
4. With reference to the graph and passage, suggest why it is foolish to predict future birth and fertility rates on the basis of evidence from the past five years. (5)
5. What do the graphs at the end of the passage indicate about the possible effects of the pill and legal abortion on fertility rates? (4)

5 Why do women live longer than men?

In all Western societies and for all age groups the death rate for females is significantly below that for males. Why this should be so is far from clear. Research in this area is limited and it is not possible to reach any firm conclusions. The following passage examines some of the suggestions that have been made to explain sex differences in mortality.

Death rates of males compared to females (female rates taken as 100)

age in years

	0-5	5-10	10-15	15-20	20-25	25-35	35-45	45-55	55-65	65-75	75-85	85+
1846-50	116	103	95	91	104	94	99	113	112	111	109	107
1966-70	130	150	156	253	223	156	139	164	206	191	153	125

(from 'The surplus of women' by Barbara Preston, **New Society**, 28 March 1974, p. 762; reproduced with permission)

The table shows that the death rates of males compared to females have changed since the last century. In 1846–50 a higher proportion of women than men died between the ages of 10 and 45. Many women died in childbirth and from diseases related to childbirth. Also more women than men died from tuberculosis. Since 1850 the death rate for both sexes has declined significantly but the decrease has been greater for females. This is partly due to fewer pregnancies and developments in ante-natal and post-natal care which have reduced deaths associated with childbirth. The extent of tuberculosis has been greatly reduced as a result of better nutrition, advances in medicine, improved ventilation in homes and a reduction of air pollution.

By 1926–30 the death rate for males was higher than the rate for females in every age group. By 1971 a boy aged one could expect to live, on average, to the age of 69.4 years, a girl to the age of 75.4 years. The growing gap between male and female death rates has been attributed to three main causes of death 1) heart disease (by far the most important) 2) lung cancer 3) bronchitis and emphysema (a disease of the lungs). These diseases kill more men than women. They are strongly associated with smoking. In the case of heart disease before the age of 65, the risk for smokers is two or three times greater than for non-smokers. Considerably more men smoke than women.

A variety of explanations has been advanced to account for sex differences in mortality. Some researchers argue that biologically based or genetic differences between the sexes are an important factor. They point to the fact that more males than females die in the womb and in the first year of life and claim that this indicates that genetic factors are important. It has also been suggested that hormone differences between the sexes explain the relatively low rate of heart disease among women. However, there is as yet no firm evidence to prove that sex differences in mortality are biologically based.

A second type of explanation sees gender roles as a major reason for the differences in male and female death rates. The culturally defined roles of men are seen to expose them to greater risks of death than the roles ascribed to women. For example, it is socially more acceptable for men to smoke and drink. Men are supposed to shrug off ill-health and not give in to illness. This may explain why women report more illness than men, see the doctor more often and spend more time in hospital. Men are socialized to be more aggressive than women and to take greater risks. This may account for the fact that in Britain in 1971 over twice as many males than females died in road accidents. However this may be simply due to the fact that more men drive cars and motorcycles.

As Section 10 has shown, there are 'men's jobs' and 'women's jobs' in the labour market. Some researchers claim that sex differences in mortality are job related. The US Metropolitan Life Insurance Co. lists the following most dangerous jobs in order of danger. Most come under the heading of 'men's jobs'.

1) sponge diving
2) motorcycle racing
3) trapeze and high-wire artists
4) structural steel workers
5) lumbermen
6) bank guards
7) munitions and explosives workers
8) coal miners

Typical male illnesses from middle age onwards appear to be related to stress. These include heart disease and stomach ulcers. It has been argued that certain jobs produce a high level of stress and that men are much more likely to be found in such jobs. Thus the business executive and the professional, striving for success in a competitive world, may well be under considerable pressure. If they are middle-aged, overweight, work too hard and smoke, they are in a high risk group. Some researchers speculate that the problem of stress is made worse by the fact that males in Western society are not as free to express their emotions as females. Lack of emotional outlet can increase stress.

The movement of women into areas of society traditionally occupied by men may have unfortunate consequences for their health. Figures from the USA show that heart disease and lung cancer are increasing among women. This may be due to the rising number who smoke and work in high stress jobs.

(adapted from 'The surplus of women' by Barbara Preston, **New Society**, 28 March 1974, 'The family, marriage and its relationship to illness' by Ann Oakley in **An Introduction to Medical Sociology** edited by D. Tuckett, Tavistock, London, 1976, **Medical Sociology** by William C. Cockerham, Prentice-Hall, Englewood Cliffs, 1978 and 'Sex, illness and medical care' by Constance A. Nathanson in **Health, Illness and Medicine** edited by G.L. Albrecht and P.C. Higgins, Rand McNally, Chicago, 1979)

1. How can the information in the table be used to show that differences in male and female death rates are not solely due to genetic or biological factors? (3)
2. Men smoke more than women.
   a What reason for this is given in the extract? (1)
   b How might smoking be related to stressful occupations? (2)
   c What link is suggested between smoking and the high male death rate? (2)
3. Women take better care of themselves than men.
   What evidence is contained in the passage which may support this statement? (3)
4. Why are the dangerous occupations listed in the passage usually defined as 'men's jobs'? (3)
5. Briefly outline the suggested relationship between occupational stress and the high male death rate. (3)
6. The Women's Liberation Movement is a threat to women's health.

Briefly discuss this statement with reference to evidence in the passage. (3)

6 The age structure of the population

The population of Western industrial societies has steadily grown older. This process is known as the 'ageing of the population'. Compared to Third World and pre-industrial societies, Western countries have a small proportion of children, a high proportion of old people and a fairly large intermediate group sometimes known as the 'working age group' made up of people from 15–64 years of age. The following population pyramids illustrate the ageing of the population of England and Wales. They are followed by a passage which examines some of the reasons for changes in the age structure of the population and some of the consequences of these changes.

England and Wales: population pyramids for 1881, 1931 and 1981

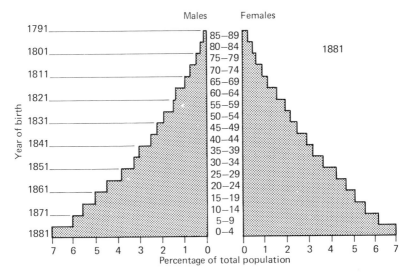

(The figures in the middle of the pyramids show the different age groups. The figures at the bottom of the pyramid show the age groups as a percentage of the population as a whole. Thus in 1981, the age group 0–4 years made up just over 6% of the population).

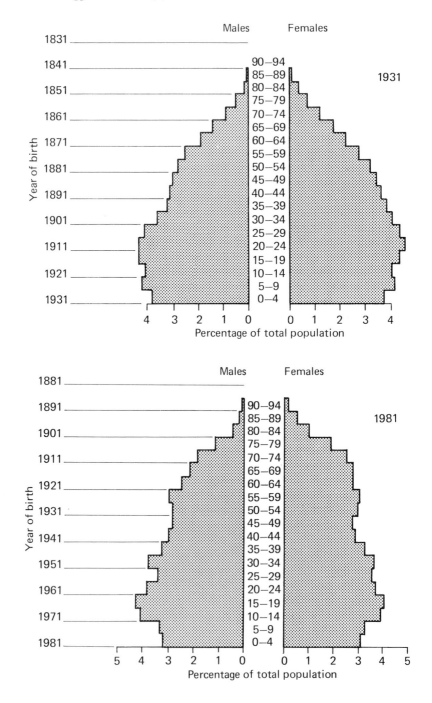

Common sense suggests that the main reason for the ageing of the population is that old people are living longer. However this has only a slight influence on the age structure of the population. In fact the life expectancy of a person aged 70 has increased by only four years since the beginning of this century. The reduction in mortality has led to an increase in the life expectancy of every age group, not just the elderly. In this century the main decline in mortality has been for infants and children. This would lead, if it continued at the same rate, to a rejuvenation of the population. The population would grow younger as increasing numbers of infants and children survived. Why then is the population ageing? The main factor is a decline in fertility. Women are producing fewer children. This means that the proportion of young people in the population grows smaller and the proportion of old people increases. The result is an ageing population.

Although the average life expectancy of a person aged 70 has only increased by four years this century, a lot more people are reaching their seventieth birthday. The decline in infant and child mortality has resulted in a much higher proportion of young people eventually reaching old age. Thus in Britain in 1951, 6.6 million people, 13.6% of the population, were over retirement age, by 1981 the number is estimated to be 9.5 million, 17.7% of the population.

The elderly are often seen as a problem in Western society. With the ageing of the population this 'problem' is seen to be growing. In many pre-industrial societies the elderly are regarded in a very different light. Their status is high, their knowledge is valued, their advice sought and they often hold positions of power and responsibility. In such societies where the pace of change is slow, the knowledge and experience of old people is extremely valuable. In today's industrial societies where the pace of change is rapid, the emphasis is on new skills, new ideas and new techniques rather than traditional knowledge. Some have argued that as a result of this the value and therefore the status of old people falls. A large elderly population will therefore be seen as a problem, as a drain on the nation's resources with little to offer in return.

In Britain men retire at 65, women at 60. They have been phased out, so it is sometimes claimed, to make room for younger people with energy and fresh ideas who can keep pace with a fast changing society. But retirement may simply be another word for unemployment. The lowering of the retirement age, the increasing numbers of people accepting early retirement (and indeed the raising of the school leaving age) may well be an attempt to provide jobs for the rest of the population. The view of the elderly as obsolete, incompetent and 'past it' may be unjustified. This is recognized in the United States where it is illegal to discriminate in jobs against people under 70. Pressure groups like the Grey Panthers fight for the right of the elderly to work and may well have helped the election of a President in his 70s, Ronald Reagan. Rather than seeing old people as a problem, the real problem may be Western economic systems which have so far been unable to provide jobs for everybody who wants to work.

There is no doubt that the present method of dealing with an ageing population is very costly. In Britain about a third of the social welfare budget goes to the elderly, most of it in the form of pensions. Old people occupy half of all National Health Service beds and the average cost to the state for care and treatment of a person over 75 is seven times that of a person of working age. Despite the money spent on the elderly, around two million old people live at or below the poverty line.

The modern nuclear family is not well suited to care for the elderly. The increasing geographical mobility of the work-force means that old people are often separated from their children. The growing number of working wives means they have less time to care for ageing relatives. The decline in fertility means fewer younger relatives at the very time the numbers of old people are growing. Isolation is a serious problem for many old people. About a third live alone and over a third of those over 75 have outlived their children.

(adapted from **Human Societies** by Geoffrey Hurd, Routledge & Kegan Paul, London, 1973, **A Happier Old Age**, HMSO, London, 1978 and 'Old Age', **New Society**, 19 November, 1981)

1. What percentage of the population (to the nearest whole number) does the youngest age group form in a) 1881 and b) 1981?   (2)
2. What percentage of the population (to the nearest whole number) does the age group 60–64 form in a) 1881 and b) 1981?   (2)

3. The changing shape of the population pyramids indicates an ageing population. Show that this is the case with some reference to information from the pyramids. (3)
4. Advances in medical science which have kept **old** people alive longer are the main reason for the ageing of the population. Criticize this statement with reference to information in the passage. (3)
5. Briefly suggest why the knowledge and experience of the elderly would be valuable in a hunting society. (3)
6. In terms of an ageing population, how might the Western economic system, rather than the elderly as such, be seen as the problem? (3)
7. State financial support for the elderly is insufficient. What evidence does the passage contain to support this statement? (1)
8. Why are many old people lonely? (3)

7 Migration

As defined by the government, an immigrant is a person who enters a country with the intention of living there for a year or more – having lived outside the country for at least a year. An emigrant is a person who leaves a country with the intention of living abroad for a year or more – having lived in the country for at least a year. The migration statistics from which the following chart is compiled are based on these definitions.

Net migration: United Kingdom 1901–1984

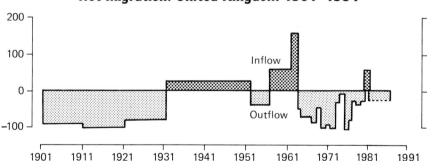

(Net migration is the difference between immigration (inflow) and emigration (outflow). It may be positive (+) in which case more people enter than leave the country or negative (–) in which case more people leave than enter)

(from **Social Trends 16**, HMSO, London, 1986, p. 22. Chart reproduced with the permission of the Controller of Her Majesty's Stationery Office)

Citizenship of immigrants 1984

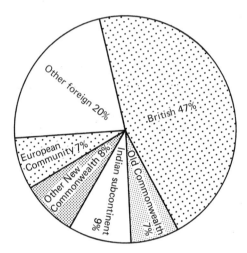

(the Indian subcontinent consists of India, Bangladesh and Pakistan)
(compiled from figures in **Social Trends 16**, HMSO, London, 1986, p. 27)

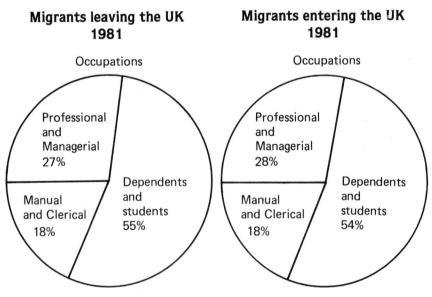

Migrants leaving the UK 1981	Migrants entering the UK 1981

(compiled from figures in **Annual Abstract of Statistics**, HMSO, London, 1985, p. 20)

The traditional picture of a migrant is someone leaving his homeland to start a new life in a far away country. This still happens but today many migrants are simply moving from one country to another for a limited period. They may be students, lecturers, politicians, businessmen or workers on a contract abroad, many of whom have every intention of returning home after a few years. When they do return they will be immigrants in terms of the official definition. During the 1970s no fewer than one third of immigrants into the UK were people born in the UK. Similarly, about one third of emigrants from the UK were born abroad.

From 1901 to 1931 there was a net outflow of people from the UK averaging 80,000 a year (i.e. there were 80,000 more emigrants than immigrants a year). From 1931 to 1951 there was a net inflow due mainly to refugees from Europe. There was a return to net outflow from 1951 to 1956. From 1956 to 1961 there was a net inflow due mainly to immigrants from the New Commonwealth, particularly from the West Indies and the Indian subcontinent (the New Commonwealth includes all Commonwealth countries apart from Canada, Australia and New Zealand which together are known as the Old Commonwealth). Since 1961 (except for 1983–84) there has been a net outflow with Britain returning to its traditional role as an exporter of people.

With the exception of people expelled from a country, such as Jews from Nazi Germany and Asians from Uganda, people come to Britain for much the same reason as they leave. They hope for a better job, an improved standard of living, they may have family ties abroad, they may be restless or dissatisfied with their own country. Some of these reasons probably also account for migrants returning to their country of origin. Figures for West Indian migration suggest that the experience of Britain was not what many had hoped for. From 1970 to 1980 53,000 West Indians migrated to the UK but 54,000 returned to the Caribbean.

(adapted from **Population** by Charles Gibson, Basil Blackwell, London, 1980 and 'International migration: recent trends' in **Population Trends 18**, HMSO, London, 1979)

1. Consider the following statements in the light of the above evidence.
   a Immigrants are black, emigrants are white.   (7)
   b Immigrants are unskilled, emigrants are skilled.   (4)
   c Britain is being swamped by immigrants.   (5)
2. Suggest two reasons why the West Indians who returned to the Caribbean might have been dissatisfied with their experience of British society.   (4)

8 Population changes – United Kingdom

The population of the United Kingdom has grown from just over 38 million in 1901 to over 56 million in 1984. Figure 1 illustrates this growth and includes a projection, based on 1983 figures, of future population size. Figure 2 shows the factors – births, deaths and migration – which have produced these changes in population size. Natural increase refers to the growth in population caused by an excess of births over deaths. Figure 3 looks at the numbers of live births from 1945–1980 and compares them with various projections made at different times.

Figure 1 Population size and projections – United Kingdom

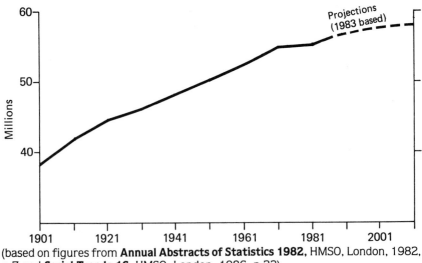

(based on figures from **Annual Abstracts of Statistics 1982**, HMSO, London, 1982, p.7 and **Social Trends 16**, HMSO, London, 1986, p.23)

Figure 2 Population changes and projections – United Kingdom

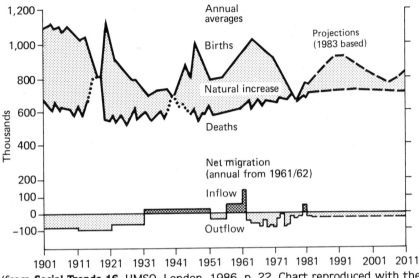

(from **Social Trends 16**, HMSO, London, 1986, p. 22. Chart reproduced with the permission of the Controller of Her Majesty's Stationery Office)

Figure 3 Actual and projected live births in England and Wales

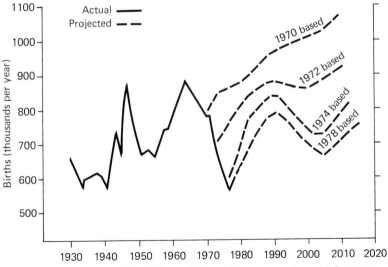

(from **Monitor PP2 79/2**. Office of Population Censuses and Surveys, HMSO, London, 1979)

1. Briefly outline the changes in population size shown in Figure 1.
(3)
2. Assess the effect of migration on changes in population size (Figure 2).
(3)
3. Why did the population of the United Kingdom increase from 1901 to 1980?
(6)
4. From the evidence in Figure 3, now much confidence should be placed on projections of population changes? Present information from the figure to support your answer.
(4)
5. Briefly suggest why governments need to make predictions about changes in the population.
(4)

9 The social effects of the fall in mortality

Death, as the following extract shows, is no longer at the centre of human life.

At the end of the seventeenth century, the life of the average family man, married for the first time at 27, could be summed up thus: born into a family of five children, he had seen only half of them reach the age of 15; he himself had had five children of whom only two or three were alive at his death.

This man, living on average until 52, will have seen about nine people die in his immediate family (not counting uncles, nephews and first cousins), among whom would have been one grandparent (the three others being dead before his birth), both his parents and three of his children.

Nowadays the situation of the average man of 50 is as follows born into a family of three, at 26 he married a girl of 24. The only deaths he has seen have been those of his four grandparents. And he still has one chance in two of living a further 26 years.

In the past, in one out of every two cases, the death of young children occurred before that of their father, and half the remaining children saw their father die before attaining their majority. The average age of the children at the death of their first parent was 14.

In the future, the 'average' man will be 55 or 60 when his father dies. This means that the funds of the family inheritance will almost constantly be in the hands of men and women over 60; about half the private wealth of a nation will be in the hands of old people over 70.

(Fourastie, quoted in **Population** by R. Pressat, Penguin, Harmondsworth, 1973, pp.51–2)

1. Discuss the possible effects of these changes on society and on the lives of individuals.   (20)

Section 14 Urbanization

Towns and cities are a recent development. For 99.9% of its history the human race lived in hunting and gathering bands. These bands led a nomadic existence, moving from place to place, with little in the way of shelter other than tents and brush huts. Jericho, the oldest known city, was built around 10,000 years ago and by 1500 BC towns and cities were spread from Turkey in the west to India in the east.

A town can only exist if there is sufficient food to feed its inhabitants. A hunting and gathering economy does not produce enough food to support a large urban population. In certain areas it has proved possible for small, settled populations to 'live off the land'. For example a permanent population living in stone houses was established in Syria about 10,000 years ago in an area of high natural production – wild grains, fish and animals. However, it was the invention of agriculture which provided the foundation for urban life. Farmers were able to produce enough food both for their own needs and to support urban populations.

The establishment of towns and cities is not, however, the same thing as an urbanized society. A society only becomes urbanized when the majority of its population lives in towns and cities. Britain was the first country to urbanize. The following passage examines this process.

1 Urbanization in Britain

In eighteenth century Britain (1700–1800) most people lived in rural areas and the economy was mainly agricultural. In 1750 the proportion of the population living in communities of 5000 or more was probably not over 16%. By 1851 this proportion had risen to over 50%, by 1900 to 75%. The growth of towns and cities was due to two main factors – migration and natural increase. Migration from rural to urban areas was extensive. In 1851 less than half the inhabitants of

George Cruikshank's (1829) view of urbanization – farm animals, haystacks and trees flee from the march of bricks and mortar.

Manchester, Liverpool and Glasgow had been born in those cities. Natural increase (the excess of births over deaths) also contributed to the growth of urban populations. The migrants tended to be young adults with a higher than average proportion of people in the child bearing age group. The combined effects of migration and natural increase can be seen from the following figures. In 1811 the population of Liverpool was 115,000. By 1851 it had risen to 453,000, an increase of 338,000 of whom 222,000 were migrants.

The move to urban areas was due to a 'push' from the countryside and a 'pull' from the towns. The enclosure movement (enclosing small, scattered landholdings into larger, compact units), new farming techniques (new crops, new systems of crop rotation and selective breeding of sheep and cattle) and the increasing use of new types of agricultural machinery (seed drills, new types of ploughs and threshing machines) led to increased output and a reduction in the labour requirements for agriculture. This provided the food for a rapidly growing urban population and the labour for an industrializing nation. Small farmers and agricultural labourers were 'pushed' off the land – the proportion of the workforce employed in agriculture declined from 33% in 1831 to 15% in 1871 to 7.6% in 1911.

The 'pull' to the towns was due to industrialization and the expansion of trade and commerce. The growth of the big cities such as Liverpool and Glasgow was due partly to the development of overseas trade. However the bulk of urbanization was due to industrialization. It was the application of power – first water power and then steam power in the 1780s – to machinery that changed the unit of production from the family workshop to the factory. Workforces were concentrated around factories in the towns. Typical of these developments were the cotton towns in south-east Lancashire, the woollen towns in Yorkshire, metal-working and engineering in the Midlands' towns and the iron and coal towns of South Wales. The increasing demand for labour and the relatively high wages 'pulled' migrants from rural areas into the towns and cities.

Urban life for the new industrial working class was harsh by today's standards. This is how Dr. Ferriar described cellar dwellings in Manchester in 1796:

Gustave Doré's engraving of Bluegate Fields, London in the 1870s.

Each consists of two rooms under ground, the front apartment of which is used as a kitchen, and though frequently noxious by its dampness and closeness, is greatly preferable to the back room: the latter has only one small window, which though on a level with the outer ground, is near the roof of the cellar; it is often patched with boards or paper, and in its best state is so much covered with mud as to admit very little either of air or light. In this cell, the beds of the whole family, sometimes consisting of seven or eight, are placed. The floor of this room is often unpaved: the beds are fixed on the damp earth. But the floor, even when paved, is always damp. In such places, where a candle is required even at noon-day, to examine a patients, I have seen the sick without bed-steads, lying on rags; they can seldom afford straw.

Particularly during the first half of the nineteenth century, urban life for the mass of the working class was characterized by overcrowding in inadequate housing on unpaved and unlit streets with open sewers, high death rates and widespread poverty. It was not until the second half of the nineteenth century that some of the basic amenities of urban living began to appear (see Section 13:2).

(adapted from **An Economic and Social History of Britain since 1700** by M. W. Flinn, Macmillan, London 1963; **The First Industrial Revolution** by Phyllis Deane, Cambridge University Press, Cambridge, 1965 and **The First Industrial Nation** by Peter Mathias, Methuen, London, 1969).

1. When did Britain become an urbanized society?   (1)
2 a What is migration?   (2)
   b What is natural increase?   (2)
   c How much of the growth in Liverpool's population between 1811 and 1851 was due to (1) migration (2) natural increase? (2)
3. a What are 'push' and 'pull' factors?   (4)
   b Briefly outline the 'push' and 'pull' factors that contributed to urbanization in Britain.   (6)
4. Using evidence from the passage suggest why the death rate in urban areas was high particularly during the first half of the nineteenth century.   (3)

2 The 'loss of community'

Sociology as an academic discipline was born in the nineteenth century. Its founding fathers grew up in a rapidly changing society. They were impressed, concerned and sometimes frightened by what they saw as massive social upheavals caused by industrialization and urbanization. They wished to understand and explain this process. Some of their ideas along with more recent developments from them are examined in the following passage.

For many of the early sociologists the change in their societies was not simply a change in locations from rural to urban settlements. It was a change in social relationships. They saw the whole texture and fabric of the new urban life as fundamentally different. There was a change from the close-knit, 'natural' life of the village to the fragmented impersonal, 'artificial' existence of the city. There was a 'loss of community'.

The German sociologist Ferdinand Tönnies (1855–1936) spelt this out in his distinction between the **gemeinschaft** relationships of traditional society and the **gesellschaft** relationships of industrial society. Gemeinschaft means community and refers to social relationships based on close personal ties centered on the family, the neighbourhood and the church. People have a sense of belonging to the community in which they have been born and raised. By comparison gesellschaft relationships lack depth and warmth, they are superficial, impersonal and calculating. People relate to each other in terms of their roles as shopkeeper, policeman and teacher not as members of the same community who have grown up together and shared many of the same experiences.

Emile Durkheim (1858–1917) saw a similar change when he distinguished between the **mechanical solidarity** of traditional society and the **organic solidarity** of modern industrial society. Traditional society is based on mechanical solidarity. Its unity comes from a shared culture, it is based on tradition and face-to-face relationships. People are united in a social group because they are basically similar. Modern industrial society is held together by organic solidarity. Its parts are different but each is necessary for the functioning of society – just like the different parts in a petrol engine. Industrial society has a specialized division of labour with each occupational group dependent on others. People are becoming increasingly different, fewer aspects of culture are shared and life is centered on the individual rather than the community. Although Durkheim welcomed this change, feeling it would provide more freedom for peole to live their own lives, he feared its consequences. In particular he saw the rapid social change of the nineteenth century producing a situation of **anomie** or normlessness. Traditional norms and social controls were breaking down and had yet to be replaced by new ones. As a result individuals were becoming increasingly rootless, isolated and dissatisfied. Anomie and the breakdown of traditional social controls was seen in the rising rate of suicide, crime and social disorder in urban society.

In America sociologists were making similar contrasts between traditional rural and modern urban life. In his famous essay 'Urbanism as a Way of Life' (1938) Louis Wirth argues that the city dweller tends to be nervous and insecure, he is lost in the crowd and life lacks the depth and meaning of traditional rural society. Relationships with others at work, in shops and on the street are short-lived, shallow, practical and rational.

More recently these sweeping statements about the 'loss of community' have been questioned. Firstly, there is considerable doubt about the rosy picture of rural life presented by some sociologists. Raymond Williams points out that the peasantry in pre-industrial England often lived in poverty, exploited and oppressed by local landowners. He sees the harmony and solidarity of village life as little more than 'a mutuality of the oppressed' – people clung together because they were all stuck in the same rut.

Secondly, the picture of isolation and 'lack of community' in the city has been questioned by a range of studies. Writing in the 1950s about Bethnal Green, a working class borough in the East End of London, Young and Willmott state 'There is a sense of community, that is a feeling of solidarity between people who occupy the common territory which springs from the fact that people and their families have lived there for a long time.' Bethnal Green in the 1950s was a place where 'everybody knew everybody else', where people were born, raised and died on the same or adjoining streets, where relationships between kin and neighbours were often close, supportive and longstanding (see Section 9:4). In **The Urban Villagers**, the American sociologist Herbert Gans describes similar 'village-like' working class and ethnic communities in Boston and New York.

The idea of a 'loss of community' is based in part on an idealised and romantic picture of village life. More recent research has shown that close-knit communities can be found in both rural and urban settlements.

(adapted from **Urban Sociology** by Martin Slattery, Causeway Press, Ormskirk, 1985)

1. Briefly explain the idea of 'loss of community'. (4)
2. The picture of 'traditional society' provided by Ferdinand Tönnies suggests a much more pleasant way of life than that of urban/industrial society. In what ways does it appear more pleasant? (4)
3. Durkheim both welcomed and feared what he saw as the change from organic to mechanical solidarity. Why? (4)
4. How does Raymond William's view of pre-industrial England differ from Tönnies' picture of traditional society? (4)
5. The discovery of 'urban villages' casts doubt on the idea of a 'loss of community'. Explain. (4)

3 Internal migration and de-urbanization

Official statistics on the extent of urbanization are difficult to interpret. The definition of an urban area is complex and debatable. In addition the definition used in 1981 was different from that used in previous years. However whichever definition is used the same general trends appear. These trends are examined in the following passage.

The results of the 1981 census show that nearly 90% of the population of England and Wales lives in urban areas. Despite this high percentage there is an indication that a process of de-urbanization is occurring, a movement of population from urban to rural areas. Since the 1971 census there has been a movement away from larger urban centres – for example the number of people living in areas with a population of over one million fell by 7% between 1971 and 1981. Over the same period the numbers living in smaller urban areas (those with fewer than 50,000 inhabitants) increased by nearly 10%, while the numbers living in rural areas rose by just over 5%. East Anglia, a mainly rural area, has been the region with the fastest population growth – 1.5 million in 1961 rising to 1.9 million in 1983. This growth was due mainly to immigration from other parts of the country (internal migration).

In the 19th century the pattern of migration was from the countryside to the town. In 1885 E. G. Ravenstein published his **Laws of Migration** based on a study of the 1881 census. He stated that

- most movements were over short distances
- any long distance moves usually ended in a large urban centre
- the urban population was less likely to move than the rural population.

Urban centres attracted migrants and tended to hold them.

In the 20th century the pattern of migration changed. It is now one of movement between towns, from town to countryside and of longer distance moves. This is partly due to better transportation (which means that family ties can be more easily maintained) and better information about different parts of the country, especially about jobs.

Changes in industry account for many of the changes in migration patterns. The older industrial areas such as the North West are losing population as traditional manu-facturing industries such as shipbuilding, engineering and textiles decline. New industries able to utilise electricity and oil are not tied to traditional industrial areas near the coalfields as they often where in the last century. There has been a movement of population to the South and the East were job opportunities are greater. Those areas are closer to European markets and have seen the fastest growth in service industries where most of the new jobs have been created in the last 25 years (see section 16:3). The same push/pull factors largely account for the movement from large to small towns and to rural areas. During the past 25 years the decline in manufacturing jobs has been greatest in Britain's largest cities. This decline has been particularly rapid in inner city areas which is part of the reason for the 'flight from the inner cities'. In contrast manufacturing employment has fallen little if at all in small towns and has actually increased in rural areas.

Living standards for most people have risen steadily since 1945. Many people can now afford to move to retirement homes in areas of their choice. Towns on the South coast such as Torquay, Bournemouth and Brighton are favourite spots as are areas such as Dorset and Devon. The surroundings are pleasant and the climate relatively mild. Such migrants may move considerable distances.

The following table shows how the distribution of population in England has changed between 1911 and 1981.

This change is due largely to migration rather than differences in birth and death rates.

Standard Regions of England – Percentage of population 1911 and 1981

	1911	1981
North	7.8	6.3
North West	16.1	13.0
Yorkshire and Humberside	10.7	9.9
West Midlands	9.1	10.5
East Midlands	6.3	7.8
East Anglia	3.3	3.8
South West	7.4	8.8
South East	32.6	34.2

(from **Population Trends** No.36, HMSO, London, 1984)

The following figure shows population changes in various types of urban and rural areas in England and Wales between 1971 and 1981.

Population change, England and Wales 1971–1981

Population, 1981 (millions)   Population change, 1971-81 percentages

London 6.7   −9.9%

Conurbations 11.2   −4.6%

Other large cities 2.8   −5.1%

Smaller cities 1.7   −3.2%

Industrial towns 6.7   + 3.0%

New towns 2.2   + 15.1%

Resorts & retirement areas 3.3   + 4.9%

Partly rural areas 9.5   + 7.0%

Rural areas 5.0   + 10.3%

(based on a table in **The State of the Nation** by S. Fothergill and J. Vincent, Pan Books, London, 1985, p. 10)

(passage adapted from **Social Trends 15**, HMSO, London, 1985, **Population Trends 36**, HMSO, London, 1984.)

1. What is internal migration? (2)
2. East Anglia's population growth is mainly due to internal migration. How else can a population grow? (3)
3. How have patterns of internal migration changed since the last century? (3)
4. Between 1911 and 1981 which region of England experienced
   a the largest growth in its share of the population? (2)
   b the largest decline in its share of the population? (2)
   c suggest reasons for these changes. (5)
5. Briefly summarize the evidence for de-urbanization. (3)

4 The inner city

The 1980s brought recession, industrial decline, rising unemployment, a growth in poverty and public spending cuts. This has affected the nation as a whole but the harshest effects have been felt by those living in the inner cities. The problems of the inner city were focussed by the riots of 1981 and 1985. They have been intensified and brought to a head by the recession. But, as the following passage shows, they are not new.

> The inner city has a long history. It has existed since the birth of the industrial town. This is how Engels described Manchester Old Town in 1844.
>
>> Everywhere, half or wholly ruined buildings, some of them actually uninhabited, which means a great deal here, rarely a wooden or stone floor to be seen in the houses, almost uniformly broken, ill-fitting windows and doors, and a state of filth. Everywhere heaps of debris, refuse and offal; standing pools for gutters, and a stench which alone would make it impossible for a human being, in any degree civilised, to live in such a district.
>>
>> (quoted in Slattery, 1985, p. 59)
>
> Over 130 years later the Liverpool Inner Area Study provided a remarkably similar description of Liverpool's inner city.
>
>> In 1975, eleven per cent of land in the study area was lying vacant, much of it the cleared sites of terraced houses. For those who have to live with the day to day

reality of large, rubble-strewn sites the impact is immediate, unsavoury and depressing. Packs of half wild dogs scavenge among bags of abandoned household refuse. Pools of water collect where badly fitted cellars have subsided. Children build fires with cardboard cartons and the abandoned timber from demolished houses and play among the piles of brick, rubble and broken glass. Half bricks provide a ready and almost endless supply of ammunition for the frequent destruction of the windows of surrounding houses. Mattresses, furniture, gas cookers, prams and even cars that have outlived their usefulness are dumped.

(quoted in Slattery, 1985, p. 60)

Mattresses, prams and cars are not the only things dumped. The inner cities are a dumping ground for people.

For the inner city is a sump for the disadvantaged of every kind, a place to which those with the fewest resources sink, and from which those who gain any freedom of choice escape. It is a place of deprivation, of toil and struggle and isolation, a knacker's yard for society's casualties, a breaker's yard where the pressure of need grinds people against each other and wears them down.

(Harrison, 1985, pp. 30–31).

Inner cities are urban areas with the highest concentrations of bad housing, unemployment, poverty and crime. They are the sites of the older, declining industries – clothing, textiles, shipbuilding and docking. The decline in these industries has led to the shedding of labour and a relative fall in wage rates. The result is rising unemployment and lower incomes. Housing is a mixture of old Victorian terraces now reaching the end of their useful life and more modern council estates, often of the worst possible design. Inner city areas have higher than average concentrations of unskilled and semi-skilled manual workers and high levels of unemployment. People live there because they cannot afford to live anywhere else.

Something of the pressures and problems of inner city life can be seen from the following quotations taken from Paul Harrison's study of Hackney, a deprived area in London. A woman describes the problems of low income.

'When we have to break into the rent money to pay the milk, that really gets us arguing, and once we start, we're down on each other's throats all night. It isn't fair that we have to suffer like this. We don't ask much out of life, just a little money to buy food and decent clothes.'

An unemployed man talks about the future.

'I got no plans, I just take it as it comes. What's the worth of thinking ahead? The only time you can think ahead is if you've got money. If you made plans, you'd only be disappointed. They wouldn't work out any way.'

An old age pensioner talks about her fears of burglary.

'After my last break-in I had a special chain and alarm bell fitted, but I still think about burglars all the time. I lie in bed at night and worry. I think, what if they got in? If my alarm bell went off at night, I'd die of fright.

My son set it off once by mistake, and I nearly had a heart attack.'

Paul Harrison argues that the problems of the inner city are not primarily caused by the city itself or by the people who live there. Their lives are shaped by events outside the inner city, by economic and political processes beyond their control. Inner city life is lived by people at the bottom of the class structure, people who are powerless to change their situation, people the rest of the country has turned its back on and would prefer to forget. Class is the problem and the only real solution is more equality, a redistribution of income and wealth. People need money to escape from inner city life. Harrison concludes,

> But I doubt whether any policy aimed at particular deprived areas can solve the inner-city problem, because the local problem is the symptom of national diseases. Improve one particular location, and another inner-city area would burst forth elsewhere. Dress and heal the open sore in Hackney, and another will erupt in Tottenham or Leyton. As long as British society continues to generate an under-class on low incomes with insecure jobs or no jobs, and without adequate education, new inner-city areas will continue to arise wherever housing is significantly worse than average.

(adapted from **Inside the Inner City** [revised edition] by Paul Harrison, Penguin, Harmondsworth, 1985 and **Urban Sociology** by Martin Slattery, Causeway Press, Ormskirk, 1985)

1. Inner cities are 'dumps' in more ways than one. Briefly explain this statement.   (4)
2. Why is unemployment particularly high in the inner cities?   (4)
3. Why is life in the inner cities stressful?   (6)
4. The problems of the inner cities cannot be solved by the people who live there. Why not?   (6)

Section 15 Work and Leisure

This section goes from what many people see as one extreme to the other – from work to leisure. It begins by looking at different types of production technology – the technology used to produce goods – and examines their influence on people's experience of work. It moves on to a more general consideration of the question of job satisfaction which sociologists have examined from several different viewpoints. Although to many people work and leisure are very different things, research has indicated that they may be closely related. The section goes on to consider the view that the work people do has an important influence on their leisure activities.

1 Assembly line production

Production technology – the technology used to produce manufactured goods – can have an important influence on the behaviour and attitudes of workers and the amount of satisfaction they derive from their work. The following extract taken from Arthur Hailey's novel **Wheels** looks at the assembly of motor cars on a production line. It reflects the findings of a number of sociologists who have studied assembly line production.

> But neither pay nor good fringe benefits could change the grim, dispiriting nature of the work. Most of it was physically hard, but the greatest toll was mental – hour after hour, day after day of deadening monotony. And the nature of their jobs robbed individuals of pride. A man on a production line

lacked a sense of achievement; he never made a car; he merely made, or put together, pieces — adding a washer to a bolt, fastening a metal strip, inserting screws. And always it was the identical washer or strip or screws, over and over and over and over and over and over and over again, while working conditions – including an overlay of noise – made communication difficult, friendly association between individuals impossible. As years went by, many, while hating, endured. Some had mental breakdowns. Almost no one liked his work.

Thus, a production line worker's ambition, like that of a prisoner, was centred on escape. Both a temporary breakdown of the line and absenteeism provided partial escape; so did a strike. All brought excitement, a break in monotony.

(from **Wheels** by Arthur Hailey, Souvenir Press, London)

1. Identify three reasons given in the passage for the dispiriting effect of assembly line work. (3)

2. With some reference to the extract, suggest why assembly line
   workers often feel powerless.   (3)
3. Identify the three ways noted in the passage which allow 'partial
   escape' from the problems of working on the line.   (3)
4. Briefly suggest why these methods of escape provide at least
   short-term relief for the workers.   (3)
5. Why do pay and 'good fringe benefits' appear so important to
   assembly line workers?   (3)
6. Why are relationships between assembly line workers and
   management often hostile?   (3)
7. With some reference to the passage briefly suggest how
   assembly line work might influence the worker's life beyond the
   shop floor.   (2)

2 Craft technology

The American sociologist Robert Blauner claims that workers will
experience satisfaction from their work if 1) they feel they are able
to control their work 2) they find a sense of purpose and meaning
in their work 3) they feel a part of a social group at work and 4)
they become involved and are able to express themselves in their
work. These ways of experiencing satisfaction from work are
largely unavailable to the assembly line workers described in the
previous extract. In Blauner's terminology they are 'alienated' or
cut off from their work. He argues that their alienation is due to
the production technology used in the assembling of motor cars.

Blauner contrasts assembly line production with craft
production using the craft printer as an example. His study was
conducted before mechanical typesetting was widely used.
Blauner found that the craft printer's experience of work was very
different from that of the assembly line worker. He argues that
this is due mainly to the different production technologies
employed.

> Printing technology is still relatively 'underdeveloped' with
> much of the work done by hand rather than machine. The
> essential feature of a craft technology is the lack of stan-
> dardization of the product. Printers turn out new editions of
> newspapers, new magazines and new books every day. Since

the product they work on is constantly changing, it has been more difficult to standardize the work process.

In a craft technology, the worker sets his own pace of work because he must be able to take special pains when the process requires it. Since operations aren't standardized and craftsmen are responsible for a high quality product they need time to 'putter' and to perfect their work. When hand compositors are working up a page form they must insert an unspecified number of empty metal lines or spaces on various columns of the page so that the lines of type are spread evenly. When pressmen make ready the presses and page forms for final printing, they must make a large number of elaborate and unpredictable adjustments. A printing craftsman not only sets his own work rhythm, he is free from pressure on the job.

The freedom to determine techniques of work, to choose one's tools and to vary the sequence of operations is part of the nature and traditions of craftsmanship. Because each job is somewhat different from previous jobs, problems continually rise which require a craftsman to make decisions. Traditional skill thus involves the frequent use of judgement and initiative, aspects of a job which give the worker a feeling of control over his environment.

Craftsmen generally have considerable freedom of physical movement since they do not work on conveyor belts or other machines which control their pace. Printers can usually walk anywhere they want, not only on the shop floor but also to editorial offices and other parts of the plant.

Craft technology does not involve the elaborate subdivision of work characteristic of mass production. A craftsman may no longer be a 'jack-of-all-trades' who makes the entire product himself; still his work is always quite varied and he continues to work on a large segment of the product. His craft training is very broad rather than narrowly specialized.

(from **Alienation and Freedom** by Robert Blauner, University of Chicago Press, 1964, pp. 35, 36, 45, 50)

1. Compared with assembly line workers, craft printers have considerable control over their work.
   a Show that this is the case with reference to the extract.   (4)

    b Why does this control mean that printers work under less pressure than car assemblers? (2)

2. Craft printing requires the 'frequent use of judgement and initiative'.

    a Explain this statement using examples from the extract. (3)

    b Why does this make craft printing a relatively interesting and involving job? (3)

3. Assembly line workers have very specialized and narrow tasks.

    a How does this differ from the work of craft printers? (2)

    b As a result of this why might craft printers derive more meaning and sense of purpose from their work? (3)

4. Craft printers often take a pride in their work. Briefly suggest why this is so. (3)

3 Micro-chip technology

Fiat proudly boasts that its cars are 'hand-built by robots'. Journalists can now type their stories directly into a computer which can prepare them for printing. The assembly line worker and the printer are steadily being made redundant by micro-chip technology. The heart of this technology is a small silicon chip the size of a shirt button. It has the power to perform detailed and complex operations. Examples of micro-chip technology include pocket calculators, cash points at banks, word processors, computer controlled machine tools and robots.

    Craft technology was the typical form of production in pre-industrial society. Goods were largely produced by hand. Industrialization brought mechanization and mass production. Mechanization refers to the use of machines to assist the production process. Thus assembly lines are mechanized – cars are moved from one point to another on the line by machine power. Machines are often used for mass production – the manufacture of large quantities of identical products. Mechanization is taken a step further by automation. Automated production has traditionally been used in the oil and chemical industries. The raw materials enter the production process, the various stages of manufacture are automatically controlled by machines, and the finished product emerges 'untouched by human hand'. The introduction of micro-chip technology means that increasingly complex production processes can now be automated.

Renault R9s move down the assembly line where industrial robots perform the welding with a precision that humans could never match.

Books and articles have poured from the presses predicting the effects of micro-chip technology both on work and on society in general. The following extracts focus on particular instances of the effects of this technology.

> When it is finished early next year, a highly computerised plant in Somerset will be run by one white coated supervisor, who will rarely get his hands dirty and spend most of his time sitting in front of a computer console. He will be helped by just four other workers.
>
> A conventional factory of the same size would require several more machinery operators. It would also need clerical staff, warehousemen and people who push pieces of metal from one machine to another. All these people are absent from the Somerset plant. Thanks to computer technology, its staff of five will do the work of 20. With the new equipment, the five will make £1 million worth of goods per year; an average of £200,000 per person. For the rest of the company's 2000 employees the comparable figure is £17,000.

Initially the machines in the workshop will turn out parts for just one product – bomb release mechanisms for the Tornado military aeroplane. But the machines operate according to computer programs which can be varied by tapping a few buttons on a keyboard. So the equipment is flexible enough to make thousands of other components that could be fitted to products as diverse as engines and pressure valves.

The company's manufacturing director thinks that the labour saving computerised system at the plant will set the pattern for much of British industry. 'I've no doubt that the manufacturing business has got to become increasingly mechanized and automated. Unfortunately, in Britain's present environment this will cause social problems.'

Unemployment could result if engineers install similar hardware in the rest of Britain's engineering industry. Firms could decide to stay with conventional manufacturing techniques that need more people. But that would not reduce the unemployment problems. According to the plant manufacturing director firms that do not automate face troubled times due to competition from others that introduce advanced technology. Many of the former will go bankrupt and again will have to lay off their workers.

(from 'Britain advances in computerised factories' by Peter Marsh. This first appeared in **New Scientist**, London, the weekly review of Science and Technology, 19 March 1981, pp. 751–3)

'How to improve your sec's life' says the caption on a recent ad for Canon's AP Series electronic typewriter. This is a machine which can store up to 20 A4 pages of text electronically, and print it out in immaculate script at the touch of a button.

The crude sexism of the ad's slogan contains the implication that micro-electronics are good for you – or at least for your secretary. This impression is backed up by lavish and glossy publicity material from lots of manufacturers about the office of the future – the so-called 'paperless office', in which elegant young secretaries sit in air-conditioned splendour, smiling into visual display units.

Of course, the future may not turn out to be like the ads. But even if it does, not everyone will be satisfied, least of all women. To understand why, we need to look in more detail at the most important of the new office technologies – word processing.

A word processor is basically a combination of a small computer, a TV set, a typewriter keyboard, and a printer which is about the same size as a modern electric typewriter. Text is typed into the computer via the keyboard, but instead of being printed directly by the printer, is displayed on the TV screen. If desired, it can also be stored electronically on small magnetic discs (called 'Floppy discs' in the trade). The fact that it's stored electronically rather than on paper means that the text is very easy to edit and manipulate: mistakes can be corrected, new material inserted and blocks of text deleted, in a flash.

However the typing pool will not disappear. The only difference will be that the typing job will now have been rather comprehensively deskilled, because skills such as good layout, accurate keystroking and spelling, correct centring of headings – things which give typists pride in their work – will be devalued: they will be programmed into the machine which usually has, among other things, an automatic spelling-correcting programme. In this sense, the new technology reduces the gap between good and bad typists, and thereby eliminates incentives to improve or widen one's skills.

(from 'The processor takes over' by John Naughton, **The Observer**, 14 November 1982, p. 25)

1. a What social problems does the managing director foresee as a result of the increasing automation of British industry? (2)
   b Despite these problems why does he believe that this development is essential? (3)
2. a The word processor means that the job of a typist will be de-skilled. What evidence does the extract provide to support this statement? (3)
   b What effects might this have on job satisfaction? Give reasons for your answer. (4)
   c What effects might deskilling have on typists' bargaining power and wages? Give reasons for your answer (4)
3. Many decisions taken by workers on the shop floor can now be made by others and directly programmed into computers. How

might this affect the power of management? Give reasons for
your answer.   (4)

4 Deskilling

The previous passage introduced the idea of deskilling – reducing
the skill required to perform a task. Since the early 1970s there
has been a large amount of research and debate about the question
of deskilling. The following passage provides a brief introduction
to this area.

In 1974 the American sociologist Harry Braverman published
his ideas about deskilling. Writing from a Marxist point of
view he argued that the main concern of capitalism is profit.
Profits can be increased by reducing labour costs – by
reducing the numbers of workers employed, by paying them
less and by making them work harder. This can be done in
various ways including (1) introducing new technology which
replaces workers by machines (2) reducing the skill needed for
work (deskilling) – unskilled workers are cheaper to employ
than skilled workers (3) increasing management control in
order to get more work from the workforce. Deskilled
workers are easier to control because they can be easily
replaced and their tasks can be designed from above by
management. Skilled workers have more power – they have
greater control over their work, they cannot be easily
replaced and so they can bargain more effectively with
management.

Braverman argues that the history of capitalism is a history
of deskilling, of building workers' skills into machines and
cheapening labour by substituting skilled for less skilled
work. The result is the 'degradation of work' – workers are
degraded, they lose skills, creativity and control over their
work.

Many researchers reject Braverman's view of an evil
capitalist system steadily deskilling workers, grinding them
underfoot and squeezing profits at their expense. However
they do recognise that deskilling does occur, especially with
the introduction of microtechnology. The micro-chip is a

device for copying intelligent human responses. More than any other form of technology it has the capacity for (1) deskilling work and (2) replacing workers. Thus computerised photo-composition in printing has made the traditional craft of compositing obsolete. As one worker said, 'It took me six years, perhaps eight, to learn how to be a good comp and operator. You could take any competent typist from out on the street and I maintain that within two months she would be doing my job.' There are many examples of micro-technology destroying skilled jobs and replacing them with less skilled. The introduction of semi and fully automatic telephone exchanges has resulted in the loss of large numbers of manufacturing jobs. Most craft skills and machinists have been eliminated completely and complex assembly skills have been reduced by smaller and simpler tasks such as wiring.

But microtechnology does not necessarily lead to deskilling. Some workers learn new and higher level skills. A process of 'reskilling' can occur. There are examples of workers programming machines themselves and so raising the level of skill in their jobs. Nor does microtechnology necessarily lead to greater efficiency. If the interest is taken out of work the result is often high labour turnover and absenteeism. Some managers are aware of this problem as the following quotation from a manager in charge of word processing at **Cadbury** shows.

> We must take more account of the job satisfaction element in the future of word processing. On a shared logic system such as ours, the operators are keying in bits and pieces of data dictated to them without ever seeing the finished results of their work in hard copy. We cannot regard typists as automatons; somewhere along the line technology must be applied to making the work interesting as well as efficient.

The cooperation of the workforce is needed for efficiency. To gain this programmes of 'job enrichment' have been created with the aim of increasing interest and involvement in work. They include enlarging jobs (increasing the number of operations performed by each worker) rotating jobs (moving workers from one job to another), increasing worker participation in decisions which affect their work and 'quality circles' (small groups of workers who meet to discuss and solve production problems). At one extreme job enrichment has been seen as a con-trick to encourage workers to accept 'wage-slavery', at the other extreme it has been seen as a means of really improving the quality of workers' lives.

(adapted from **Labour and Monopoly Capitalism** by Harry Braverman, Monthly Review Press, New York, 1974 and 'Work' by Paul Thompson in **Developments in Sociology** Vol. 2 edited by Michael Haralambos, Causeway Press, Ormskirk, 1986)

1. What does the term 'deskilling' mean? (2)
2. How might deskilling lead to higher profits? (4)
3. Why is microtechnology a greater threat to jobs and skills than previous forms of technology? (4)
4. Simply introducing microtechnology does not necessarily lead to increased efficiency. Explain with reference to the passage. (4)
5. Briefly explain how job enrichment can be seen as
   a a con-trick (3)
   b a means of improving the quality of workers' lives. (3)

5 Alienation

So far the extracts in this section have suggested that the amount of satisfaction a person derives from work is influenced by production technology. Marxist theory provides a very different perspective. It argues that if workers are employed by a privately owned company, then they will be alienated no matter what form of production technology they work with. Thus the assembly line worker and the craft printer will both experience alienation if they work in private industry. Neither will be able to derive real satisfaction and fulfilment from his work. Marxist views on alienation are examined in the following passages.

The village blacksmith shop was abandoned, the roadside shoe shop was deserted, the tailor left his bench, and all together these mechanics (skilled workers) turned away from their country homes and wended their way to the cities wherein the large factories had been erected. The gates were unlocked in the morning to allow them to enter, and after their daily task was done the gates were closed after them in the evening.

Silently and thoughtfully, these men went to their homes. They no longer carried the keys of the workshop, for workshop, tools and keys belonged not to them, but to their master. Thrown together in this way, in these large hives of industry, men became acquainted with each other, and frequently discussed the question of labour's rights and wrongs.

Terrance Powderly,
Grand Master Workman, Knights of Labor,
"Thirty Years of Labor", 1889

(quoted in **Schooling in Capitalist America** by Samuel Bowles and Herbert Gintis, Routledge & Kegan Paul, London, 1976, pp. 56-7)

Karl Marx believed that only in a communist society could a person experience true satisfaction and fulfilment from work. In a communist society industry is owned by the people rather than by private individuals. The wealth produced by workers is shared by everybody on the basis of 'to each according to his need'. People therefore work for society as a whole and, since they are members of society, they also work for themselves. In doing so they satisfy their own needs and also the needs of others. Work in a communist society allows people to express their basic human needs – care and humanity for others. As a result workers experience a deep satisfaction from their labour and alienation is a thing of the past.

In capitalist societies such as the USA and the countries of Western Europe, much of industry is privately owned. The owners invest capital (money) in companies in return for a share of the profits. Marx believed that this system resulted in the exploitation of workers. Wealth was produced by their labour but a part of this wealth was taken from them by the owners of industry in the form of profit. People cannot find real satisfaction by working in a system which is based on their own exploitation. In Marx's words, 'the alienated character of work for the worker appears in the fact that it is not his work but work for someone else, that in work he does not belong to himself but to another person.' As a result the worker 'does not fulfil himself in his work but denies himself, has a feeling of misery, not of well-being, does not develop freely a physical and mental energy, but is physically exhausted and mentally debased. The worker therefore feels himself at home only during his leisure, whereas at work he feels homeless.'

(adapted from **Karl Marx: Selected Writings in Sociology and Social Philosophy** edited by T.B. Bottomore and M. Rubel, Penguin, Harmondsworth, 1963)

1. a Who is 'the master' mentioned in the first extract? (2)
   b Why is he referred to as 'the master'? (3)
2. Why do Marxists regard workers in capitalist society as 'wage slaves'? (4)
3. Why do Marxists argue that both craft printers and assembly line workers are alienated if they work in private industry? (4)
4. How might communism end the alienation of the worker? (4)
5. Workers in many communist societies do not appear to be particularly satisfied and fulfilled. Provide evidence to support this statement from your knowledge of communist societies e.g. Russia, Poland and East Germany. (3)

6 Industrial sabotage

Industrial sabotage may be defined as any action aimed at the destruction of the workplace, the plant or machinery used at work or the goods produced. The following extract looks at examples of industrial sabotage.

They had to throw away half a mile of Blackpool rock last year, for, instead of the customary motif running through its length, it carried the terse injunction 'Fuck Off'. A worker dismissed by a sweet factory had effectively demonstrated his annoyance by sabotaging the product of his labour. In the Christmas rush in a Knightsbridge store, the machine which shuttled change backwards and forwards suddenly ground to a halt. A frustrated salesman had demobilized it by ramming a cream bun down its gullet. In our researches we have been told by Woolworth's sales girls how they clank half a dozen buttons on the till simultaneously to win a few minutes' rest from 'ringing up'. Railwaymen have described how they block lines with trucks to delay shunting operations for a few hours. Materials are hidden in factories, conveyor belts jammed with sticks, cogs stopped with wire and ropes, lorries 'accidentally' backed into ditches. Electricians labour to put in weak fuses, textile workers 'knife' through carpets and farm-workers cooperate to choke agricultural machinery with tree branches.

(from 'Industrial sabotage: motives and meanings' by Laurie Taylor and Paul Walton in **Images of Deviance** edited by S. Cohen, Penguin, Harmondsworth, 1971, p. 219)

1. How might a Marxist explain industrial sabotage in capitalist society? (4)
2. Suggest why the jamming of conveyor belts by assembly line workers is a typical example of industrial sabotage. (4)
3. a How might a person feel after having committed an act of industrial sabotage? (3)
   b With some reference to the extract briefly explain why he might feel this way. (4)
4. Suggest two ways, other than industrial sabotage, by which people can express dissatisfaction with their experience of work. Briefly explain your choices. (5)

7 Work, leisure and family life

In the early 1950s a study of the relationship between the work, leisure and family life of coal miners was conducted by Dennis, Henriques and Slaughter in the mining town of Featherstone in Yorkshire. Like a number of similar studies their research indicated that the nature of work influences leisure activities and family life. However a word of caution is necessary. Featherstone is a mining town in which miners form an occupational community. Miners who are less concentrated in occupational communities, such as those in Nottinghamshire, may well have a rather different lifestyle which is less influenced by the nature of their work. In addition, the Featherstone study was conducted in the early 1950s in a traditional working class town. The miners' lifestyle may be due as much to traditional working class sub-culture as to mining itself.

Despite improvements in working conditions, coal miners believe that 'pitwork can never be other than an unpleasant, dirty, dangerous and difficult job'. Many dislike and are even hostile towards their work. Nevertheless men are proud of their status as miners. The strength and skill required for the job are seen as a reflection of the miner's manhood and they are held in high regard in the community.

Mining is a dangerous occupation with a high rate of injury and death. One man's mistake can lead to the death of others. As a result miners develop a sense of unity, of group solidarity, with their first loyalty being to their workmates. A miner's wages are partly determined by the productivity of his work group. This encourages everybody to pull their weight and cooperate as members of a team. Miners share experiences which to some extent set them apart from other workers. They work in extreme and demanding conditions which produce a high level of stress.

The leisure activities of the miners in Featherstone revolve around drinking in pubs and workingmen's clubs with their workmates. Leisure is vigorous, boisterous and frivolous with little thought given to tomorrow. In the company of their workmates miners live for the moment, 'let off steam' and spend much of their time drinking and gambling.

Miners' wives rarely work outside the home due partly to the traditional belief that a wife's place is in the home and partly to the lack of job opportunities for women in the area. Their role is mainly domestic and many are proud of their performance as housewives. Dennis, Henriques and Slaughter write, 'Housewives boast of their attention to the needs of their husbands, and of how they have never been late with a meal, never confronted a returning worker with a cold meal, never had to ask his help with household duties.' Husbands, for their part, feel that it's a 'poor do' if they do not receive this kind of attention. After work they return home to be fed, to get cleaned up, changed and rested and then they are 'off out' with their mates.

(adapted from **Coal is our Life** by N. Dennis, F. Henriques and C. Slaughter, Eyre and Spottiswoode, London, 1956)

1. Why is mining regarded as a 'man's world'?   (3)
2. Why is a miner's first loyalty to his workmates?   (4)
3. Suggest how the nature of work may influence the miner's leisure activities.   (7)
4. a How does a miner see his wife's role?   (2)
   b How might the nature of work influence the way he sees his wife's role?   (4)

8 Work and patterns of leisure

The British sociologist Stanley Parker argues that leisure activities are 'conditioned by various factors associated with the way people work'. He suggests that the amount of autonomy people have at work (the amount of freedom to take decisions and organize their work), the degree of involvement they find in work and level of satisfaction they derive from work are directly related to their leisure activities. Parker bases his findings on a series of interviews he conducted with bank clerks, child care officers and youth employment officers plus published material on a range of occupations studied by sociologists (including the study of coal miners outlined in the previous passage). He sees the relationship between work and leisure falling into three main patterns: the extension pattern, the neutrality pattern and the opposition pattern.

Parker admits that 'considerably more research needs to be done' to confirm his findings. His caution is justified since more recent research indicates that the connection between work and leisure is not as close as his study suggests.

In the **extension pattern** work extends into leisure. Work and leisure activities are similar and work is a central life interest rather than family and leisure. People who follow this pattern have relatively little time for leisure activities as such. Studies of managers in the USA give a picture of all work and no play with a working week of over 60 hours. Non-work time was often spent reading trade journals or keeping fit with the aim of improving performance at work. Even when leisure was used purely for relaxation, nearly three-quarters of the managers in one survey stated that they saw 'leisure time as a refresher to enable you to do better work'. The extension pattern is associated with occupations providing high levels of autonomy, involvement and job satisfaction. Such occupations include those of managers, businessmen, doctors, teachers, social workers and some skilled manual workers.

In the **neutrality pattern** a fairly clear distinction is made between work and leisure. Activities in the two areas differ and family life and leisure, rather than work, form the central life interest. The neutrality pattern is associated with occupations providing a medium to low degree of autonomy, which require the use of only some of the individual's abilities and where satisfaction is with pay and conditions rather than work itself. Hours of leisure are long compared to the extension pattern and are used mainly for relaxation. Leisure is often family-centred involving activities such as the family outing. Occupations typically associated with the neutrality pattern include clerical jobs and semi-skilled manual jobs.

In the **opposition pattern** work is sharply distinguished from leisure. Activities in the two areas are very different and leisure forms the central life interest. Hours of leisure are long and used mainly to recuperate from and compensate for work. The opposition pattern is associated with occupations providing a low degree of autonomy, which require the use of only a limited range of abilities and which often produce a feeling of hostility towards work. The opposition pattern is typical of unskilled manual work, mining and distant water fishing.

(adapted from 'Work and leisure' by Stanley Parker in **The Sociology of Industry** edited by S. R. Parker, R. K. Brown, J. Child and M. A. Smith, George Allen & Unwin, London, 1967)

1. Which patterns do the following activities fall into? Briefly explain your answers.

    a Having a few drinks to escape from work. (2)
    b Wining and dining clients at a restaurant. (2)
    c Taking the children to the zoo. (2)
2. Suggest why many teachers and social workers extend work into leisure. (3)
3. Considering the types of occupations in the neutrality pattern, suggest why work is not extended into leisure. (3)
4. Why do people whose leisure falls into the opposition pattern need to recuperate from and compensate for work? (3)
5. A survey by John Child and Brenda MacMillan of 964 British managers showed that they worked some 20 hours a week less than American managers. They used their relatively long hours of leisure for relaxation and enjoyment. Playing and watching sport, home improvement and hobbies such as photography were major leisure time activities.
    a How can this evidence be used to question Parker's argument? (2)
    b How can the concept of culture be used to explain the differences between British and American managers? (3)

Section 16
Unemployment and the Future of Work and Leisure

Most people's lives are divided between work and leisure. But for a sizeable and growing minority there is a third alternative – unemployment. This section begins with an examination of the problem of defining and measuring unemployment. It looks at the social characterstics of the unemployed and considers the effects of unemployment on men, women and young people. The section also examines changes in employment patterns and the future of work and leisure.

1 Unemployment – definition and measurement

The following passage looks at two questions. (1) What is unemployment? (2) How much unemployment is there is the UK? As the passage indicated, the answers to these questions are not straightforward.

> In the United Kingdom the unemployed are officially defined as those claiming unemployment benefit. The unemployment rate is the number of unemployed as a percentage of the total of employed and unemployed people. However, there is considerable argument about the 'true' extent of unemployment as compared to government figures. For example the TUC (Trades Union Congress) believes that the government has seriously underestimated the actual figure. According the the Department of Employment there were

3,276,861 people unemployed in October 1985. Yet the TUC puts the 'true' figure at around 4.5 million. Why is there such a large difference between these estimates?

Firstly, up to November 1982, the unemployed included all those registered as unemployed at job centres whether they were claiming unemployment benefit or not. Since then official figures have been based only on those actually claiming unemployment benefit. Many of the unemployed are not entitled to benefit. This is often true for married women. They may have been out of employment for some time – for example producing and rearing children – and not kept their national insurance contributions paid up. As a result they are not entitled to unemployment benefit. Or, their previous earnings were below the level at which employers pay national insurance. Again they are not eligible for benefit. Many part-timers and home workers come into this category. The TUC estimates that at least 250,000 people would be added to the unemployment statistics if the 1982 method of calculating unemployment had been retained.

The TUC claims that a second government measure has artificially cut unemployment by a further 200,000. In March 1983 men over 60 who were claiming long-term supplementary benefit were no longer required to sign on at job centres. They ceased to become part of the unemployment statistics.

Thirdly, special training schemes like YTS (Youth Training Schemes) and the Community Programme further reduce the official level of unemployment. According to the TUC they involve another 450,000 who might otherwise register as unemployed.

Finally some people who are entitled to unemployment benefit simply do not claim. They are therefore not included in the official figures.

Thus the numbers of unemployed and the unemployment rate will depend on how unemployment is defined.

The following table provides official statistics on unemployment from 1961 to 1984. It also shows the number of job vacancies notified by employers to job centres (only about one third of all vacancies are notified to job centres).

Unemployed claimants and vacancies : annual averages

	United Kingdom			Thousands and percentages	
	Unemployed (thousands)			Unemployment rate (percentages)	Vacancies (thousands)
	Males	Females	Total		
1961	231	61	292	1.3	214
1971	647	104	751	3.3	131
1976	1,006	296	1,302	5.5	122
1979	930	366	1,296	5.3	241
1980	1,181	484	1,665	6.8	143
1981	1,843	677	2,520	10.4	97
1982	2,133	784	2,917	12.1	111
1983	2,219	886	3,105	12.9	145
Year ending mid-1984	2,176	925	3,101	12.9	156

(from **Social Trends 15**, HMSO, London, 1985, p. 69)

(passage adapted from 'Women and Society' by Sarah Fildes in **Developments in Sociology** Volume 1 edited by Michael Haralambos, Causeway Press, Ormskirk, 1985 and 'New Society Database' in **New Society**, 8 November 1985, p. 268)

1. Bearing in mind that only about one third of all vacancies are notified to job centres, how many people in mid-1984 would be officially unemployed if all vacancies were filled?   (2)
2. According to some researchers various categories of people should not be included in the unemployment statistics. They include:
   (a) claimants who are not really looking for jobs,
   (b) those who have jobs 'on the side' in the 'black economy' and who are claiming benefit illegally,
   (c) 'job changers' who are out of work for 4 weeks or less.
   Briefly consider the justification for excluding each of these groups from the official unemployment statistics.   (9)
3. Assess the TUC claims that the government has underestimated the 'true' figure of unemployment.   (7)
4. Why do you think the government redefined unemployment in the early 1980s?   (2)

2 Who are the unemployed?

Unemployment is not spread evenly throughout the population and across the country. The unemployed tend to be particular categories of people living in certain parts of the United Kingdom. These points are illustrated in the following passage.

> The following table shows the spells of unemployment of a sample of nearly 7000 men aged 18–64 during the twelve months before they were interviewed in the 1983 General Household Survey. It shows that the 18–24 age group has the highest level of unemployment. Non-whites are more likely to be unemployed than whites, manual workers more likely than non-manual. Within the manual working class, semi-skilled and unskilled workers are more likely to experience unemployment than skilled workers.

Male unemployment in the previous 12 months : by age, by colour, and by socio-economic group, 1983

	Great Britain			Percentages and numbers
	No spells of unemployment	1 spell of unemployment	2 or more spells of unemployment	Sample size (= 100%) (numbers)
Males aged (percentages):				
18–24	65	28	7	1,167
25–39	84	14	2	2,554
40–59	88	11	1	2,664
60–64	83	16	1	602
All males aged 18–24	82	15	2	6,987
Colour (percentages)				
White	83	15	2	6,289
Coloured	71	28	1	272
Socio-economic group (percentages)				
Professional/employers and managers	94	5	1	1,546
Intermediate/junior non-manual	89	9	1	1,101
All non-manual	92	7	1	2,647
Skilled manual	83	15	2	2,749
Semi-skilled/unskilled manual	68	28	4	1,468
All manual	77	20	3	4,217

(from **Social Trends 15**, HMSO, London, 1985, p. 73)

Unemployment by region

21.0 N Ireland

15.2 Scotland

18.8

16.1 North

15.7 West Midlands

16.8 North West

12.5 East Midlands

14.8 Yorks and Humber

10.1 E. Anglia

9.7 South East

11.7 South West

Wales

1984 annual average rates in UK %

(adapted from 'New Society Database' in **New Society**, 8 November 1985, p. 268)

Unemployment varies from region to region. Northern Ireland is the worst affected with a rate of 21% in 1984 compared to a UK average of 13.1%. At the other end of the scale the South East had an unemployment rate of 9.7% in 1984.

One of the most worrying trends is the increase in the length of time people are unemployed. This is shown in the following chart (the break in the graph is due to the changes in the official definition of unemployment examined in the previous passage). The number of long-term unemployed – claimants

Unemployment by duration

(from **Social Trends 16**, HMSO, London, 1986, p. 72)

unemployed for more than a year – increased by 15% between April 1983 and April 1984 while total employment increased by only 2%.

1. a Which age groups have the highest and lowest levels of unemployment?   (2)
   b Briefly suggest why.   (4)
2. a Which socio-economic groups have the highest and lowest levels of unemployment?   (2)
   b Briefly suggest why.   (4)
3. a Which regions have the highest and lowest levels of unemployment?   (2)
   b Briefly suggest why.   (4)
4. Why is long-term unemployment growing at a faster rate than unemployment as a whole?   (2)

3 Changes in employment patterns

Since unemployment was recognised as the major social problem of the 1980s. ITV's **News at Ten** has had a regular item on job gains and job losses. The gains tend to be in high tech industries, supermarkets, hotels and catering, the losses in engineering, iron and steel and motor vehicle manufacture. As the following extract shows, this trend has been developing over many years.

A comparison of the 1961 and 1981 censuses shows a major change in the occupational structure. During this period professional, managerial and intermediate white collar jobs (e.g. clerical work) increased by nearly 46%. There has been a significant decline in the numbers of manual workers. There were a million fewer skilled manual workers in 1981 compared to 1961 – a decline of 20%. The number of semi-skilled manual workers fell by over 11%, with the biggest drop – 35% – among unskilled manual workers.

Labour is shifting from agriculture, mining, shipbuilding, textiles, engineering and the old 'smokestack' industries such as iron and steel and moving into the so-called 'sunrise'

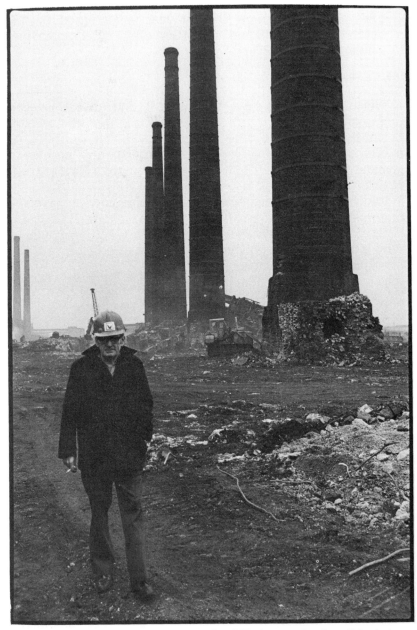

Smokestacks at East Moors steelworks Cardiff, about to be demolished. A man who has spent all his working life as a steel worker at East Moors is now employed to demolish it.

industries of high technology and the service sector – insurance, banking, health, education, hotels and catering. The recession and foreign competition have put many manufacturing companies out of business. Those that remain are shedding labour in order to reduce costs and remain competitive. Manufacturing firms are reducing the numbers of workers on the shop floor and installing new technology that requires more technicians and professionally qualified staff. The Austin Rover chairman Harold Musgrove has forecast, 'The day is nor far off when entire areas of our plants will run automatically with minimal human supervision night and day, seven days a week'. The combined effects of a smaller and increasingly automated manufacturing base can be seen from the following figures. Over a million jobs were

Employment changes, Great Britain 1978–1983 (thousands)

'traditional' industries	job losses	job gains
motor vehicles	− 179	
textiles	− 173	
iron & steel	− 110	
coalmining	− 51	
shipbuilding	− 42	
machine tools	− 23	
'growth' industries		
computer manufacture		+ 15
pharmaceuticals	− 0.5	
radio, radar, electronics	− 11	
aerospace	− 21	
instrument engineering	− 25	
services		
insurance, banking, finance & business services		+ 363
health		+ 360
education		+ 269
hotels, restaurants, pubs, catering etc.		+ 225
shops & wholesalers		+ 85
entertainment & recreation		+ 58
garages		+ 47
public administration		+ 22
post & telecommunication	− 21	
transport	− 197	
all other services		+ 327

(based on tables in **The State of the Nation** by S. Fothergill and J. Vincent, Pan, London, 1985, p. 32) lost from British manufacturing in 1980–82 alone, compared with 1.5 million over the ten years from 1970 to 1980. Changes in patterns of employment are shown in the table on the previous page.

Although the growth in service jobs has been large 1.5 million between 1971 and 1983 – it has fallen well behind what is needed to significantly reduce unemployment. Present trends do not indicate a change in this pattern. Cuts in public spending have reduced the expansion of jobs in education, the health service and in central and local government. In addition the expansion of services has led to the employment of growing numbers of part-time women whereas industry has been shedding full-time jobs for men. Thus hotels, catering, sport and recreation, the growing leisure and tourism industries employ mainly sales, clerical, cleaning and unskilled staff. Many jobs are part-time, seasonal, low paid and filled by women. This trend can be seen in the following table.

Employment change, Great Britain 1971–1981 (thousands)

	Women	Men
industry		
full-time	− 534	− 1,576
part-time	− 76	no change
services		
full-time	+ 322	+ 200
part-time	+ 1,087	+ 124

(based on a table in **The State of the Nation** by S. Fothergill and J. Vincent, Pan, London, 1985, p. 32)

Despite the growth in female unemployment, increasing numbers of women are finding work. The proportion of the civilian labour force made up of women increased from 37 to 41% between 1971 and 1983. Most part-time workers are women – 4 million out of the 4.7 million workers in part-time employment in 1983. Whereas in 1983 only 5.9% of male employees were part-time, the figure for women was 44.6%.

(adapted from 'Leisure' by Kenneth Roberts in **Developments in Sociology** Volume 2, edited by Michael Haralambos, Causeway, Ormskirk, 1986 and **Social Trends 15**, HMSO, London, 1985)

1. High technology industries are sometimes known as 'sunrise industries', traditional manufacturing industries as 'sunset industries'. Briefly suggest why.   (2)
2. According to the table
   a Which industries had the highest job gains and job losses?   (2)
   b Which services had the highest job gains and job losses?   (2)
3. Briefly explain why job losses have occurred in traditional industries.   (4)
4. Amongst manual workers the largest job losses have occurred in the unskilled manual group. Suggest why this is so.   (4)
5. Why are women more likely to be part-time workers than men?   (3)
6. It has been forecast that male unemployment will increase, femal unemployment decrease. Why might this be so?   (3)

4 The effects of unemployment

What does work mean to people? Obviously it varies from person to person and, as Section 15 shows, from occupation to occupation. It may also vary according to whether a person is young, middle-aged or approaching retirement, whether or not they have dependent children, whether or not they are self-employed and so on. Despite this variation, the experience of unemployment suggests that there is a broad measure of agreement about the meaning of work. Many of the effects of unemployment seem common to all groups of unemployed adults. These are examined in the following passage.

> The spare-time produced by unemployment is spent in bed, watching television, listening to the radio, reading and gardening. Pastimes become cheaper and less commerical – people don't have the money for expensive hobbies and nights out. On average the incomes of the unemployed are 40% below their normal earnings. Gradually 'luxuries' like holidays, the car and evenings in the pub have to be abandoned. Even such do-it-yourself hobbies like home decorating (which in the past saved money) become too expensive.
> Unemployment is tedious and depressing. Mental health

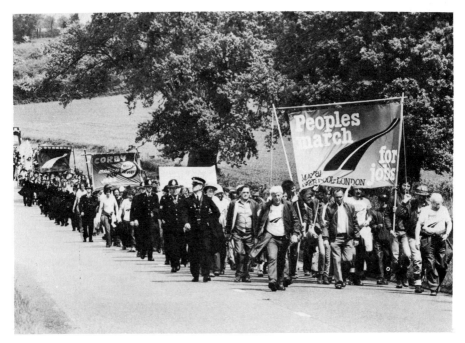

One of the few organized protests by the unemployed – The People's March for Jobs from Liverpool to London, 1981.

suffers. People are isolated – they have less contact with friends than when they were working. Some even describe signing-on as a highlight in an otherwise drab existence.

Then there is the stigma of unemployment. Public opinion polls show that most people see the unemployment problem as the result of economic conditions and government policy. Yet this does not prevent individuals from feeling that unemployment is their own fault for being unqualified, too lazy, too choosy or unable to impress an employer. Even if they don't believe this, they will feel that others see them in this way.

Loss of work means a drop in social status and self-esteem. Often the unemployed feel useless and worse – a burden on the community. Practically every time they meet somebody the first question is, 'Have you found a job yet?' Admitting failure is painful. This is another reason why the unemployed often withdraw from mixing with friends and neighbours.

The severity of the effects of unemployment usually increases the longer people are out of work. Those recently unemployed tend to see themselves as 'between jobs' and 'looking for work' rather than as part of the long-term, 'hard-core' unemployed.

The middle class unemployed face many of the same problems. They often have savings and golden handshakes to soften the blow but they have further to fall than redundant manual workers. Unemployment is less common and in some ways less easy to live with in middle class communities, so much so that some people hide their situation from friends, neighbours and even their own families.

(adapted from 'Leisure' by Kenneth Roberts in **Developments in Sociology** Volume 2, edited by Michael Haralambos, Causeway Press, Ormskirk, 1986)

1. The experience of unemployment shows what work means to people. With reference to the passage briefly outline the meaning of work. (5)
2. a Why do people have less contact with friends when they are unemployed? (2)
   b How might this affect them? (2)
3. With reference to the passage suggest why the rapid growth in long-term unemployment in particular is a cause for concern. (4)
4. Why do many unemployed people feel 'useless'? (4)
5. How might the class position of the unemployed affect their experience of unemployment? (3)

5 Women and unemployment

Until recently unemployment amongst women has been largely ignored. It has been seen as a problem for men. Unemployment results in the loss of a major source of income. The unemployed man therefore loses his traditional status as the breadwinner and provider and this may result in the weakening of his position as head of the family. He also loses a job, a major source of male identity and self-esteem. By contrast, unemployment for a woman has been seen as a minor problem. Her identity and self-esteem lie not in the world of work or in the role of provider but primarily in her roles as mother and housewife.

The following passage questions this traditional view of women and unemployment.

> A major survey on women and employment published in 1984 (**Women and Employment: A Lifetime Perspective** by Jean Martin and Ceridwen Roberts) found that unemployed women 'react to being without paid employment in much the same way as studies show unemployed men do'. Thus the traditional view that an unemployed woman can return quite happily to her domestic 'duties' was shown to be false.
>
> A study entitled **Redundant Women** (1984) by Angela Coyle examined the effects of unemployment on women made redundant in two clothing factories, one in Castleford, the other in Harrogate. She argues that the picture of unemployed women returning to the shelter and support of the male breadwinner fails to take account of divorced, separated and widowed women, many of whom have dependent children to support. Further, where husbands were employed, the loss of the wife's earnings caused economic hardship. Her income was not simply 'pin money'. In addition the wife has lost something more personal – financial independence within the family, the loss of which can result in a 'personal crisis'. Nor does it appear that women can happily revert to their 'appropriate' roles of housewife and childcarer. Some of the redundant women did immerse themselves in domestic work but it was only a short term solution. After a while they felt isolated. They missed their friends and the interest and change of scenery that paid employment provided. Work was not some kind of marginal activity tacked on to their domestic roles: it was a central part of their lives. Coyle concludes,
>
>> As for men, unemployment for women is often experienced as a crisis of automony (freedom to live their own lives), as a loss of independence, and here women's domestic role is no compensation. On the contrary work for women has been seen as their ROUTE OUT of domestic and financial dependence. Consequently, the family may soften the blow of job loss, but in the end the family appears to be the trap.
>
> (Adapted from 'Women and Society' by Sarah Fildes in **Developments in Sociology** Volume 1 edited by Michael Haralambos, Causeway Press, Ormskirk, 1985)

1. Why does Angela Coyle say that 'in the end the family appears to be the trap' for unemployed women? (5)
2. Women have as much right to paid employment as men. Discuss this view with reference to the passage. (5)
3. When female unemployment is taken seriously it will be a major breakthrough for women's liberation. Briefly discuss. (5)
4. The survey by Martin and Roberts found that unemployed women place a much greater importance on having a job than other non-working women. Suggest why this might be so. (5)

6 Youth unemployment

Young people are more likely to be unemployed than members of other age groups. Their experience of unemployment is in many ways similar to that of adults. However, in certain respects, youth unemployment is different. This difference is examined in the following passage.

In 1984 a team of researchers led by Paul Willis conducted a study of youth unemployment in Wolverhampton. The overall unemployment rate in the city was 20% but among the 16 to 24 year olds, one in three was out of work. Willis makes the following points about the effects of unemployment on young people.

For young people in today's society getting a job is a major step towards becoming an adult. Without employment the transition from adolescence to adulthood is broken. Young people are left in limbo, in a state of 'suspended animation' unable either to look forward to or make the transition to adult status. According to Willis, widespread youth unemployment has created a 'new social condition'. For many young people the lack of a job and a wage prevents freedom and independence from parents, it postpones planning for marriage and becoming a consumer. This has 'devastated' young people's sense of the future.

In place of the normal transition to adulthood, unemployed young people experience long periods of poverty, dependency on their families, on state welfare and state training and

Young people in Wolverhampton. Among 16 to 24 year olds one in three is out of work.

employment schemes. Life becomes increasingly centered on the home. Leisure activities that cost money are ruled out and in any case leisure without work is pointless. Many young people withdraw from normal social life and experience 'a strange sense of inactivity'. Isolated at home they become bored, frustrated and demoralised which often leads to stress and conflict within the family.

The 'new social condition' created by youth unemployment means that young people are literally going nowhere. They are suspended in limbo between adolescence and adulthood, unable to move from one to the other.

There are other studies, however, which present a less pessimistic picture of the effects of youth unemployment. They show that in some respects young people are not isolated when out of work – they often spend more not less time with their friends. They continue to be interested in going out, clothes and music, but simply spend less money on these things – local discos replace city centre night spots. With support from their families and without domestic responsibilities, they are often in a better position than adults to cope with unemployment. Many have never had a job so they don't suddenly lose a lifelong occupational identity. The fact that youth unemployment has become so widespread tends to reduce the stigma. And they are able to share the experience with others in the same situation. The poverty of youth unemployment is somewhat different from that of adult unemployment. Even the transition from school to unemployment means a rise in personal income.

Despite evidence which suggests that the effects of unemployment are less severe for young people, there is no suggestion that they actually enjoy being out of work. Like the vast majority of people they want a job and, like adults, they suffer rather than enjoy the experience of being unemployed.

(adapted from 'Youth unemployment, a new social state' by Paul Willis in **New Society**, 29 March 1984, pp. 475–477; 'Future? What future?' by Douglas I. Smith and Howard Williamson in **Youth in Society**, November 1985, pp. 11–14 and 'Leisure' by Kenneth Roberts in **Developments in Sociology** Volume 2, edited by Michael Haralambos, Causeway Press, Ormskirk, 1986)

1. Why do many young people see leisure without work as pointless? (5)
2. What is the 'new social condition' created by youth unemployment? (5)
3. What effects might spending time with others in the same situation have on young people's experience of unemployment? (3)
4. Why do the young people in the Wolverhampton study experience 'a strange sense of inactivity'? (5)

7 The future of work

Section 16:3 identified a number of changes in employment patterns. Firstly, the decline in manual and the growth of non-manual occupations. For the first time in history there are now more white collar jobs – 52% in 1983 – than manual occupations. Secondly, reflecting this change, the decline in employment in the primary (agriculture and mining) and secondary (manufacturing) sectors of the economy and the expansion of the tertiary sector (services). Thirdly, a growth in part-time work – jobs largely filled by women. Fourthly, a steady growth in unemployment. Will these trends continue? What is the future of work? These questions are examined in the following passage.

Whenever new production technology is introduced prophets of doom and prophets of hope have produced widely differing pictures of the future. Mechanisation, automation and more recently microelectronics have led on the one hand to dismal prophecies of mass unemployment with a growing section of the workforce permanently replaced by computers. On the other hand the optimists look forward to a move from 'dirty' jobs in the old traditional industries to 'clean' jobs in high technology industry and the service sector. This will lead on the one hand to a more highly automated and more productive manufacturing industry resulting in a more prosperous nation; on the other hand to a more caring society with the expansion of health and social services and a more enjoyable society with the growth of leisure industries.

Early fears about the impact of the micro-chip have yet to be realised. The economic recession has destroyed far more jobs than the chip. However, all the indications suggest that jobs will not return in manufacturing industries. Automation will probably increase and the workforce continue to decline. For example the Detroit car industry plans to introduce 25,000 robots over the next five years which will replace 80–90,000 workers. Nor is there any indication that the new high-tech 'sunrise' industries will take up the slack. It is estimated that high technology industries in the USA will only produce between 750,000 and a million jobs in the next ten years. And this is less than half the number of jobs lost from US manufacturing industry in the period 1981–1983 alone.

Will the service sector be the saviour of employment? Indications from the USA, which often points the way for Europe, suggest that this is a possibility. About two-thirds of the US workforce is now employed in the service sector. This is where the new new jobs are growing – in business services, health, food and drink, finance and insurance. This is the pattern in the UK though the pace of job creation has been slower. But, despite the growth of the service sector, job gains there have not yet kept pace with job losses in the rest of the economy. Most predictions see this trend continuing. One estimate sees male unemployment rising from 15% to over 18% in 1990 with the female rate declining from 9% to 7%.

Much of the predicted decline in female unemployment is seen to result from a continuing increase in part-time employment. One in five workers in the UK are now part-time, their numbers having doubled in the past twenty years. The figure for 1990 is expected to be one in four. Part-timers are usually low paid with few fringe benefits. They are less likely to get sickness benefit, paid holidays or occupational pensions. They have less job security and can be taken on or laid off rapidly depending on the demand for the company's goods or services.

Some researchers believe that they have discovered a growing trend in employment practice between 'core' or 'primary' and 'peripheral' or 'secondary' workers. Core workers tend to be qualified, skilled, well paid, full-time with good terms and conditions of employment and secure jobs.

The outer, peripheral workers are likely to be low-paid, often temporary and part-time with little job security. Some employers see this as a way of cutting labour costs and of increasing the flexibility of the company to rapidly adjust to changes in demand. However there are fears that this trend may create a new stratum of second class citizens on the fringes of the labour market.

(adapted from 'Society Today: The future of work' parts 1 and 2 in **New Society**, 25 October 1985 and 8 November 1985)

1. Briefly outline the prospects for jobs in
   a Traditional manufacturing   (4)
   b High technology industry   (4)
   c Services.   (4)
2. Explain the differences between the projected male and female unemployment rates.   (3)
3. Should the trend towards part-time employment be welcomed?
                                                                       (5)

8 The future of leisure

With the development of microtechnology the optimists look forward to a golden age of leisure. The 5 day, 40 hour week will be a thing of the past. Save for the occasional spell of work, people will have the freedom to enjoy a life of leisure. This will not of course happen overnight. People will have to be educated for leisure and there needs to be a large investment in sport and leisure facilities.

But, as this section has indicated, unemployment is not the same as leisure. There are few if any signs that the unemployed regard their situation as leisure. As present they do not appear to be compensating for unemployment with 'leisure' activities. Employment appears to provide a type of status, identity and sense of personal worth that leisure activities cannot offer.

The pessimists are forecasting an age of enforced unemployment for a large section of the population. Part of the workforce will enjoy the fruits of the new technology while the rest will be unemployed, their skills unwanted and unneeded. The following rather pessimistic note is sounded by the famous science fiction writer Arthur C. Clarke, author of **2001**.

In the world of the future, the sort of mindless labour that has occupied 99% of mankind for much more than 99% of its existence, will, of course, be largely taken over by machines. Yet most people are bored to death without work – even work that they don't like. In a workless world, therefore, only the highly educated will be able to flourish, or perhaps even survive. The rest are likely to destroy themselves and their environment out of sheer frustration. This is no vision of the distant future; it is already happening, most of all in the decaying cities. So perhaps we should not despise TV soap operas if, during the turbulent transition period between our culture and real civilisation, they serve as yet another opium for the masses. The drug, at any rate, is cheap and harmless, serving to kill time for those many people who like it better dead.

(quoted in 'Society Today' p. 1, in **New Society**, 29 November 1979)

The future of work and leisure?

1. What does Arthur C. Clarke mean by 'mindless labour'?   (3)
2. Why are most people bored without work?   (3)
3. Why does Arthur C. Clarke see education as essential for survival in a workless world?   (3)
4. What events in the 'decaying cities' is Clarke referring to?   (3)
5. Why does Clarke suggest that TV soap operas may have an important role to play in the 'transition period'?   (4)
6. Briefly suggest what Arthur C. Clarke might mean by 'real civilisation'.   (4)

Section 17 Crime and Deviance

Deviance refers to those acts which do not conform to the norms and values of a particular society. Crime refers to those activities which break the law and are subject to punishment applied by officials appointed by the state. All crime is deviant yet many deviant acts are not defined as criminal. For example attempted suicide, Mohican haircuts and alcoholism are often seen as deviant but they are not crimes in Britain today.

The first passage in this section looks at the culture of the Bushmen of the Kalahari Desert. It shows that what is considered normal and deviant varies from one society to another. The following three extracts indicate how little is known about crime and therefore about criminals. They suggest that official statistics on crime seriously underestimate the actual extent of crime. In view of the lack of knowledge about crime it may be premature to explore the causes of crime. However considerable work has been done in this area. A small part of this research is looked at in a passage dealing with crime in relation to social class. This is followed with an examination of white collar crime which again shows how little is known about the extent and nature of crime in Western society. The focus of the section now changes. Rather than asking why people commit crimes, the question changes to why certain people come to be defined as deviant and/or criminal. This question is looked at in terms of labelling theory. The section closes with an examination of the relationship between ethnicity and crime, a subject that has attracted considerable media attention in recent years.

1 Deviance and culture

Crime and deviance are culturally defined. As culture changes, so do definitions of deviant and criminal activities. At certain times in Western society it was considered deviant for women to smoke, use make-up and consume alcoholic drinks in public. Today this is no longer the case. In the same way definitions of crime change over time. Sexual relations between people of the same sex were once a criminal offence in Britain. Since 1969 homosexual acts between consenting adults over twenty-one in private have no longer been illegal.

Different cultures have different norms and values. As a result what is considered normal and deviant will vary from one society to another. This can be seen from a comparison of our own society with that of the Bushmen of the Kalahari Desert in southern Africa. Their traditional way of life is briefly described in the following passage.

> The Bushmen live in small family bands rarely numbering more than twenty people. They have a hunting and gathering economy – the men hunt and the women gather edible roots and berries. The Bushmen are nomadic – they roam from place to place in search of food and water. They have few possessions and build tiny dome shaped huts made of grass.
>
> Bushmen dress in the skins of animals. Men wear only a leather loincloth, women a small leather apron and a cape made from a whole animal hide. Sometimes they wear sandals but mostly their feet are bare. Bushmen waste nothing. When they kill an antelope most of the meat is dried to preserve it but sooner or later every last bit is eaten down to the gristle inside the ears and sometimes even the hide. Blood from the kill is collected in a shallow hole lined with skin then scooped out in handfuls and drunk. Bones are cracked open for marrow and worked into arrow points to kill more antelope.
>
> Bushmen are polygynous – a man may have two or more wives. He is allowed to have as many wives as he can afford – which depends on how well he hunts. Co-wives are often sisters. Girls marry young – around 8 or 9 years old to a husband in his teens. However sexual intercourse is not permitted until the wife reaches puberty. The husband always goes to live with his wife's family. Divorce is a straight-forward matter – the couple simply announce their divorce and separate.
>
> Many Bushmen women have decorative scars on their foreheads and thighs. The cuts are made while they are young

Bushman hunter.

with a knife or an axe blade, then charcoal is rubbed in. One woman explained that it was worth the pain – she had been extremely ugly and the scars had improved her looks.

Bushmen rarely fight with each other and go to great lengths to avoid quarrels and disagreement. In particular they try to prevent jealousy and for this reason the few possessions they have are constantly circulating round the group. No one keeps a good knife for long even though they may really want it because they will become the object of envy. Their culture insists that food, water and material possessions are shared. Without this they may not survive the famines and droughts of the Kalahari Desert.

(adapted from **The Harmless People** by Elizabeth M. Thomas, Penguin, Harmondsworth, 1969)

1. What norms of dress in Bushmen society would be viewed as deviant in Western society? (3)

2. The Bushmen would consider some of our eating habits extremely wasteful. Briefly suggest why.   (2)
3. If English parents behaved like Bushmen parents they might well be taken to court by the National Society for the Prevention of Cruelty to Children. Why?   (2)
4. What aspects of marriage and divorce among the Bushmen would be defined as illegal in the UK? Briefly explain why they would break the law.   (5)
5. Why would many of our norms and values regarding property be considered immoral and deviant by the Bushmen? Give examples in your answer.   (4)
6. Briefly outline why certain aspects of Bushmen culture make sense in a desert environment.   (4)

2 Official statistics on crime

Statistics on crime for England and Wales are published annually by the Home Office. They are compiled from information provided by local police forces. The police record all crimes known to them and those which have been detected or 'cleared by arrest'. Many crimes are not known to the police and only a proportion of those known are cleared by arrest. Of those arrested some are not prosecuted – they may be simply cautioned or released through lack of evidence. A sample of convicted criminals is not therefore likely to represent the criminal population as a whole.

> The following table comes from an investigation into crime rates conducted by Keith Bottomley and Clive Coleman. It was carried out in a medium sized industrial city in the North of England – given the name Northern City. The table is based on a random sample of indictable (serious) crimes recorded by the police in Northern City in 1972. The overall detection rate and the detection rate for each type of crime are similar to the figures for England and Wales at this time.
> Burglary refers to entering a building illegally with intent to commit a crime. Robbery refers to depriving a person of property by violence or threat of violence. Theft refers to illegally taking another's property. Fraud refers to illegally

Classification of offences as detected or undetected: Northern City, 1972

Offence	Total recorded as known to police	Undetected Number (%)	Detected Number (%)
Violence against the person	103	14 (14)	84 (81)
Sexual offences	26	8 (31)	17 (65)
Burglary and Robbery	776	596 (77)	178 (23)
Theft (excluding shoplifting)	1197	783 (65)	408 (34)
Shoplifting and Handling stolen goods	276	19 (7)	257 (93)
Fraud and Forgery	75	9 (12)	66 (88)
Criminal Damage	53	44 (83)	9 (17)
Total	2506	1473 (59)	1019 (41)

deceiving a person e.g. a clerk who fiddles the accounts to dishonestly obtain money from his or her employer.

(from **Understanding Crime Rates** By Keith Bottomley and Clive Coleman, Gower, Farnborough, 1981, p. 96)

1. What percentage of crimes known to the police were detected? (2)
2. Which two categories of crime had the highest detection rate? (2)
3. Which two categories of crime had the lowest detection rate? (2)
4. Suggest two reasons why the numbers of burglaries, robberies and thefts known to the police are relatively high compared to other offences. (4)
5. Suggest two reasons why the cases of fraud known to the police are relatively low compared to other offences. (4)
6. Many sociologists have based their explanations of crime on investigations of the social background of convicted criminals. In view of the evidence in the table, what problems are involved in basing explanations on this information? (6)

3 Victim studies

For various reasons the majority of criminal offences do not appear in police statistics. Probably the most common reason is that members of the public often do not report crimes to the

police. Evidence to support this view is provided by 'victim studies',
two of which are examined in the following extract.

The table below shows the results of a survey into the extent
of crime in three precincts (areas) of Washington DC in the
USA. People were asked if they had been a victim of crime in
the past year. The table compares the crime rate based on the
survey results with the crime rate based on official police
records.

**Comparison of police rate and survey rate in three precincts
of Washington DC**

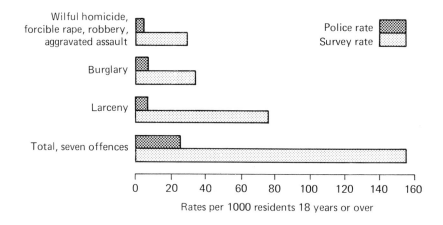

(Larceny is the American equivalent of the English term theft)

A national survey of the victims of crime based on a sample
of 10,000 households in the USA produced results similar to
the Washington DC survey. Among other things it asked
people who had been victims of crime, but had not reported it,
why they had not done so. The results are given in the
table opposite.

1. a To the nearest 20, what was the police rate and the survey
      rate for the seven offences in the Washington research?   (2)
   b On the basis of the figures in your answer to part a), how
      much greater was the survey rate than the police rate?   (2)

Victim's most important reason for not notifying police (in percentages)

Reasons for not notifying police

Crimes	Percent of cases in which police not notified	Felt it was private matter or did not want to harm offender	Police could not be effective or would not want to be bothered	Did not want to take time	Too confused or did not know how to report	Fear of reprisal
Robbery	35	27	45	9	18	0
Aggravated assault	35	50	25	4	8	13
Simple assault	54	50	35	4	4	7
Burglary	42	30	63	4	2	2
Larceny ($50 and over)	40	23	62	7	7	0
Larceny (under $50)	63	31	58	7	3	0
Auto theft	11	20	60	0	0	20
Malicious mischief	62	23	68	5	2	2
Consumer fraud	90	50	40	0	10	0
Other fraud (bad checks, swindling, etc.)	74	41	35	16	8	0
Sex offences (other than forcible rape)	49	40	50	0	5	5
Family crimes (desertion, non-support, etc.)	50	65	17	10	0	7

(Tables from 'Crime in America: The President's Commission on Law Enforcement and Administration of Justice', abridged in **Delinquency, Crime and Social Process** edited by Donald R. Cressey and David A. Ward, Harper & Row, New York, 1969, pp. 13 and 14)

2. According to the Washington survey, which of the seven crimes was most underestimated by police records? (2)
3. On the basis of the Washington research, should sociologists rely on police statistics if they wish to discover the extent of crime? Briefly summarise the evidence which supports your answer. (4)
4. According to the second table,
    a Which type of crime are victims most likely to report to the police? (2)
    b Which type of crime are victims least likely to report to the police? (2)
5. What was the most common reason for not reporting cases of burglary? (2)
6. In cases of assault and family crimes suggest why a relatively high percentage of victims did not report the offence because they 'felt it was a private matter or did not want to harm the offender'. (4)

4 The crime rate

The publication each year of statistics on crime by the Home Office produces a predictable storm of protest. There is an outcry about the 'rising tide of crime' and the Home Secretary of the day is often accused of being too soft on the criminal. However as the following passage indicates, crime statistics must be approached with considerable caution. The graph shows the trend in notifiable offences (formerly known as 'indictable' crimes) recorded by the police in England and Wales from 1900 to 1984. Notifiable offences include violence against the person, sexual offences, burglary, robbery and theft, fraud and forgery and criminal damage. Motoring offences make up the bulk of crimes which fall ·outside the category of notifiable crime.

**Notifiable offences in England and Wales recorded by the police
1900–1984**

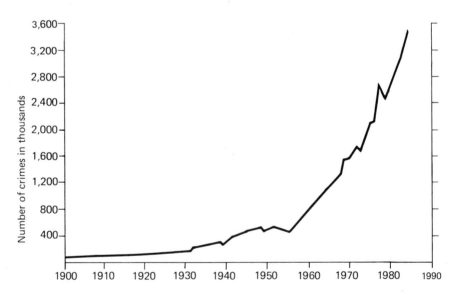

(adapted from 'Patterns of lawbreaking' by Allison Morris, p. 7, in **The
(Lawbreakers** edited by Allison Morris, BBC Publications, London, 1974,
Social Trends 15, HMSO, London, 1985, p.71 and **Social Trends 16**, HMSO,
London, 1986, p.183)

As the previous extract has indicated, crimes known to the police may give little or no indication of the actual extent of crime. Recent research suggests that the amount of crime in England and Wales might be up to 10 times that recorded by the police. The possible relationships between trends in actual crime and trends in recorded crime are illustrated in the following diagrams. The shaded areas indicate the 'dark figure' of crime, that is crimes not known to the police.

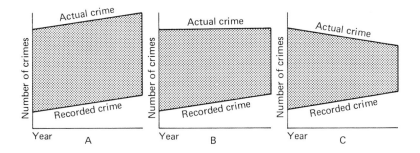

(from 'Patterns of lawbreaking' by Allison Morris, p. 7, in **The Lawbreakers** edited by Allison Morris, BBC Publications, London, 1974)

An increase in recorded crime may not indicate an increase in the extent of crime. People may be more willing or have more reason to report crimes. For example, in the case of burglaries, more may be reported for insurance purposes. Another possibility is that the police may simply be recording more incidents as crimes. One study showed that in Oxford 6% of reported offences were written off by the police as 'no crimes' compared with fewer than 2% in Salford.

Changes in the recorded rates of particular crimes may reflect a change in police policy rather than an actual increase in those crimes. In the four years before Sir John McKay was appointed Chief Constable of Manchester there were only three prosecutions for male importuning (soliciting for immoral purposes). After his arrival there were 30 in 1959, 105 in 1960, 135 in 1961 and 216 in 1962. On July 1, 1976, James Anderton was appointed Chief Constable of Manchester. That year 55 search warrants were executed under the Obscene Publications Acts and there were proceedings in 25 cases. In 1977 there were 287 warrants and 134 proceedings and in 1978, 151 warrants and 91 proceedings. The changes in the recorded rates for the above crimes probably indicate far more about the concerns of the Chief Constables than any change in the extent of these crimes.

This passage suggests that fears about a rising tide of notifiable crime may be exaggerated. A closer look at 'notifiable crimes' shows that many are far less serious than they first appear. Robbery, for example, may refer to a bank holdup or the forcible removal of a child's dinner money by one of his classmates in the schoolyard. About 95% of 'notifiable crimes' are property offences but about two thirds of these involve property worth less than £100. Crimes of violence with firearms have risen sharply during the 1970s. In 1978 the figure was 2,759 in England and Wales. But 2,417 were committed with air-weapons, most by 14–17 year olds. Air pistols and rifles are dangerous but not nearly so dangerous as firearms. Yet crimes involving their use are included in official statistics under the heading of crimes of violence with firearms. Fears about the rising crime rate may be justified but it is important to remember that notifiable crime covers offences from breaking a window and stealing a bicycle to armed bank robbery and murder.

(adapted from 'Hysteria and the crime rate', **The Guardian**, March 15, 1982, p. 14 and 'The great myth of the detective' by Peter Evans, **The Times**, March 25, 1982, p. 12)

1. Outline the trends in notifiable crime shown in the graph.   (2)
2. Describe the relationships between actual and recorded crime shown in the diagrams.   (3)
3. Give two reasons for a rise in the rate of recorded crime which are not related to changes in the rate of actual crime.   (4)
4. Suggest why the recorded rate of certain crimes in Manchester suddenly increased.   (4)
5. Notifiable offences may not always be as serious as they appear. Briefly discuss this statement.   (3)
6. The **Sun** newspaper in a series of articles on crime referred to 'Britain's shocking crime wave' and told its readers that 'Britain is a nation that walks in fear'. Why might such comments be irresponsible?   (4)

5 Crime and social class

Criminal behaviour does not appear to be spread evenly throughout society. It seems to be concentrated within certain social groups. Thus official statistics indicate that members of the working class are more likely to break the law than members of other social classes. A number of sociological theories have been developed to explain social class differences in crime. The following passage examines one such theory put forward by the American sociologist Albert Cohen.

Before Cohen developed his theory one of the standard explanations for social class differences in crime went as follows. In Western society a high value is placed on individual achievement and materialism. The successful person reaches the top of his chosen career, lives in a large, detached house, drives an expensive car and has a substantial bank balance. However, relatively few members of the working class have the opportunity to achieve this kind of success. Most have few if any educational qualifications and work in 'dead-end' jobs with little or no opportunity for promotion and advancement. Their way to the top is largely blocked. As a result there is greater pressure placed on them to find alternative ways of becoming successful. Crime offers one such way. A bank robbery can provide all the trappings of success.

This theory does help to explain certain crimes such as burglary and robbery which can result in material gain. But consider the following example taken from a study of a teenage gang in Glasgow.

The lads burst into the reading room in a public library. Dan and Bill began setting fire to the newspapers on display while Tim and some of the others pushed books off tables and emptied the shelves of encyclopedias and reference books. Dave tried to set fire to the newspapers which old-age pensioners were reading. On the way out the boys punched and kicked an attendant in a green uniform. This was a source of great amusement and they could hardly run for laughing.

It is difficult to see how this incident can be explained by the theory outlined above. It involved no material gain – the boys stole neither money nor property. Statistics suggest that this type of crime is committed by young working class males. Albert Cohen offers the following explanation.

Many crimes appear, at first sight, to be motiveless – there seems to be no sensible or practical reason for them. Even when theft is involved, the articles are sometimes of little or no value to the thieves. A group of teenagers may steal light-bulbs from a shop and run down a busy street smashing them as they go. Cohen sees this type of activity as stealing 'for the hell of it'. There is an enjoyment of the discomfort it produces for others, a delight in defying the rules of society. It involves spite and malice, contempt and ridicule, challenge and defiance.

Cohen begins his explanation in much the same was as the theory which began this passage. With low educational qualifications and dead-end jobs the road to the top is blocked for many working class boys. In terms of society's standards their status is low and as a result they experience 'status frustration'. They are frustrated and dissatisfied with their status. Rather than turning to crime in an effort to be successful in material terms, they look to crime as a means of gaining status and prestige. Thus the successful thief gains respect from other members of his group, the joy rider is highly regarded by his peers, the good fighter is admired by his friends. A 'delinquent subculture' has been created which turns many of the norms and values of the wider society upside down. Bad becomes good. In terms of this subculture a person can achieve something, he can be successful, at least in the eyes of his peers. The main motive for crime now becomes prestige rather than material gain. In this way the problem of status frustration is at least partly solved. At the same time crime offers the chance to hit back at the wider society which has denied many working class boys the opportunity to become successful.

(adapted from **Delinquent Boys** by Albert K. Cohen, The Free Press, Glencoe, 1955 and **A Glasgow Gang Observed** by James Patrick, Eyre Methuen, London, 1973, p. 77)

1. Why does the explanation of working class crime given in the first paragraph fail to explain the behaviour of the Glasgow boys?   (4)

2. Briefly suggest how the types of crime described by Cohen can

be seen as 'the D stream's revenge'? (4)
3. a What is status frustration? (2)
 b Why are working class boys more likely to experience status frustration than middle class boys? (3)
 c How does the 'delinquent subculture' help to solve the problem of status frustration? (3)
 d In view of your previous answer, suggest why the types of crimes discussed by Cohen are often committed by groups or gangs. (4)

6 White collar crime

Although official statistics indicate that crime is concentrated in the working class this may not be the case. There is a growing body of evidence which suggests that the extent of white collar crime may be significant. Edwin Sutherland who pioneered the study of white collar crime defines it as 'crimes committed by persons of respectability and high social status in the course of their occupations'. It would therefore include the crimes of ex-President Richard Nixon and his associates in the Watergate Affair and the possible involvement of Prince Bernhardt of the Netherlands in the Lockheed bribery scandal in which the American company paid bribes in order to secure orders for its aircraft. Lower down the scale white collar crime includes factory owners breaking safety regulations, council officials taking bribes from building firms in return for contracts, lawyers fabricating evidence for the benefit of their clients and accountants 'cooking the books' and embezzling money from their employer. The following passage, based in part on the work of Edwin Sutherland, examines white collar crime.

White collar crimes are difficult to detect. Many are 'crimes without victims'. In cases of bribery and corruption, both parties involved may see themselves as gaining from the arrangement, both are liable to prosecution and neither, therefore, is likely to report the offence. Many white collar crimes, even if detected, do not come to court and so escape public attention. In the case of embezzlement, banks or building societies may come to a private arrangement with the staff concerned. Offenders may be sacked and given time to pay back the money they have stolen. They escape prosecution which avoids publicity and preserves public confidence in the good name of their former employer. Violations of factory leglislation rarely result in prosecution. Usually factory inspectors simply notify a firm that a particular matter 'requires attention'. Misconduct by professionals such as doctors or lawyers is often dealt with behind closed doors by their professional associations. Usually they are reprimanded, in exceptional cases their licence to practice is withdrawn. In most instances the public never hears about the offence and the good name of the profession is maintained. In cases of tax evasion the offence often results in nothing more than an 'official demand' for payment. The matter is neatly summarized by Willie Sutton, an American bank robber, who stated, 'Others accused of defrauding the government of thousands of dollars merely get a letter from a committee in Washington asking them to come in and talk it over. Maybe it's justice but it's puzzling to a guy like me.'

When suspected white collar criminals are apprehended and brought to court they are treated rather differently from other defendants. Sutherland gives the following reasons for this. Firstly, judges have a similar social background to many white collar criminals. They tend not to think of politicians, businessmen and professionals as 'criminal types'. They often hand out lenient sentences feeling that only light pressure is needed for reform. Secondly, compared to the burglar and the mugger, white collar criminals are not considered to be a danger to the public. They are therefore more likely to be fined or put on probation. They therefore escape prison and the stigma it brings and can more easily return to normal life. Thirdly, the victims of white collar crimes are not seen to be harmed as seriously as the victims of many other crimes. If an accountant has been defrauding a building society the loss to each individual depositor may be tiny. Fourthly, the media tend not to portray white collar crime as serious. Indeed it is sometimes presented in a sympathetic light. For example when VAT inspectors 'raid' a businessman's home they can appear as the 'villains of the piece'. Sutherland suggests that mass media portrayal of white collar crime is influenced by the fact the media are owned by businessmen who may themselves break the law.

(adapted from ' "Is white collar crime" crime'? by Edwin H. Sutherland in **The Sociology of Crime and Delinquency** edited by M. E. Wolfgang, L. Savitz and N. Johnston, John Wiley and Sons, New York, 1962 and **Sociology of Deviant Behaviour** by Marshall B. Clinard, Holt, Rinehart & Winston, New York, 1974)

1. Why is burglary more likely to be reported than bribery? (4)
2. Give three reasons why many white collar criminals whose offences have been detected do not come to court. (3)
3. What evidence is there in the passage which suggests that it may be easier for a white collar criminal to regain his standing in the community than it would be for other convicted criminals? (6)
4. Suggest why the 'top' white collar criminals such as ex-President Nixon often escape prosecution. (3)
5. White collar crimes are a lot more serious than their treatment suggests. Briefly discuss this view. (4)

7 Labelling theory (1)

So far this section has looked at explanations for why people commit criminal acts. However it has not asked how and why certain people and certain acts come to be defined as deviant or criminal. Labelling theory provides answers to these questions.

Defining an act as deviant or criminal is not a simple, straightforward process. Take the act of nudity in Western society. Nudity in the bedroom between husband and wife is usually considered normal. Should a stranger enter the room then continued nudity in his or her presence would be seen as deviant. Yet in some situations such as nudist camps or certain holiday beaches nudity in the presence of strangers would be considered perfectly normal by those present. A spectator at a cricket match who 'streaked' across the pitch might be viewed as a 'bit of a lad' but dressed in a mackintosh and exposing himself on a street corner he would probably be

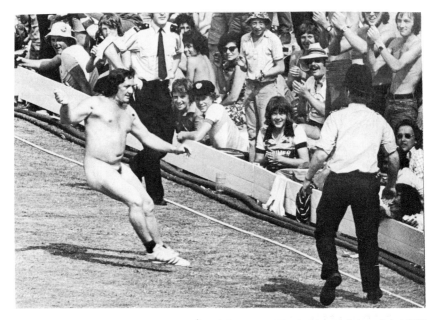

Lords Cricket ground during a test match between England and Australia, 1975. The streaker was removed by police to the amusement of the crowd and play continued.

regarded as 'some kind of pervert'. He might be arrested for indecent exposure and charged with a criminal offence.

Thus there is nothing normal, deviant or criminal about the act of nudity. It all depends on how others interpret, define and label the act. Whether or not it is defined as deviant will depend on who commits the act, when and where it is committed, who observes it and the interaction between the various people involved.

This type of reasoning led to the development of labelling theory by the American sociologist Howard Becker. He argues that deviance and crime are simply acts which are labelled as such. In his words, 'The deviant is one to whom the label has successfully been applied; deviant behaviour is behaviour that people so label'. This leads to questions which previous approaches to crime and deviance had not fully considered. In particular, why is there a tendency for certain types of people and certain kinds of activities to be labelled as deviant? To answer this question we must examine those who define others as deviant. Thus with respect to crime we must look at the ways in which police, probation officers and the courts define crime and criminals.

In an important study of probation officers in California, Aaron V. Cicourel tried to discover why some boys but not others were defined as delinquents. It was the probation officer's job to decide whether or not to charge boys who had been arrested, with a criminal offence. Cicourel found that this decision was influenced by their view of the 'typical delinquent'. In terms of this view a delinquent was likely to come from a broken home, have a poor school record, reject authority, belong to an ethnic minority group, come from a low income background and live in an inner city area. If a boy's background corresponds to this picture he is more likely to be charged with a criminal offence, and, if found guilty, labelled as a delinquent. By comparison the middle class white boy is more likely to be warned and released without charge. He does not fit the picture of the 'typical delinquent'. In addition his parents with their 'respectable' background are often able to convince the probation officer that their child's act was not really delinquent, that it was excusable – he was ill; under strain; he got in with a bad crowd; it's not his usual behaviour; he's really sorry for what he's done; he's got a bright future to look forward to; and so on.

In this respect a delinquent is a person who is defined as such. It's not so much what he's done but the way others define both him and his actions. Whether or not a person is labelled as deviant depends on the interaction and negotiation that takes place between those involved.

(adapted from **Sociology: Themes and Perspectives** (2nd edition) by M. Haralambos with R. M. Heald, Bell & Hyman, London, 1985, pp. 429–430, 434–435)

1. Briefly state why the definition of an act as deviant is not simple and straightforward. (4)
2. A person kills another person. Examine the various ways in which this action might be defined. (4)
3. You are caught taking goods out of a supermarket without having paid for them. How might you avoid being seen as a thief? (4)

4. In view of Cicourel's study it is not surprising that official statistics show that most delinquents come from working class backgrounds. With reference to the passage explain why this is so. (4)
5. Briefly criticise labelling theory as an explanation of crime. (4)

8 Labelling theory (2)

The previous passage looked at how and why certain people are defined as deviant. This passage considers the effects that such labelling may have on their lives.

A label defines an individual as a certain kind of person. It is a 'master status' in the sense that it overshadows all the other statuses possessed by an individual. If a person is labelled as criminal, mentally ill or gay such labels tend to override his status as father, husband, worker, friend and neighbour. The deviant label becomes the dominant status. Others tend to respond to him in terms of the label and assume that he has the characteristics associated with the label. Thus if a person is labelled a thief, behaviour which was once seen as normal – a late night, a new video, a change of car – may well be seen in a new light.

A person's self-concept, the way he sees himself, comes largely from the way others respond to him. Labelling may well produce a self-fulfilling prophecy – a person will tend to see himself in terms of the label and act accordingly (see Section 10:8 for a discussion of the self-fulfilling prophecy). There are a number of possible stages in this process.

First a person is publicly labelled as deviant. This may lead to rejection by family and friends, he may lose his job and be forced out of the neighbourhood. This may encourage further deviance. For example a drug addict may turn to crime to support his habit since employers may refuse to give him a job. Those labelled as deviant may seek out others in the same situation. They provide understanding and support since they share his problems. Within this group a deviant subculture may develop in which a deviant lifestyle is a major concern. This can be seen in certain gay communities particularly in the

United States. The self-fulfilling prophecy has now come to pass. Those forced into 'deviant communities' now see themselves as different from the wider society and act accordingly.

This process is not inevitable. Drug addicts do give up their habit and re-enter conventional society; ex-convicts do get jobs and go 'straight'. However, once labelled, there is pressure on the individual to follow the route described in the previous paragraph – there is pressure on the label to stick.

(adapted from **Sociology: Themes and Perspectives** [2nd edition] by M. Haralambos with R. M. Heald. Bell & Hyman, London, 1985, pp. 430–431)

1. Why is a label sometimes described as a 'master status'?   (3)
2. How might labelling theory help us to understand some of the problems faced by ex-convicts?   (4)
3. One pupil has been labelled as a troublemaker. Another is seen as well-behaved. Both do the following things.
   –arrive late for a lesson
   –talk when they are supposed to be working in silence
   –fail to hand in their homework.
   a Bearing in mind the way the pupils are seen, how might teachers interpret the behaviour of each?   (4)
   b What effect might the teachers' reactions have on the progress of the two pupils in school?   (4)
4. People in 'deviant' communities' sometimes re-define their deviance as a problem of the wider society. Thus gays in the United States often argue that homosexuality is a problem invented by heterosexuals (non-gays).
   a What do they mean by this?   (2)
   b What justification is there for this argument?   (3)

9 Crime and ethnicity

In recent years the media has given considerable attention to the subject of ethnicity and crime. It has focussed on what has been seen as the link between 'street crime', ethnicity and the inner city. The following passage looks at some aspects of this question.

Reports in the press and on television give a picture of

pensioners living in fear of their lives as they walk the streets of the inner city. While there may be some truth in this, their fear may well be due as much to media reports as to the extent of crime. 'Mugging' – thefts from people involving some form of personal assault usually in public places – has caught the public imagination. Officially there is no such crime – it comes under the heading of 'robbery and violent theft'. The media have tended to portray 'mugging' as a 'black crime' and cases which hit the headlines often involve frail old white ladies as the victims. Official statistics provide a very different picture of the typical victim. Figures for London in 1982 show that the chances of being assaulted on the streets were more than 50 times higher for Asians and 30 times higher for Afro-Caribbeans than for whites. The people most likely to be 'mugged' were not elderly women but those in the 21–30 age group with assaults more common on men than women. Crimes that get called 'mugging' make up less than 1% of all notifiable offences recorded by the police; 'robbery and other violent theft' amount to only 3%. Yet the headlines give a very different impression – 'mugging' apparently sells newspapers.

Home Office figures released in 1984 show that in London Asians made up 2% of those arrested for street robbery, Afro-Caribbeans 52%. Since the non-white population of London is just under 14%, this would seem to indicate a high proportion of blacks involved in 'street crimes'. But before drawing this conclusion a number of points must be considered.

1) The figures are based on victims' perception of the colour of their attacker – this perception may not be accurate.

2) The figures do not allow comparison with other types of crime since the colour of offenders is only recorded for 'robbery and other violent theft' (i.e. 3% of notifiable offences).

3) Many other crimes such as fraud may be mainly 'white' crimes since whites have more opportunity to commit such crimes. Blacks may be more likely to commit street crimes for similar reasons. However the fact that statistics link colour and street crimes can give the impression that blacks are 'more criminal' than whites.

4) The 1984 Home Office report shows that police are far

more likely to 'stop and search' blacks than whites. Between 30 and 40% of all arrests came from such stops. This may account at least partly for the high proportion of blacks arrested for street crimes.

The police stop people they believe are behaving 'suspiciously'. The behaviour of young Afro-Caribbeans often appears suspicious to white policemen. Paul Harrison provides the following account of why people are stopped from his study of Hackney, an inner city area in London. Four policemen give their reasons.

> (*PC Rod Bateman*) 'Anything out of the ordinary. It's the sixth sense you pick up.'
>
> (*Colin Dryden*) 'They say the hairs on the back of your neck stick up. I'd stop someone acting suspiciously in house doorways, near cars, or at bus-stops.'
>
> (*PC Paul Wilson*) 'Any younger blacks in a Jewish street, that would draw my attention.'
>
> (*PC Simon Herrema*) 'In the early hours of the morning, we'd stop almost anyone walking the streets doing anything out of the ordinary. If we see a couple of young lads, white or black, driving a car at 2 in the morning, it's always worth while stopping them.'
>
> It is an unfortunate fact of cultural diversity that many young Afro-Caribbeans, innocent or otherwise, behave in a way that makes those hairs stand up on white policemen's necks. They tend to hang around in the street more. More of them are out partying in the small hours. Many run away on principle when they see a police officer – which most police also take as a sign of guilt, as they cannot understand why any law-abiding person could possibly wish to avoid meeting them. But this is not simply a matter of cultural mis-interpretation. For while in many cases these signs are innocent, they are also, often, the places, the times and the patterns of behaviour that do, regardless of race, fit in with actual or imminent crime.

(adapted from **Sociology Update 1983, 1984, 1985** by Martyn Denscombe; quotation from **Inside the Inner City**. (revised edition) by Paul Harrison, Penguin, Harmondsworth, 1985, p. 359)

1. How can newspaper reports on 'mugging' be seen as irresponsible? (4)
2. Why do reports on 'mugging' apparently sell newspapers, particularly tabloids like **The Sun**. (4)

3. Many crimes are 'crimes of opportunity'.
     a What does this mean? (2)
     b How might it partly account for the high level of black street crime? (3)
4. How might labelling theory help to explain the high proportion of blacks arrested for street crimes? (7)

Section 18 Religion

Religion may be defined as a belief in some form of supernatural power which influences or controls the lives of human beings and the world of nature. This section examines the role of religion in society from a number of different viewpoints. It also considers the claim that religion is steadily declining in importance in modern industrial society.

1 Religion and society

Religion has often been seen as a means of strengthening and reinforcing social norms and values. In doing so it contributes to order and stability in society. Religious ceremonies have been seen as a means of uniting a social group and so producing social solidarity. Religion is different from all other aspects of society because it involves a belief in supernatural power. Because of this many sociologists argue that it can make a unique and vital contribution to the wellbeing of society. These points are examined in the following passage.

> Supernatural power means literally power above and beyond the forces of nature. It is, for example, the power of the Christian God who is believed to be omniscient – all knowing, and omnipotent – all powerful. Such power is beyond the normal powers which are found in the world of nature and the society of man. It is a special kind of power which does not obey the normal rules which operate in the natural world. Thus the Christian God has no beginning and no end. He does not experience birth and death like men and women. He is supernatural, he lives on another plane.
>
> A belief in supernatural power is the basis of religion. It sets religion apart from the everyday world.
>
> Religion involves the creation of the sacred. When something is made sacred or sanctified it is set apart, given a

special meaning and treated with reverence, awe, respect and sometimes fear. Thus the beliefs of the Christian religion and its symbols such as the cross and communion wine are sacred. Mistreatment of the sacred, such as vandalising a church, causes deep revulsion and shock for those who believe.

Religion includes a set of beliefs and practices which the faithful are required to hold and follow. Thus the Christian religion includes the Ten Commandments which among other things instruct members to honour their parents, not to commit adultery, not to steal and not to kill. These commandments are backed by supernatural power. Those who follow them may be rewarded with an afterlife of eternal happiness in a land flowing with milk and honey. Those who break them may suffer an afterlife of eternal damnation. Religious beliefs can therefore have considerable control over the behaviour of people in society.

The influence of religion on social life can also be seen from religious rituals and ceremonies. Many sociologists argue that such events can unify people in society. They produce social unity or social solidarity. In a religious ritual a social group comes together to express its faith in common values and beliefs. People often recite prayers and sing songs which spell out these shared beliefs. In doing so they experience a sense of collective identity and a feeling of belonging. This unity is backed by the power of religion which gives the gathering a sense of awe and reverence. The atmosphere is highly charged, emotions are touched and the ceremony is raised above the level of a normal social event. By participating in a religious ritual people feel a part of something larger than themselves and become aware of the moral bonds which unite them.

(adapted in part from **Sociology** by Leonard Broom and Philip Selznick, 6th edition, Harper & Row, New York, 1977).

1. a The norms and values of society are often similar to religious beliefs. If this is the case, how can religion strengthen and reinforce social norms and values? (4)

   b How does this contribute to order and stability in society? (3)

2. a What beliefs of the Christian religion reinforce the norms and

values of marriage and family life?   (3)
  b A church marriage sanctifies the union between two people.
    How might this strengthen the marriage?   (3)
3. How does a religious ritual help to unite a group of people?   (3)
4. Religion does not always contribute to order and unity in society. In fact it can do just the opposite. Briefly discuss this view using at least one example to support it.   (4)

2 Religion and social order

In every society certain events and situations produce stress, worry and anxiety. If these emotions were not kept in check, social order might be threatened. Imagine a society in which people were constantly tense and anxious – it is difficult to see how things could run smoothly. The anthropologist Bronislaw Malinowski argues that one of the main functions of religion is to check and reduce emotions which threaten to disrupt society. He also believes that religion strengthens social solidarity or unity in society. Religious ceremonies involve people coming together to worship as a community. Joining together in a common faith and often in mutual support helps to unite a social group.

Malinowski spent several years studying the people of the Trobriand Islands which are off the coast of New Guinea in South-East Asia. The Trobriands consist of a number of small atolls – ring shaped coral reefs surrounding a lagoon. The waters of the lagoon are calm since they are protected from the open sea by a barrier reef which acts as a breakwater. The islanders fish in the lagoon by dropping poison into the water. The fish are stunned, they float to the surface and are scooped into canoes. In Malinowski's words, within the lagoon, 'fishing is done in an easy and absolutely reliable manner by the method of poisoning, yielding abundant results without danger and uncertainty'.

The same is not true of fishing in the open sea. Tropical storms are common. They may overturn or break up the frail outrigger canoes resulting in injury or loss of life. In the lagoon the islanders can always predict a reasonable catch. Sometimes they return empty-handed from an expedition beyond the barrier reef. They have to rely mainly on luck hoping that their nets strike a shoal of fish.

Before fishing in the open sea the islanders perform a religious ceremony. However, no religious ritual is associated with fishing in the lagoon.

(adapted from **Magic, Science and Religion and Other Essays** by Bronislaw Malinowski, Anchor Books, New York, 1954).

1. Why is religion associated with fishing in the open sea but not in the lagoon?   (6)
2. Malinowski claims that in all societies religion is associated with one or more of the 'life crises', that is birth, puberty, marriage and death.
   a How might the emotions that death produces disrupt normal social relationships?   (4)
   b How might religion check and reduce these emotions?   (5)
   c How might a funeral ceremony strengthen social solidarity?   (5)

3 Religion – The opium of the people

Karl Marx described religion as 'the opium of the people'. Opium is an hallucinatory drug which gives a feeling of wellbeing. It produces illusions which distort reality. Marx believed that religion gives a false picture of society. It prevents people from seeing the truth. It provides an illusion of happiness and offers an imaginary escape from problems.

Marx believed that religion helps to keep the poor and oppressed in their place. He saw it placing 'imaginary flowers on their chains'. This kept their chains hidden and made them easier to wear. By offering comfort and support religion made their suffering more bearable. By appearing to give solutions to their problems, religion tended to prevent them from taking practical steps to solve those problems. In particular it discouraged them from trying to overthrow their oppressors.

The following passage provides evidence which can be used to support Marx's views. It describes the religious music of many black Americans who have been a downtrodden minority in United States' society.

Religion as the opium of the people

Throughout the USA black churches have resounded with the
sound of gospel music. In Detroit the Reverend C.L. Franklin,
father of the famous soul singer Aretha Franklin and pastor
of the Bethel Baptist Church, has raised congregations to
fever pitch with his preaching and gospel singing. So intense
is the feeling that he arouses that nurses are regularly on
hand to tend members of his flock overcome with emotion.
People leave the church feeling cleansed, their burdens lifted,
recharged and ready to face the problems of a new week. At a
Madison Square Garden gospel concert in New York City,
Mahalia Jackson, the Queen of Gospel, sings 'Just over the
Hill', a song about going to heaven. As she sinks to her knees,
singing with intensity and jubilation, women in the audience
shriek and faint. Gospel music, in the words of one of its
singers, 'stirs the emotions'.

A member of the Ward Sisters, a famous black gospel group
states, 'For people who work hard and make little money,
gospel music offers a promise that things will be better in the
life to come.' According to Thomas A. Dorsey, one of the
founders of modern gospel music, 'Make it anything other

than good news and it ceases to be gospel.' Many gospel songs ring with joy, excitement, anticipation and conviction about reaching the 'blessed homeland' and 'waking up in glory'. Life on earth might be hard, painful with little hope for improvement but life after death is nothing but good news.

God not only promises eternal salvation and perfect happiness. He also provides support and direction for life on earth. Typical lines from gospel songs include, 'Take your burdens to the Lord and leave them there', 'God will carry you through', 'Since I gave to Jesus my poor broken heart, he has never left me alone', and 'What would I do if it wasn't for the Lord'. The songs often say as much to the singers as their audiences. The gospel singer Dorothy Love refused to sell her song 'I've Got Jesus and That's Enough' to a rock and roll song company. Her reason: 'That's my whole story. I'd be selling out everything I am.'

(adapted from **The Gospel Sound** by Tony Heilbut, Simon and Schuster, New York, 1971 and **Right On: From Blues to Soul in Black America** by Michael Haralambos, Eddison, London, 1974).

In the late 1950s and early 1960s some black preachers came out of their churches and on to the streets. Led by the Reverend Martin Luther King, the Southern Christian Leadership Council, an organization of black churches in the southern states of the USA, directed mass protest against racial discrimination. Partly due to its campaign, the American government passed civil rights laws which declared discrimination on the basis of skin colour to be illegal.

(adapted from **The Negro in Twentieth Century America** edited by J.H. Franklin and I. Starr, Vintage Books, New York, 1967)

1. Why does Marx compare opium with religion?   (4)
2. a What are the emotional effects produced by gospel music? (3)
   b What are the messages contained in the words of gospel music?   (3)
   c How might the emotional effects and the message of gospel music help to keep blacks at the bottom of the stratification system?   (6)

3. Explain how the evidence in the second passage can be used to argue that Marx's theory of religion does not always apply.   (4)

4 Secularization

At first glance the future of religion in Britain and in many other Western societies is not bright. Dwindling congregations, churches up for sale and in a state of disrepair, increasing numbers of people married in registry offices and fewer children attending Sunday school suggest a steady decline in the influence of religion. Evidence such as this has led a number of researchers to argue that Western societies are undergoing a process of secularization which means they are becoming increasingly secular or non-religious. Those who argue that secularization is occurring claim 1) that participation in organized religion is declining, for example fewer people attend church, 2) that religion has less influence on society as a whole, for example the churches are no longer responsible for educating the young and 3) that people are no longer guided by religious beliefs in their everyday lives, for example the will of God is not an important consideration affecting their decisions.

However it is very difficult to measure the strength of religious belief. Simply because church attendance has declined does not necessarily mean that people are any the less religious. They may well have turned to 'privatised religion', preferring to worship in the privacy of their own homes. Also, because the state has taken over many of the social welfare responsibilities of the church, such as caring for the poor, does not necessarily mean that religion has lost influence in society. It may well be that the strength of Christian beliefs, such as the importance of caring for the poor, has led the state to take over these responsibilities. The evidence can therefore be interpreted in a number of ways and the case for secularization is far from proven.

The following passage is based on the work of the British sociologist Bryan Wilson. He is one of the strongest supporters of the view that secularization is occurring in Western societies.

> The signs of a decline in religion became increasingly clear after World War II which ended in 1945. War memorials lost many of the religious symbols with which they were

traditionally adorned. Indeed they were often not put up at all. In 1947 the BBC, which had traditionally stood firm on the side of the Church of England, abandoned its policy of not broadcasting opinions hostile to Christianity.

Except for ceremonies like the coronation and the opening of Parliament, the church is rarely seen or heard on the national stage. At the close of the last century a Prime Minister's correspondence gave serious attention to church opinion. In 1937 the bishops had an important voice in the abdication of Edward VIII who wished to marry a divorcee. In recent years we have seen the occasion when the Prime Minister was 'too busy' to see the Archbishop of Canterbury. No longer do people look to the pulpit for guidance and information. They are more likely to turn to television, books, newspapers and magazines. Control of social welfare has long since passed to armies of specialists employed by the state who educate, counsel, cure, rehabilitate and care for the poor and the aged.

The clergy are steadily moving down the social scale. Even in the 1950s their wages were similar to those of many professional workers. Today many number amongst the low paid with unskilled manual workers often earning considerably more. Church buildings are suffering a similar fate. They were built, elaborately decorated and repaired in a much poorer society. Yet in today's more affluent society even their basic fabric is often not maintained.

Religion seems less and less to guide people's thoughts and direct their actions. They no longer appear to ask 'What is God's will?' so much as 'What shall I do to get on?' They seem less concerned about death and the after life than about happiness here and now. The church's traditional disapproval of divorce, artificial techniques of birth control, sexual relationships outside marriage and homosexuality appears to have little impact. If anything changing attitudes in society about these and other matters have changed the church's views. More and more the church seems to follow rather than lead.

The decline in the church's influence on people's beliefs and actions is reflected in participation in organized religious activities. In 1950, 67% of children in England were baptised in the Church of England, in 1973 only 43%. In 1953, 6.5% of the population took Easter Communion in the Church of England but 20 years later the figure had dropped to 4%. The same trend is apparent in the Roman Catholic and non-conformist (e.g. Methodist and Presbyterian) churches. Information from public opinion polls mirrors this trend. In the early 1950s, 90% claimed to believe in God; by the mid 1970s this figure was down to 64%.

However it would probably be a mistake to conclude that religion is doomed. There is, and probably always will be a deeply committed minority of religious people. However for the vast majority religion is becoming simply an 'optional extra'.

(adapted from 'How religious are we?' by Bryan Wilson, **New Society**, 27 October, 1977)

1. What evidence does the extract contain to suggest that religion is becoming less effective as a mechanism of social control?   (3)
2. a What are the occupational groups referred to by the phrase 'armies of specialists'?   (2)
   b What functions has the church lost to these specialists?   (2)
3. What evidence does the extract provide to indicate that the political influence of the church has declined?   (3)
4. a What evidence does the extract contain which suggests that people are less willing to provide financial support for the church?   (2)
   b How can this be seen as evidence of secularization?   (2)
5. Briefly explain how the following views can be used to argue against the case presented in the extract.
   a People have turned from organized to 'privatised' religion. (3)
   b In earlier times church attendance was often regarded as a sign of respectability.   (3)

Index

advertising 30-32
affluent workers 89-91, 171
Afro-Caribbeans
  and crime 114-115, 393-395
  and educational
    attainment 239-244
  and life chances 102-103
  and migration 312-313
  and occupation 102-103
  and relations with police 114-116
  and subculture 101, 108-112,
    240-241
  and unemployment 102-103, 116
  and urban riots 113-117
alienation 337, 345-347
anomie 325
animal behaviour 5
Asians
  and crime 394
  and educational
    attainment 239-244
  and family 187-189, 206-208,
    289-292
  and life chances 102-103
  and migration 312-313
  and occupation 102-103
  and subculture 101, 108-110,
    206-208, 240-241
  and unemployment 102-103
  and urban riots 113-114
assembly line production 335-337
autobiographies 26-28, 32-37, 59,
  60-63
automation 339-341, 361, 370-371

birth rate
  and social class 298-300
  in England and Wales 297-303
birth control 289-290, 298-300,
  302-303
black Americans 32-37, 63-66, 101,
  106-107, 231
Blackfoot Indians 26-28, 60-63
Bushmen 376-377

caste 73-75, 206
Cheyenne Indians 6-8, 11, 21

class, social (see also middle class,
    working class)
  and birth rate 298-300
  and crime 385-389
  and educational
    attainment 225-234
  and embourgeoisement 89-91
  and health 86, 227-228
  and income 80-81
  and life chances 85-86
  and occupation 76, 84-85
  and poverty 89, 128-132, 148-149
  and socialization practices 21, 226
  and speech patterns 229-231
  and voting behaviour 91, 170-173
  and wealth 82-83
  background of MPs 179-181
  importance of 95
  Marxist view on 77-79
  Registrar-General's classification
    of 76
  subcultures 87-88
compensatory education 127,
  232-233
comprehensive system (of secondary
    education) 127, 252-254
conjugal roles 198-202, 211-212,
  276-277
contraception (see birth control)
craft technology 337-339
crime 375, 378-395
  and ethnicity 114-115, 393-395
  and social class 385-389
  and victim studies 379-381
  and youth 260-262, 385-386, 391
  official statistics on 378-384, 394
  rate 380, 382-384
  white collar 387-389
culture (see also subculture) 1-3,
  6-17
culture of poverty 126-128

death rate
  in England and Wales 292-295
  in Third World 289-290
  social effects of fall in 316-317
delinquency 260-262, 385-386, 391

democracy   155-158, 161
deviance   375-376, 389-393
deskilling   341-342, 343-345
de-urbanization   326-329
divorce   204, 208-212
dual labour market   103, 371-372

education   219-254
   and ethnicity   239-244
   and gender   245-249
   and poverty   227-228
   and role in society   219-224
   and social class   225-234
   and speech patterns   229-231, 233
   as agency of socialization   219-220
   as preparation for work   219-220,
      222-224
   compensatory   127, 232-233
   in nineteenth century   139, 219
   Marxist views on   222-224
   organization of secondary   250-254
elaborated code   230-231
embourgeoisement   89-91
ethnicity   97-117
   and crime   114-115, 393-395
   and educational
      attainment   239-244
   and family   206-208
   and life chances   102-103
   and subculture   101, 108-112
   and urban riots   113-117
   definition of   101
extended family   190-198

family   183-217
   alternatives to   215-217
   and ethnicity   206-208
   and industrialization   190-193
   and social control   19-22, 26-28
   and socialization   19-22, 26-28, 169
   Asian   187-189, 206-208
   breakdown of   208-212
   changing role in society   184,
      186-187, 189-190
   conjugal roles in   198-202,
      211-212, 276-277
   critical views of   213-215
   diversity of   202-208
   extended   190-198
   in pre-industrial society   184-185,
      268-269, 290-292
   in relation to work and
      leisure   348-350
   in Third World   187-189, 290-292
   nuclear   190-191, 198-199,

      202-205, 213-215
   one parent   203-205
   role of women in   194-197,
      198-202
   symmetrical   198-199
   working class   190-198
fertility   297-303
feudal system   70-73
fringe benefits   81, 84-85

income (distribution of)   80-81, 131,
   149
infant mortality   86, 295
initiation ceremonies   255-257
inner cities   330-333
   and riots   113-117
   unemployment in   332
   welfare in   150-153
instinct   1-2, 3-4
interest groups (see pressure groups)
internal migration (see migration)
interviews   46-50, 58
interviewer bias   47-50

job enrichment   344-345

kibbutz   215-217

labelling theory   389-393
language (see speech patterns)
life chances
   and education   225-249
   and ethnicity   102-103, 239-244
   and gender   246-249, 304-306
   and social class   85-86, 225-234
leisure
   and family life   198, 348-351
   and unemployment   363, 369,
      372-373
   future of   372-373
   in relation to work   348-351

Marxism
   and alienation   345-347
   and education   222-224
   and politics   161-164
   and power   161-164
   and poverty   128-129
   and religion   400-402
   and social class   77-79
   and work   77-79, 129, 345-347
mass media
   and crime   384, 388-389, 393-394
   and politics   28-29, 158-161,
      164-168

and poverty 132-134
and role of women 30-32, 273-274
and social control 28-32
and youth 263, 264
Mbuti pygmies 15-16
means test 140, 144
mechanization 339
microtechnology 339-345, 361,
370-372
middle class
birth rate 298-299
conditions of employment 84, 131
crime 387-389
educational attainment 225-226
life chances 85-86, 225-226
Registrar-General's classification
of 76
socialization practices 226
social mobility 92-93
speech patterns 229-231
subculture 87-88
unemployment 356
voting behaviour 170-173
migration 311-314
internal 319, 321, 326-329
mortality (see death rate)

newspapers 132-134, 158-160,
166-168
norms 9-10
novels 59, 60, 63-66
nuclear family 190-191, 198-199,
202-205, 213-215

official statistics 59, 60, 66-68
on crime 378-384, 387, 394-395
on income distribution 68, 80-81
on poverty 67, 130-131
on suicide 68
on unemployment 67, 353-359
on wealth distribution 82-83
old age
and family life 191, 310
and population structure 307-310
status of 60-61, 310
opinion polls 176-179

participant observation 62-67
peer groups 16, 25-26, 27-28, 216,
233-234
pilot studies 57-58
political parties 156, 170-176
political socialization 166-169
population 289-317
and Third World 289-292

changing age structure of 307-310
changing size (UK) 314-315
positive discrimination 232
postal questionnaires 56
poverty 119-135
absolute 121-125
and educational
attainment 227-228
and mass media 132-134
and social class 128-132
and welfare state 137-153
culture of 126-128
Marxist views on 128-129
measurement of 67, 121-125,
130-131
official statistics on 67, 130-131
relative 124-125, 130
solutions to 127-128, 129,
148-149
war on 127
power 155-164
distribution of in Western
societies 155-158
Marxist views on 161-164
pressure groups 156-157, 158-161
primary sources 39-59
public opinion polls (see opinion polls)

questionnaires 55-57
and opinion polls 176-179

race 97-100
racialism 32-36, 106
racism 32-36, 63-66, 104-107
cultural 105
in police force 114
in schools 241, 242-244
institutional 106-107
Rastafarians 112
religion 397-405
and caste system 74-75
and secularization 403-405
and social control 22-24, 397-402
and social solidarity 397-398, 399
future of 403-405
Marxist views on 400-402
restricted code 230-231
riots 113-117
roles 10-12, 15-16

sampling procedures 50-55, 177
secondary sources 59-68
self-concept 236
and ethnicity 240-241

and unemployment 364, 365–366, 367, 369
self-fulfilling prophecy 236–238, 392
significant others 26–28
social class (see class, social)
social control 19–37
  and education 222–224
  and family 19–22
  and mass media 28–32
  and peer groups 25–26, 27–28
  and politics 161–164
  and racialism 32–36
  and religion 22–24
  and socialization 19–22, 26–28
  and significant others 26–28
  and welfare state 137–139
socialization 13–17, 19–22, 26–28
  and education 219–220
  and family life 16, 19–22
  and peer groups 16, 25–26, 27–28, 216
  and mass media 28–32, 166–168, 273–274
  and religion 22–24, 397–402
  and significant others 26–28
  and social control 19–22
  for gender roles 30–32, 247–249, 273–276
  in kibbutz 215–217
  political 166–169
  social class differences 226
social solidarity 8, 219, 397–398, 399
social stratification 69–95
  and caste system 73–75
  and ethnicity 102–107
  and feudal system 70–73
  and social class 76–95
speech patterns 229–231, 233
status 10–12
  achieved 11
  ascribed 10–11, 73
status frustration 236, 386
streaming 234–236, 237–238, 242–244
subculture
  and delinquency 386
  and ethnicity 101, 108–112
  and poverty 126–128
  and social class 87–88
  and youth 255, 259–264

television 30–32, 164–166
tripartite system (of secondary education) 145, 250–254

unemployment
  and ethnicity 102–103, 116, 356
  and inner city 116, 332
  and social class 356
  and welfare state 137–138, 140–142, 144, 149, 152
  and women 355, 362, 365–366, 371
  and youth 367–369
  by duration 358–359
  by region 357–358
  definition and measurement 67, 353–355
  effects of 363–369
  extent of 67, 353–355
  future of 359–361, 370–373
  long-term 358–359, 365
urbanization 319–333

values 6–8
victim studies 379–381
voluntary organizations 146–148
voting behaviour 91, 170–176
  and age 174–176
  and gender 174–176
  and social class 91, 170–173

welfare state 132–134, 137–153, 163, 199
  criticisms of 148–153
  establishment of 142–143
  foundations of 140–142
  origins of 137–139
wealth (distribution of) 82–83, 132
West Indians (see Afro-Caribbeans)
white collar crime 387–389
women 267–287
  and divorce 211–212
  and education 245–249
  and family 194–197, 198–202, 272, 276–277
  and industrial society 270–287
  and labour market 270–272, 278–287, 362, 371
  and mass media 30–32, 273–274
  and pre-industrial society 188–189, 268–269
  and unemployment 355, 362, 365–366, 371
  biological theory of role 267–268
  cultural theory of role 268–276
  life expectancy 304–306
  religious definitions of role 23
  socialization of 30–32

work   335-351, 359-362, 370-373
  and alienation   337, 345-347
  and deskilling   341-342, 343-345
  and production
    technology   335-342, 343-344,
    361, 370-372
  and women   270-272, 278-287,
    362, 371
  conditions of   84-85, 131
  future of   359-362, 370-373
  in relation to leisure   348-351
  Marxist views on   77-78, 345-347
working class
  birth rate   299-300
  conditions of employment   84-85,
    131
  crime   260-262, 385-386
  educational attainment   225-234
  embourgeoisement   90-92
  family   190-198
  health   86, 227-228
  life chances   85-86, 92-93,

    131-132, 227-228
  Marxist views on   77-79
  poverty   89, 128-132
  Registrar-General's classification
    of   76
  socialization practices   21, 226
  social mobility   92-93
  speech patterns   229-231
  subculture   87-88
  unemployment   356
  voting behaviour   91, 170-173

youth   255-265
  and crime   260-262, 385-386, 391
  and mass media   263, 264
  and social class   259-262, 385-386
  and unemployment   367-369
  culture   255, 259-263
  in industrial society   257-265
  in pre-industrial society   255-257
Youth Training Scheme (YTS)   67, 354